THE BROKEN CRESCENT

The "Threat" of Militant Islamic Fundamentalism

Fereydoun Hoveyda

A National Committee on American Foreign Policy Study

PRAEGER

**Westport, Connecticut
London**

Library of Congress Cataloging-in-Publication Data

Hoveyda, Fereydoun.
    The broken crescent : the "threat" of militant Islamic fundamentalism / Fereydoun
Hoveyda.
       p. cm.
    "A National committe on American Foreign Policy study."
    Includes bibliographical references and index.
    ISBN 0–275–95837–X (alk. paper)—ISBN 0–275–97902–4 (pbk.)
    1. Islamic fundamentalism.   2. Islam and politics.   3. Religion and politics.   I. National
Committee on American Foreign Policy.   II. Title.
BP60.H73   1998
320.5'5'0917671—dc21   97–40886

British Library Cataloguing in Publication Data is available.

Library of Congress Catalog Card Number: 97–40886
ISBN: 0–275–97902–4 (pbk.)

First published in 1998

Praeger Publishers, 88 Post Road West, Westport, CT 06881
An imprint of Greenwood Publishing Group, Inc.
www.praeger.com

Printed in the United States of America

The paper used in this book complies with the
Permanent Paper Standard issued by the National
Information Standards Organization (Z39.48–1984).

10 9 8 7 6 5 4 3 2 1

This book is not about Islam, one of the great
Abrahamic religions that claims a billion followers.
It is about "militant Islamic fundamentalism," a
movement that uses religion for political ends.

"Allah conceived Islam as a religion. Men have
transformed it into politics."

—Muhammad Said al-Ashmawy (Egyptian judge),
"Islamism against Islam"

"The emerging new scientific power is already apportioning
the future parts. . . . Are we [Muslims] going to specialize in
the industry of whirling dervishes?"

—Jamal Eddine Bencheikh (professor at the Sorbonne)
in *Le Monde*, Paris, April 7, 1989

"The State becomes God when it is not able to carry out its
human tasks."

—Georges Bernanos (French writer and essayist),
Les Enfants Humiliés

"I do the wrong, and first begin to brawl
The secret mischiefs that I set abroach
I lay into grievous charge of others
. . . then I sigh and with a piece of Scripture
Tell them that God bids us do good for evil . . .
And thus I clothe my naked vilainy
With old ends stolen forth of holy writ
And seem a Saint when most I play the devil"

—Shakespeare's Gloucester
in *Richard III*

Contents

Preface

Since the tragic attacks of September 11, 2001, I have received numerous e-mails from readers who consider *The Broken Crescent* as a *prescient* book. While I am thankful for their compliments, I must own that I totally lack the qualities of clairvoyance and other fortune telling abilities. What I did in 1998 amounted to present facts, personal experiences, and an analysis of the phenomenon of Islamic fundamentalist militancy against the backdrop of the Muslim world's history. I tried to explain to the best of my ability its causes and consequences.

Like the vast majority of Americans, I welcomed the rapid and forceful response of the administration. Nevertheless I do not feel completely at ease with "Operation Enduring Freedom." Indeed, by labeling bin Laden and his associates "sheer terrorists" and dismissing the ideology that animates them, it seems to me that the President and his aides are neglecting the most important dimension of the scourge they want to eradicate. Indeed bin Laden's recruits are not mercenaries or ordinary killers. Like their leader, they are indoctrinated believers who think of themselves as Allah's foot soldiers with reserved facilities in Paradise. They participate in a holy war. They are "Jihadis." They keep high the banner of Islam.

As I have explained in *The Broken Crescent*, mainstream Islam turned fundamentalist in the Middle Ages and remained so up to now. In fact, the triumph of orthodoxy triggered the steady decline of the Muslim world at a time when the West was slowly rising out of decadence and backwardness.

Against this fundamentalist backdrop, from time to time, some intransigent believers, for religious reasons or political gains, rose (and continue to rise) to "save" Islam. They invariably call on their fellow Muslims to retrieve the purity of the religion. In recent years peoples like Khomeini and bin Laden mobilized many believers with the slogan: "Islam is in danger." Along with normal warfare, they used terrorism and encouraged it in the form of *martyrdom and suicide attacks*. In general, ordinary Muslims, while disapproving their violent methods, do not consider the militants as "terrorists." In order to differentiate them from the bulk of Muslims who are law abiding citizens, we call them *militant Islamic fundamentalists* (MIF).

In this respect, 9/11 was not a mere terrorist act, but an action of militant Islamic fundamentalists. It is therefore misleading to characterize "Operation Enduring Freedom" as a war against terrorism. It is true that, as the President and his aides repeatedly emphasize, it is not a war against Islam. But in fact it is and should be a war against MIF which is at the root of the devastating events.

World War II against three dictatorships was won not only through formidable and costly military battles on land and sea, but also through ideological confrontation. The Allies used all the information tools at their disposal in order to discredit Nazism and Fascism. In the same manner the Cold War was won largely thanks to a sustained effort to explain the values of democracy and human rights.

"Operation Enduring Freedom" cannot come to a successful end only through military operations. It needs a vast information effort in order to dispel the confusions that blur the vision of Muslim masses and allows the likes of Khomeini and bin Laden to find followers.

Judging by the popular reactions in the Muslim world, one can see the chasm that separates it from the rest of the planet. In a way, it can be said that the Muslim world has largely been locked up in the Middle Ages while the West moved on and is now entering the twenty-first century. Indeed before the twelfth century, the Muslim world was more advanced and prosperous than the West. Muslims should understand how and why this reversal of fortune happened. Obviously in the twelfth century there was no American imperialism or Israeli conspiracy. History bears witness that the decline of the world of Muslims was mainly of their own making. Indeed they jettisoned all their scientific acquisitions and condemned research and study of the laws of nature. Fanaticism and intolerance gnawed gradually at the fabric of their civilization.

As much as fundamentalism, fanaticism and intolerance are slow and enduring poisons—militant Islamic fundamentalism is a malignant and rapidly acting venom. It can cause havoc in the Western world as it did on 9/11. But it is much more lethal to the impoverished and backward Muslim world itself. This is what Muslims need to understand! If not stopped, militant Islamic fundamentalism will only add to their predicaments.

Acknowledgments

I thank the National Committee on American Foreign Policy for appointing me the first fellow of the Committee. The support and encouragement of the Committee in completing this study, especially of its chairman, William J. Flynn, and president, George D. Schwab, will never be forgotten. I also extend my gratitude to Edwina McMahon for her very skillful talents in editing the manuscript, my first written fully in English.

Introduction

Since Khomeini's seizure of power in Iran in 1979, militant Islamic fundamentalism has been rising steadily in the Middle East. More and more, its proponents resort to violence on both the national and the international levels. Indeed, they consider terrorism an efficient and inexpensive instrument of warfare that allows them to strike at the "enemy" wherever found, at little human and material cost to the attacker.

Who is the enemy? At home: "corrupt" leaders who have strayed from Allah's "right path"; outside: the Western infidels accused of conspiring to eradicate Islam from the surface of the planet.

Americans, for their part, still remember the long ordeal during which their diplomats were kept as hostages for 444 days by Iranian radical students. They also recall the bombing of the Marine barracks in Beirut in 1983; the explosion of Pan Am Flight 103 over Scotland in 1988; the New York Trade Center blast in 1993; the killing of nineteen servicemen in Saudi Arabia in 1996 . . . (to mention only a few occurrences). Knowing that the slogan "Death to America" covers walls in Islamic cities and that mobs trample the "Stars and Stripes" underfoot, Americans wonder whether Islamic fundamentalism constitutes a serious danger to them and to the West. In order to formulate an answer to this question, I shall try to explore in the following pages the origins, causes, modalities, and scope of seventh and early eighth centuries when Beduin armies hurled through Iberia and pushed northward as far as Poitiers (France), sowing panic along their trail.

"ISLAMIC TERRORISM"?

The phrase "Islamic terrorism" was coined after the 1979 hostage crisis. That year, on November 4, a group of Iranian radical students, calling themselves "followers of the line of the Imam [Khomeini]," occupied the American embassy compound in Tehran and kept as prisoners fifty-two American diplomats for 444 days.

Many Muslims were naturally outraged by a label that equates their religion with violence. Their anger seethed and increased as their coreligionists appeared in feature films on TV and theater screens as criminals attacking innocent civilians and children. It is true that racial slurs and hatred often tinged these fictional representations. But denying what an author called "Holy Terror"[1] or trying to justify it with references to real or imagined grievances does no service to Islam.

Indeed, it is a blatant fact that since 1979 (Khomeini's seizure of power in Iran), a growing number of militant Islamic groups, inspired or led by religious officials, have killed in the name of Islam. They are different from the political organizations that preceded them or coexist with them.[2]

It is true that the assassinations, suicide bombings, and other violent acts claimed in recent years by diverse fundamentalist groups have tarnished Islam's image in the West despite numerous protests against branding the religion with the brush of terrorism. Indeed, many Muslims and non-Muslims, including so-called experts and scholars, affirm that such criminal enterprises have nothing to do with "true" Islam. But what is true Islam? Can one say that Ayatollah Khomeini was not a true Muslim? Or that Sheikh Omar Abdal Rahman, convicted in a conspiracy case in the United States, is a "false" Muslim? Trying to define true Islam is a complicated matter of theological debate that cannot easily affect public opinion. To refurbish Islam's good reputation, one should rely on facts.

The reality is that the militants who resort to violence and killings do not represent the majority of Muslims. In fact, the Western media have blown up their doings and given them undue publicity. Militant fundamentalists of any religion or ideology are usually tiny minorities. The activities of a few cannot and should not affect the repute of an entire doctrine or a whole community. Most Muslims are law-abiding people who despise ter-

Having admitted the oxymoronic character of their ideal of moderate fundamentalists, they now speak of "pragmatists." While wishing them success and awaiting the results of their new enterprise, it is worthwhile to evaluate the reasons for the eighteen-year stalemate.

It has been said, time and again, that the main reason was (and remains) a persistent disregard (or ignorance) of the mind-set of the militant fundamentalists and their leaders. To this, one should add the failure to grasp the "rules of the game" of political Islam.

Curiously enough, there is no shortage of information about the Islamic world. On the contrary, a spate of published material exists. Numerous experts and think tanks are accessible. Professors from almost all Muslim countries teach in American universities. It is possible that the very abundance of information confuses policymakers. It is true that experts do not always concur; actually they often contradict one another. For instance, some see in the new wave of fundamentalism triggered by Khomeini's rise to power in Iran an absolutely unprecedented phenomenon, whereas others link it to the past. Some describe Islam as a religion that encourages violence, whereas others describe it as a profoundly humane and compassionate faith. A number of authors, both Muslim and non-Muslim, minimize the negative impact of militant fundamentalism. Instead, they extol what they call Islamic pluralism and tolerance. Moreover, many commentators and even scholars fail to underline the basic difference between Islam as a religion and its political use by activist groups.[6] In their view, Islamic movements have been seen by Westerners as more disturbing than they really are. In short, policymakers as well as laymen who are interested in understanding the nature and the consequences of the present wave of militant Islamic fundamentalism find themselves at sea in the midst of contradictory and sometimes diametrically opposed assessments.

I do not pretend to dissipate here all the existing confusion about Islam. But I hope that my narrative will provide some answers to the questions generally asked about militant fundamentalism and its impact. I have met many militant Islamic fundamentalists since my childhood. I have also visited almost all Muslim countries, Arab and non-Arab alike. Finally, I have studied Islam's history and the use of religion in political struggles. This book, therefore, draws on personal experience as well as on extensive research.

1

First Encounter with a Militant

I was four years old when I first met a militant Islamic fundamentalist. That happened in Damascus (Syria) in the late 1920s. My father was consul general of Iran. One spring night, an unusual rumpus woke me up: A guard had found a twelve-year-old boy hiding in the cellar. He was an orphan named Ahmad Badawi. He defiantly confessed that he was chased by the police because he had tried to kill the governor, targeted by the Badawi group as a collaborationist with the French enemy. Despite his age, he belonged to a fundamentalist secret association. A little later, the governor arrived with a couple of officers. After an animated discussion with my father, the governor departed with the boy. The next day I overheard my father telling my mother that the governor had pardoned Badawi and sent him to an orphanage.

THE MIDDLE EAST IN THE 1920s

In those days the Middle East lived in the throes of a profound crisis. Since the fifteenth century almost all Arabs were subjects of the Ottoman Empire, whose sultans bore the title of "caliph of the believers." By the end of World War I, the defeated empire was stripped of its Arab provinces, which were divided into several nation-states and placed under the administration of the victorious allies. The British got a mandate over Iraq and Palestine, and the French over Syria and Lebanon. In Constantinople (Istanbul), Mustafa Kemal Atatürk proclaimed a republic and dissolved the Islamic caliphate. Shaken by the sudden breakup of the "community of believers," the Arabs did not react immediately. The disappearance of their caliph left them in complete disarray. They began to wonder whether it was the end of Islam.

Great changes took place. In the Arab peninsula, the tribal chief Abdul Aziz Ibn Saud conquered Hijaz, where the two holiest cities of Islam—Mecca and Medina—are situated, forcing out the traditional Hashemite rulers, descendants of Prophet Muhammad's clan. Ibn Saud proclaimed himself king of Hijaz and Najd (his own province), which he later renamed Saudi Arabia. But because the Hashemites had led the Arab revolt against the Ottomans (with the help of Colonel Lawrence), the British awarded them with two thrones: Faisal became king of Iraq, and his elder brother, Abdallah (grandfather of the present king, Hussein), became emir and later king of Jordan, a barren territory artificially designed by Winston Churchill, then head of the Colonial Office. The French, for their part, founded two republics: Syria with a Sunni Muslim president and Lebanon with a Christian president and a Sunni Muslim prime minister.

These changes meant nothing to the Arab populations. The Muslim majority continued to consider itself as members of the community of believers and the non-Muslims as minorities living in Islamic lands. They all retained their tribal and family loyalties. To them, nationalities (Iraqi, Jordanian, Syrian, Lebanese) remained artificial and alien constructs imposed by the "infidel" occupants. As they gradually recovered from the shock of the collapse of the Ottoman Empire and the suppression of the caliphate, they began to feel more and more humiliated by their forced subjection to the rule of Christian Westerners. It was as if the Crusaders, expelled by Saladin in the twelfth century, had returned. Demonstrations, strikes, riots, and isolated terrorist activities occasionally erupted and were forcefully put down by British and French soldiers. Ahmad Badawi's attempt on the life of the governor of Damascus was by no means an isolated act.

THE RETURN OF BADAWI

I had almost completely forgotten Badawi until years later in Beirut (Lebanon), where we had moved, a Muslim cleric with an untrimmed beard called on us. Had he not named himself, we would not have recognized him. Now in his early twenties, he had set up his own fundamentalist section of the Egyptian Muslim Brotherhood.[1]

The Lebanese capital, a cosmopolitan, multiethnic, multireligious city-port, was less constrained than Damascus, where Islamic law was strictly observed. Here, outside Muslim neighborhoods, women moved freely and unveiled. They mixed with men in cafés, restaurants, cinemas, and beaches. These "anti-Islamic" ways enraged Badawi. He saw behind them a "satanic" scheme concocted by the French, in cahoots with local Christians, to wipe out Islam in the region. He invited us together with other Muslim students to attend his weekly sermon in a small suburban mosque.

His utterances were more political than religious. He warned the audience about a scheme, devised by the Jews with the help of the British, aimed at expelling the Muslims from Palestine and transforming Jerusalem, the third Muslim holy city, into a Jewish-European capital. This plan, he affirmed, was part of a vast conspiracy forged by Western Europe against Islam. The collapse of the Ottomans and the destitution of the caliphate were the first stages of the process; the Judaization of Palestine was the second. Had not Mustafa Kemal in Turkey and Reza Shah in Iran started to repeal the sharia (Islamic law) under the fallacious pretext of "modernization"? An Egyptian sheikh, Hassan al-Banna, started a movement to counter the West's "diabolical" plans. Muslims everywhere, he maintained, should strictly cling to the sharia, which was dictated by God himself to his prophet. He called on all Muslims to unite and prepare for a decisive battle against the infidels.

Like all militant fundamentalists, Badawi opposed the division of the community of believers into artificial nation-states, a Western "trick" aimed at weakening the Muslim world. Nevertheless, he hailed local nationalist politicians who were fighting the colonial authorities. Indeed, in those days, religious activists and secular nationalists worked hand in hand against the collaborationists and the foreigners. The new educated generation of tribes and "family clan" leaders embraced nationalist and modernist goals. They represented a major political force, whereas militant fundamentalists had relatively few followers. The Palestinian problem was becoming most urgent. David Ben-Gurion, who had settled there in 1907, was very active, and the British supported his Zionist objectives. Badawi shouted: "The flood of Jewish immigration should be stopped!"

Before attending his sermon, we had heard most of his arguments through our fellow students whose parents were nationalists. But it was the first time that we listened to a fundamentalist cleric calling for a jihad against the "corrupt and satanic" West and its Jewish allies. In his sermon, Badawi extolled the grand mufti of Jerusalem, Haj Amin al-Husseini,[2] the organizer of the fight against Jewish settlers and the paragon of a new type of religious leader of the first half of the twentieth century, who advocated both fundamentalist and nationalist goals.

A POLITICAL CLERIC

Haj Amin was born in 1898 in one of the two main Palestinian family clans. In 1912 he entered the famed Cairo al-Azhar Islamic university where he studied law. He then accomplished the Mecca pilgrimage, attended the Turkish Military Academy in Istanbul, and served in the Ottoman Army until 1917, when he returned to Jerusalem. He spent most of his time organizing demonstrations against Zionism. Sentenced "in absentia" to prison, he continued from exile to cast a shadow on the Palestinian stage. When the post of Grand Mufti became vacant in 1922, the then British high commissioner thought it a shrewd move to push his candidacy. Haj Amin took advantage of his lofty office to foster his own political aims.

The rise of Hitler to power in 1933 marked a turning point in the new mufti's activities. He sent a cable of congratulations to the Nazi leader and expressed support for the Jewish boycott in Germany. In doing so, Haj Amin was merely responding to a widespread sentiment among Muslims in general and Arabs in particular. Indeed, the German dictator was seeking revenge against the British and the French, the two dominant infidel intruders in the Muslim world. He could also be an ally against the Jews in Palestine. Accustomed to their own authoritarian regimes, Muslims were not bothered by Hitler's repressive and antidemocratic policies. In my school as well as in the American University of Beirut, almost everybody sided with Germany during World War II. Back in Iran, when on May 8, 1945, I announced to our family doctor the German surrender, he laughed at me and flatly denied Hitler's suicide: "He is not dead. He has gone into hiding and will return one day to deliver us from the clutches of our colonial oppressors!" In the 1940s, rumors circulated in the Middle East that Hitler had converted to Islam following a meeting with Haj Amin al-Husseini. Members of Egypt's Muslim Brotherhood firmly believed that Mussolini was an Egyptian Muslim named Mussa Nili (Moses of the Nile).[3]

In any case, Hitler's successes gave Haj Amin and his followers a great boost. Among the latter was Sheikh Ezzeddin Qassam, a Syrian born cleric expelled by the French. Haj Amin gave him a position as preacher in a Haifa mosque. In 1935, Qassam created an armed group he called the Black Hand. He launched raids against both the Jews and the British. He was eventually killed in a shootout. He became an instant hero and is remembered today as one of the first martyrs of the Palestinian "revolution." The militant Islamic fundamentalist group Hamas (of the Gaza Strip) named its military arm—which has claimed many suicide bombings in Israel—after him.

Haj Amin, for his part, proclaimed a general strike and ordered his hit men to go after internal and external enemies. But he failed to provoke a unanimous and continuous struggle against the British and the Jews. Other important family clans did not join. Undisturbed, the mufti continued to boast that he would "eject all Jews from Palestine as the prophet did in Arabia in the seventh century."

One morning in 1938, I noticed a plane with a swastika in Beirut's sky. Moments later aircraft from other countries appeared as well. The authorities were inaugurating the airport of Lebanon and Syria. The next day a rumor swept the city: Admiral Canaris of Germany had secretly met with Haj Amin al-Husseini in a private house near the capital.[4] After the declaration of war, it was no longer safe for the mufti to remain in the region. He eventually took refuge in Berlin. He returned in 1945, and despite the backing of Egypt and others, he was not able to impose himself as the spokesman for all Palestinians. Abdullah of Jordan (grandfather of King Hussein) annexed the Left Bank with the approval of local notables and fundamentalist clerics.

To come back to Badawi's sermon, the audience listened with attention but without apparent enthusiasm. Badawi was a staunch supporter of the mufti and shared his admiration for Hitler. After the sermon, he promised to remain in touch. Because he did not show up for some time, I returned to the mosque to look for him. I was told that he was traveling.

A SECULAR NATIONALIST

The June 1940 defeat of France was received by Arabs as a godsend, ending years of shameful domination by one of the Western infidels. Although the Vichy government cooperated with the Germans, Arabs looked with contempt at its military and civilian officials. Beirut's atmosphere remained tense because the city had become a nest of spies.

One afternoon, when I was leaving school, a rather elegant young man accosted me on the sidewalk. Badawi! At first, I failed to recognize him: He had shaven his beard and donned European clothes. He kept looking around as if he feared the presence of disguised enemies. We walked side by side toward my place. He said that for a couple of years he had been in Egypt and Palestine: "The Germans will soon liberate Egypt." He could not stay in Beirut because he had to carry out a very important secret mission. He lowered his voice: "Mine is a dangerous assignment. But our lives are in the hand of Allah! Come what may! I want your help: Keep this sealed envelope in a safe place. If something happens to me, a friend will contact you. Please give it to him without asking any questions. It is very important. . . . Your father saved my life in Damascus. I trust his son." He refused to reveal his destination: "The only thing I can tell is that I shall travel eastward. Watch the news. Important things are developing. Islam is going to win." He hugged me and disappeared down a lateral street. I never saw him again.

A couple of months later, a coup in Bagdad overthrew the pro-British regime. The king and the government fled, and a republic was proclaimed. The new ruler, Rashid Ali Gaylani, met Hitler in Berlin and obtained his backing. Orders were given by Vichy to the French in Syria and Lebanon to help him discreetly. The German ambassador in Tehran conveyed a message to Reza Shah urging him to provide assistance to Rashid Ali. But the overthrow of a king was not palatable to the Iranian monarch. I thought that Badawi had gone to Iraq to fight the British. This was a blatant example of tactical cooperation between nationalists and militant fundamentalists. Rashid Ali had called for a jihad against the British. Only a handful of young nationalists and fundamentalists from other Muslim countries went to Bagdad. The Iraqi revolutionaries failed to organize a mass mobilization even inside their own nation. It was probably because Rashid Ali's persona did not fit the requirements of the job. Rather short and rotund, he did not command instant respect. His aristocratic origins and his claimed links to the prophet's tribe were not enough to give him legitimacy, for the ousted king was a Hashemite descendant of Muhammad and of a family that had reigned over Mecca for centuries.

At any rate, Rashid Ali's adventure was short-lived. The British landed a whole division in southern Iraq in May 1941, and in no time the pro-Nazi regime collapsed. The monarchy was restored. Rashid Ali managed to escape through the desert. Lost and exhausted, he finally saw a cluster of tents in the endless sands. It was King Ibn Saud and his retinue. According to Arabian Desertlore , the founder of Saudi Arabia received him without asking his identity: "Drink and eat because you must be thirsty and hungry. You'll tell your story, if you desire so, later." Rashid Ali was sheltered for a short period in Riyadh. He then wended his way to Germany through Turkey. After Nasser's 1952 revolution in Egypt, he went to Cairo where the Egyptian dictator offered refuge to all the "revolutionaries" of the Arab world. After Iraq's 1958 revolution, he went to Bagdad only to discover that he was forgotten by most and considered *persona non grata* by some.

In June 1941 events such as the invasion of Russia and the British and "Free French" campaign against Vichy troops in Lebanon and Syria deflected my attention from Iraq and Ahmad Badawi. In early August the British and the Russians invaded Iran on the pretext that Reza Shah sheltered German agents. In fact, they wanted to control the Trans-Iranian Railway system, which was the only route for sending military supplies to the Red Army. Reza Shah abdicated in favor of his son, Muhammad Reza, and was sent into exile in South Africa. In late July Vichy forces surrendered, and a Gaullist high commissioner took charge of Beirut and Damascus. The whole Middle East was once again under the rule of the allies. Before the end of the year, the Japanese attack on Pearl Harbor brought the United States into the war. As a result, the balance of power changed in favor of the allies.

In March 1942, a middle-aged Muslim cleric called on me. He gave me a letter from Badawi and requested the sealed envelope. I had completely forgotten about it but found it where I had placed it (in my bookcase behind a row of hardcover books). The cleric told me: "Brother Ahmad was martyred in Iraq in the war against infidels." He opened the envelope, and his eyes glinted: It was full of British pounds!

In those days, militant fundamentalists were not admired by Arabs. My schoolmates mocked them as "backward" and preferred to join nationalist and leftist parties. Fundamentalists themselves often worked in nationalist groups. Compared to the present wave of militant fundamentalists, they were "amateurs" without real clout.

2

The Iranian Connection

Since the nineteenth century, Beirut had been an intellectual center in the Muslim world. By the late 1930s, its multiethnic, multireligious government and the relatively liberal French rule had transformed it into a haven for all sorts of refugees. Among them one could find many clerics or civilians of religious bent who had fled the forced modernization programs of Atatürk's Turkey and Reza Shah's Iran.

CLERGY VERSUS MODERNIZATION

Unlike Mustafa Kemal Atatürk, who was a highly educated officer, Reza Shah began his military career as an illiterate soldier who had to teach himself painstakingly how to read and write. Through perseverance, hard work, and daring action, he was able to reach the rank of colonel in the Russian-trained Cossack Brigade. During World War I, the British, Ottomans, and Russians occupied the country. When they withdrew in 1919, they left behind a country in the clutches of anarchy and a central government in bankruptcy. While gangs terrorized city dwellers, tribal chiefs and feudal landowners ruled almost independently in their domains. In the south, the British, who were exploiting Iran's oil resources, created their own militias. In the north, Moscow's new communist authorities were fomenting revolts.

Pro-British prime minister Seyed Zia-o-Din Tabatabai, descendant of a highly religious family, recruited "Colonel" Reza to help reestablish order, at least in the capital. Appointed war minister, Reza Khan soon understood that he was the real strong man of the regime. He discarded Seyed Zia and became prime minister in 1923. A domineering and blunt man, he persuaded the kajar shah to leave the country. He then ruled with an iron rod. Very quickly, high-ranking clerics, aristocratic bureaucrats, feudal rulers, tribal leaders, and bazaar merchants saw in him the badly needed strong man who could save them from the double menace of internal disorder and communist subversion. Reza favored a republic, but the religious establishment, frightened by Turkey's experience, preferred the old monarchic regime. In 1925 Reza became shah and founded the Pahlavi dynasty.

But to the dismay of his sponsors, he immediately undertook basic reforms similar to those of Atatürk. He arrested and eventually executed some tribal leaders and feudal landowners. Playing both ends against the center, he strove to neutralize all traditional power players. He wrested the judiciary from the hands of the clergy. He enshrined "nationalism" and "patriotism" as an alternative to religious and tribal loyalties. He imposed an unrelenting and severe system of repression.

Following in Atatürk's steps, he ordered all Iranians to wear European dresses and suits. He abolished women's veils. He prohibited the turban and replaced it first by a kind of kepi and later by Western headgear. Zealous law enforcers went so far as shaving clerics' beards. In the mid-1930s, returning from a pilgrimage to Mashad (a city northwest of Iran, where the tomb of Imam Reza, one of the twelve Shiite saints, is situated), the then young mullah Ruhollah Khomeini had to zigzag through the country and often travel by night in order to avoid the shah's "beard shavers."

Not only were his reforms erratic and chaotic, but Reza Shah also became greedy and bought large estates at artificially imposed low prices. He amassed a huge fortune for himself and his family. While trying to reduce the power of the British Oil Company (the Iranian name for the Anglo-Iranian Oil Company), he personally conducted the negotiations. After one of his numerous meetings with the monarch, the British company representative exclaimed: "There is no doubt that his majesty is after money."[1]

The religious leaders balked at the reforms they considered anti-Islamic. Some clerics organized demonstrations that were rapidly and forcefully quelled. A group of mullahs in Mashad together with some bazaar merchants took refuge in Imam Reza's shrine. An army squad broke one of the walls with heavy artillery and dislodged them. One of the merchants, named Alizadeh, managed to escape and reach Beirut.

A "CIVILIAN" FUNDAMENTALIST

He was the first Iranian fundamentalist I came to know. Our relationship started, as it were, at a monetary level. Currency transfers were strictly regulated, and mullahs and merchants performed many financial services. (As I shall explain later, the spawning of modern banks in the 1970s wrested from them a source of income and added to their discontent.) Our families in Tehran gave the amount to be sent to a bazaar merchant who asked his counterpart in Beirut to pay us. The whole operation was conducted for a fee, of course.

Some of the Iranian students were communists or free thinkers. Some approved of the shah's reforms. Notwithstanding his religious extremism and his hatred of Reza Shah, Alizadeh often invited all of us to lunch in his store. The liberal atmosphere of Beirut infected even the fundamentalist. Over the years, a kind of friendship developed between us. Alizadeh was devoted to one of the grand ayatollahs and regularly sent him a contribution (the *zakat* prescribed in the Koran). He remained typically religious, forbidding his wife and children to go to the movies. He refused vaccinations on the ground that rubbing alcohol on his skin and injecting "dead" microbes into his body were against God's commandments. He got seriously ill but survived, convinced that God saved him because he had refused vaccination. Like all Iranians, he disliked Arabs. The prophet? He had been anointed, and the rest of the Arabs learned civilization from Iran. Moreover, the Arabs should be hated because of their crime: They murdered the grandson of the prophet, Imam Hussein. In Alizadeh's views, "real" Islam was Shiism, not Sunnism. He nevertheless was ready to help the Sunni groups fight against Jewish immigration to Palestine. He sheltered members of the Muslim Brotherhood who were all Sunnis. He also supported Iranian secular nationalists who wanted to rid the country of foreign influence. He hated the British and the Russians as much as he hated Reza Shah.

Alizadeh admired Hitler, and when war broke out, he prayed for his victory. Indeed, for Iranians, the real enemies were the Russians who spread atheistic communist ideas and the British who sat on top of Iran's oil fields and interfered in their domestic affairs. At one of our luncheons in Alizadeh's Beirut store, I proposed to take a picture of him among his guests. He declined, explaining that he had eluded the shah's police after the Mashad shrine incident only because they did not have a photograph of him. He added: "Blessed be our great prophet who forbade the representation of the human face."

After the allied invasion of Iran, most of Reza Shah's reforms fell into abeyance, and turbaned clerics and veiled women reappeared in the streets of Iranian cities. Alizadeh and many others who had fled the country went back. Three years later, in 1944, having finished my studies, I returned to Iran. Through Alizadeh I met some activists who, in a way, were the fore-runners of Khomeini's movement.

War was still raging in Europe and in the Pacific. The departure of Reza Shah and the presence of three foreign armies (British, Russian, American) had softened the controls of the state over institutions and people. By 1944 a certain level of democracy existed in the capital and in some other large cities. Political parties and a more or less free press operated in Tehran. Nationalists and communists were represented in the parliament. For the first time in their long history, Iranians enjoyed a limited degree of individual freedoms, at least in the capital.

A COUNTRY STEEPED IN THE MIDDLE AGES

Outside Tehran, the whole country seemed bogged down in its remote past. Landowners ruled their estates as feudal masters had done in the Middle Ages. Peasants were treated as bondsmen (serfs) and trudged all year long in the fields and orchards. They were left in a state of semistarvation. Everywhere disease was rampant. All sorts of epidemics and maladies spread in villages and cities. Illiteracy was almost at 90 percent. Reza Shah's reforms could not change centuries of neglect in only fifteen years.

The clerics regained their traditional power and struck alliances with the landowners and the other wealthy classes of society. But they were not able to retrieve their ancient monopoly on justice and education. The presence of the Red Army gave a boost to the local communists, and the Americans were promoting democracy.

Because of the presence of foreign troops, a whole entertainment industry was thriving in Tehran. Cabarets, restaurants, bars, and dance halls had opened, and naturally numerous young Iranians joined with the foreigners. To the religious establishment, this was evil. Preachers in the mosques regularly denounced the moral "corruption" of Iranian society. Under these circumstances, a number of young religious activists created a militant fundamentalist association. It was called *Fedayin-e-Islam* (literally: "those who sacrifice their lives for the victory of Islam"). Alizadeh, whom I used to see from time to time in his bazaar store, spoke enthusiastically about the group.

A few months after my return to Tehran, during Ramadan (month of fasting), he invited me to his home to a "fast-breaking" dinner.[2] He had about thirty guests, most of them bearded young men. While we were din-ing, Alizadeh and his guests complained at length about the ill effects of the presence of so many infidel soldiers on our soil. "They corrupt morals," said a young man who had particularly stern features. "They endanger our sacred religion." Most of the guests accused Reza Shah of bringing about our predicament: Had he not built the Trans-Iranian Railway, which linked the Persian Gulf ports to the Soviet border and the Caspian Sea, the allies would not have occupied Iran. After the meal, the young man of stern features addressed us on the future of the country and Islam. He praised the nationalists who were demanding the departure of foreign armies. But that was deemed far from enough: The nation needed a complete housecleaning, from top to bottom; almost all politicians were corrupt and had sold out to their British and Russian "masters." (In those days, America, a newcomer in the region, had not yet been "satanized.") We were straying from the sharia, and that was extremely dangerous because God would punish us; the only way to save Iran and ourselves was to observe the sharia to the letter and establish an Islamic government in the country. Because the "traitors" were protected by their foreign masters, the best way to get rid of them was to kill them. He then mentioned the *Fedayin-e-Islam*, founded and presided over by a "real saint," an able and educated "brother" who had chosen as his "war name" Navab Safavi. The organization welcomed both active volunteers and donors. Among the "enemies of god" to be immediately eliminated, he mentioned a well-known writer and professor: Ahmad Kasravi, who, according to the young orator, was villifying both the clergy and Islam. Some high-ranking clerics had issued fatwas[3] condemning him to death. The Fedayin had accepted responsibility for carrying out the sentence. Kasravi would thus become the first agent of Satan to be slaughtered; many others would follow. As for the shah, if he renounced the anti-Islamic reforms of his father and obeyed the clergy, he could remain on the Peacock throne.

THE SLAYING OF AN INTELLECTUAL

Contrary to Khomeini in the 1970s, the Fedayin in the 1940s did not advocate the seizure of power. Their only concern was to erase secularist reforms and to restore "Islamic ways of life." More than they dreaded the politicians, they decried the secular intellectuals. The few democratic freedoms that the allies encouraged after Reza Shah's ouster disquieted Iranian clerics. The mushrooming of political parties and independent newspapers, they thought, would only reinforce secularism and fortify individual freedoms. As a result, intellectuals would gain credibility and arrest the grip of religion on the public. University professors, writers, and journalists had already begun to criticize the mullahs. With the suspension of all censorship, except allied military information, books and articles deriding the clerics were growing in number and circulation. It was therefore imperative to stop this dangerous trend and to discourage the development of Western-style democracy.

The Fedayin resorted to terrorism and other means of intimidation against the so-called intellectual modernizers. At the same time, they sought to cut off foreign influence. In that last domain, they considered the nationalists, who demanded the departure of allied forces and the nationalization of the British Oil Company, which constituted a "state in the state," to be "natural" partners.

One can find many instances of cooperation between militant fundamentalists and secular nationalists in recent Middle East history. The Muslim Brotherhood, for example, cooperated with Nasser and the Free Officers in the overthrow of Egypt's King Faruk. In the nationalization of Iran's oil industry in the 1950s, Prime Minister Mossadegh and the militant Ayatollah Kashani were close allies. In 1979, Khomeini chose as his first prime minister the "secular" Bazargan.

But the collaboration between fundamentalists and nationalists never lasted long. Their goals coincided only partially and always temporarily. Indeed, militant Islamic fundamentalists reject the concept of the nation-state, which they consider to be an export of the West. Their term of reference is the *umma* ("community of believers," as Muslims call the state headed by the prophet in Medina in the seventh century). For instance, Ahmad Badawi, like the vast majority of his fellow Arab Muslims, did not consider himself a Syrian, a Lebanese, or an Iraqi citizen. When asked about his nationality, he always answered: "Ana Muslim" (I am a Muslim).

Through Alizadeh I learned a lot about political Shiism and the Iranian militant fundamentalist movement. A few days after the fast-breaking dinner at his house, I asked him about the high-ranking clerics mentioned by the young militant who had issued fatwas condemning the writer Kasravi. He mentioned a few names that were unknown to me. Among them was Ruhollah Khomeini. "But these people are not high ranking," I protested. "Maybe, he retorted. But wait and see. They will shine over Iran!" He spoke of Khomeini's pamphlet titled *Kashfol Asrar* (literally: Discovery of the Secrets).[4] In one passage, the young mullah, who was to become the supreme leader of the Islamic Republic of Iran, declared Ahmad Kasravi *mahdur-o-dam* (literally: "blood worthless," meaning that his murder would not constitute a sin). In an Islamic "judicial" sentence, this was an invitation to assassination: an order to kill.[5] It was therefore the duty of any good Muslim to carry out the sentence. Why such a rage against Kasravi? He was a *seyed* (in Arabic, "mister"; in Shiism, "descendant of the prophet")[6] entitled, like Khomeini and many others, to wear a green belt (color of the House of Hashem, the prophet's clan) and a black turban (sign of mourning the assassination of Imam Hussein, grandson of the prophet), but he attacked Islam and favored secularization. Kasravi's crime was therefore graver than that of ordinary modernizers: He not only insulted the clergy but betrayed the prophet.[7]

Ahmad Kasravi was a perfect example of the "ultranationalist" Iranian intellectual who judged Islam to be a blow to Iranian civilization and the cause of its decay. He was born to a family of seyeds in Azerbaijan (northwestern province). His parents, devout Muslims, sent him to a religious seminary. But instead of becoming a mullah, he developed a deep aversion to Islamic tenets and to Islam itself, which he considered to be a religion of "nomadic and barbarous Arab tribes in a state of precivilization" imposed by force on Iranians. Having studied law at Tehran University and obtained a doctorate from the Sorbonne in Paris, he was an eminent writer who was determined to "cleanse" Iranian culture of all "Arabisms." (He avoided the use of words of Arab origin.) He criticized Sunnism as well as Shiism and accused the mullahs of building a good life for themselves at the expense of the illiterate masses. With his younger followers he launched a campaign of "de-Islamization." Advocating the total secularization of Iran, his lectures and writings were tantamount to what can be called nonreligious fundamentalism; on the political spectrum, he occupied a slot opposite to that of the militant clergy. He was eventually stabbed to death in the Justice Department, where he had been summoned to answer the accusation of insulting Islam, a punishable crime according to Iran's code. His murderer, a member of the Fedayin, was bailed out because of pressure exerted by the clergy. As one can see, Salman Rushdie's case has precedents.

My encounter in Tehran with members of the Fedayin reminded me of Badawi and the Muslim Brotherhood.

3

The Community of Devoted Fighters

In Beirut it was often difficult to distinguish fundamentalist militants from others, for all Muslim groups proclaimed the necessity of safeguarding Islamic ways of life. Moreover, they, together with Christians, fought for independence. In Egypt, where attempts at secularization and modernization went back to the early nineteenth century and a powerful political party incorporated the "nationalists" (Wafd), things were somehow different. The Muslim Brotherhood emerged in Ismailia, a town on the Suez Canal and Lake Timsah, which owed its prosperity to the British dominated canal company. A schoolteacher named Hassan al-Banna was appalled by the Western "corruption" that swept the city: Bars, brothels, and nightclubs were springing up; young Egyptians shaved their beards; women abandoned their veils and mixed with men and infidels. To Hassan, this was Sodom and Gomorrah combined.[1] Moreover, the secularist Wafd party was gaining a solid foothold in Ismailia. To Hassan al-Banna, the success of such a nationalist group represented no progress at all: If, as a result, infidels left the country, their culture would remain in the form of democratic institutions that would continue to pervert the community of believers.

NIGHT VISITORS

Born to a modest family in Muhammadia, a small town northwest of Cairo, Hassan al-Banna was exposed to fundamentalism in early childhood. His father studied at the celebrated Islamic University al-Azhar under the nineteenth-century reformer Muhammad Abdoh, a disciple of the famous Jamal ud-Din al-Afghani.[2] He was a part-time Islamic judge and ran a watch repair shop to make ends meet. He sent Hassan to a Koranic school and taught him, in addition, what he had learned from Abdoh and al-Afghani. Hassan soon became an expert in religious law. Even as an adolescent, he participated in meetings of secret religious organizations that fought against the presence of foreigners. He led his classmates in the 1919 riots that shook Egypt and eventually forced the British to recognize nominally the country's independence. At that time he joined a Sufi mystic group. But meditation and withdrawal from the world were not his cup of tea. A man of action, Hassan decided to become a teacher and so guide younger generations. He wrote a pamphlet castigating the invasion of foreign culture and calling for a return to the spiritual and political principles of the prophet and the first four caliphs.

By the late 1920s, Hassan's writings had already struck a chord with many young Muslims who were dismayed by British dominance and growing foreign influence. According to his own account,[3] one evening in March 1928, six unknown young men knocked on his door and bowed to him, saying, "You are our master and our guide." They urged him to lead them in the fight against enemies of Allah. After hours of discussions, Hassan told them, "We are all brothers in the services of Islam. We are therefore the Muslim Brotherhood." Thus the fundamentalist organization came into being. The seven conspirators were sure of following the "Right Path." Just a few years earlier, Ibn Saud conquered Mecca and Medina and established a kingdom based on "Wahhabism" (named after Ibn-Abdal Wahhab, an eighteenth-century theologian), proving beyond a shadow of a doubt that nothing could resist the combination of the holy book and the sword. The six visitors and their leader, whom they endowed with the title of sheikh, constituted the first link of a chain that grew rapidly through the Muslim world.

The fierce opposition of the Brotherhood to the powerful nationalist Wafd party caught the Suez Canal Company's attention. Under fire from this nationalist-secularist group, the company generously funded Sheikh Hassan who accepted the gifts, telling his disciples, "The holy end justifies the means." In Cairo, the royal court, for similar reasons, helped the Brotherhood's agents. By the mid-1930s, the organization possessed a solid network of press organizations and active branches in many cities. Its actions, which initially focused on combating Muslim secularists and Christian missionaries, rapidly expanded against Jewish immigration to Palestine. Young activists in other Arab countries entered into relations with al-Banna and founded branches in Syria, Lebanon, Iraq, and elsewhere. Badawi's group in Beirut was a case in point.

Apart from articulating the basic principle that sovereignty is God's, al-Banna remained vague about the specifics of a genuine Islamic government. Like other fundamentalists, he insisted on the strict enforcement of the sharia. He did not hide his admiration for Mussolini and Hitler and envisioned himself as an Islamic "just despot."[4] Impressed by the fascists' paramilitary youth groups, he created his own "battalions" (*Kataeb* in Arabic, meaning "phalanxes"). In 1938 he was proclaimed the "Supreme Guide." At this point, al-Banna called for a jihad against the "heathen, the apostates, the deviants," and all other "enemies of Allah," including all infidels. Islam's banner, he declared, should cover the whole world.

CLASH WITH COLONEL NASSER

By the start of World War II, the Brotherhood had become one of Egypt's largest and more structured political movements. It had more than 100,000 active members completely devoted to its aims and to the person of the Supreme Guide. Elated by his rapid success, al-Banna nurtured the dream of a state with the Koran as its "constitution," the sharia as its law, and himself as the absolute ruler.

Many figures on the postwar political stage such as Gamal Abdal Nasser and Anwar Sadat were at one time or another members or fellow travelers of the Brotherhood. Like the vast majority of Muslims, the organization's members prayed for Hitler's victory over the allies. When Rommel's Afrika Korps hurtled toward Egypt's border, they exulted: The end of the "anti-Islamic secular government" was at hand. Slogans covered the walls: Rommel Forward! A popular uprising seemed imminent. But the Germans' rapid advance was short-lived, and the Brotherhood's military arm did not manifest itself.

After the war, al-Banna unleashed a campaign of terror that soon became a model for other militant fundamentalist movements that were rapidly developing in the Muslim world. Cinemas were bombed, hotels set on fire, unveiled women attacked, and homes raided. Prime ministers and other pro-Western high-ranking officials were assassinated. Al-Banna was emulating his historical namesake, the Hassan, who in the last decades of the eleventh century launched his *hashashins* (assassins) against politicians and intellectuals accused of straying from "true" Islam.[5]

Young aspiring terrorists from all over the world poured into Egypt in order to learn from al-Banna's men the art of eliminating the enemies of Islam. While training terrorists and directing murders, Sheikh Hassan denied involvement in the assassinations and attacks, using what Shiite clerics call *ketman* (holy dissimulation). Indeed, deceiving infidels was admitted by all Muslims, and Shiites even extended the dissimulation to other Muslims when the security of their "cause" was at stake. But the government and the police were far from gullible. In December 1948 the Brotherhood was formally banned, and scores of its adherents were arrested, condemned, and executed. On February 12, 1949, al-Banna himself was gunned down in a Cairo street, probably by the secret police. Even those members who had volunteered to fight Israelis alongside Arab armies did not escape vexatious treatment.[6]

The organization was badly shattered after al-Banna's death. But after a relatively short period, the authorities allowed it to reemerge because they saw in it a bulwark against both the nationalists and the communists. It seems that King Farouk was instrumental in this decision as well as in the choice of Sheikh Hassan al-Hodeibi, a cleric close to the court, as the new Supreme Guide. But the militants, suspicious of the latter's so-called moderation, rallied around the more radical Saleh-al-Ashmawy who advocated "perpetual jihad." Left to themselves, the chapters in neighboring countries managed to survive and even to shelter Egyptian brothers who had fled Cairo in 1949.

Although the Brotherhood was represented among the Free Officers who overthrew the monarchy in 1952 and had contributed to destabilizing the regime, tensions arose between it and the military as early as 1953. The latter accused the organization of having links to Israel and committing conspiracy against the state. Using the pretext of an attempt on his life, Nasser outlawed the Brotherhood in 1954 and dismantled its offices and structures. Thousands of members, including Sheikh Hassan Hodeibi, the nominal Supreme Guide, were arrested. Some of the leaders were subsequently sentenced to death and hanged, forcing the Brotherhood to go underground. Splinters remained active outside Egypt, in the neighboring countries as well as in Europe. But as often happens, severe repression resulted in unintended and adverse effects. Radical elements rapidly dominated the secret organization, and Sheikh Hassan Hodeibi, in prison, had to approve the rise of a noted hard-liner to the leadership of the underground movement: Seyed Muhammad Qutb.

KHOMEINI'S PRECURSOR

The new guide was a lanky and handsome man in his late forties who had received both a religious and a modern education and occupied a post at the Ministry of Education. In 1948 he was sent to the United States to study the American educational system. He traveled extensively and was terribly shocked by what he saw: sexual permissiveness, equality of men and women, complete separation of state and church, total freedom of expression, criticism of religion, indulgence in worldly pleasures, and other things. He was appalled by the "licentiousness" that reigned everywhere. To him, the United States was steeped in paganism. He wrote his travel impressions in a booklet in which he vehemently denounced what he called Western and especially American decadence, which reminded him of the fall of Rome. In his view, Western decadence started with the Renaissance, intensified during the Enlightenment, and reached its peak with such "pseudoscientists" as Darwin and Freud because the former contended that humans descended from apes and the latter that sexuality was the essence of Adam's children. Jews, of course, were behind all this. The West was sheer damnation. In short, forty years before Khomeini, Qutb presented the United States as the Great Satan.

Upon his return in 1951, Qutb retired from the Ministry of Education and dedicated himself, as the most efficient publicist of the Muslim Brotherhood, to the "cause of Islam." His speeches and sermons drew droves of young, angry people who joined the ranks of militant Islamic fundamentalists. Qutb's views were extreme: Islam had to remain "pure" and be applied as a "total" system. It could not accept compromises with other religions whose followers should "convert." Indeed, as the last and final message of Allah, Islam had to replace Judaism and Christianity; Muslims had to conquer the whole planet. Each Muslim, man or woman, should undertake his own "personal" jihad in order to improve his Islamic qualities. All believers should assume their individual duties and accomplish the "will" of God in their daily lives.

While in prison, Qutb wrote a book, *Signposts on the Road*, in which he denounced Arab leaders such as Egypt's Nasser as nonbelievers and their governments as anti-Islamic. He called on Muslims to overthrow them. This was tantamount to a declaration of war against Nasser who, in turn, did not hesitate to respond in kind. A new wave of repression against the Brotherhood started in 1965. Thousands of militants, including Qutb himself, were arrested and tortured. In court, Qutb showed the marks of mistreatment on his body. He was hanged in prison with several of his associates.

Despite the severity of repression, the Brotherhood survived, and its followers began to call themselves the community of devoted fighters. Today, officially, the organization's leadership rejects Qutb's most extremist views. Nevertheless, members and fellow travelers continue to develop them in their writings, lectures, and sermons. Qutb is still honored as a martyr, and his books and pamphlets have been reprinted and widely distributed.

Some observers consider that Qutb strayed from traditional Islamic doctrine and even from the initial Brotherhood's philosophy, as developed by Hassan al-Banna in his manifestos. The discussions concerning Qutb and al-Banna remind one of Western policymakers' musings about the existence of possible moderates among the militant fundamentalists, obviously, an oxymoronic dream. Qutb's language might sound extremist; but in fact, he did nothing more than articulate ideas that had been aired since the early stages of Islam's expansion.

4

The Beads and the Bullets

To come back to Iran and the Fedayin-e-Islam, I learned from a friend, whose father was a high-ranking official of the police, that contacts were established between Iranian clerics and the Muslim Brotherhood's section in Iraq, despite the Shiite-Sunni rift. But who was the mysterious leader who called himself Navab Safavi?

THE "UNCLE SYNDROME"

Navab was born either in Tehran or Saveh (central Iran) around 1924. His father, Seyed Javad Mirlohi, a devout Muslim opposed to the shah's reforms, died in 1938. Navab was brought up by his uncle. This, in my opinion, is a very important biographical detail. Indeed, many Muslim leaders, religious as well as secular, have spent all or part of their childhood and adolescence in the care of an uncle (or aunt). Egypt's Nasser, for instance, lived with his uncle in Cairo; Iraq's Saddam Hussein was sent to his uncle in Bagdad. Khomeini's case is even more impressive: Orphaned shortly after his birth, he was left in the care of his aunt and her husband.[1] Very often militant biographers have invented such an uncle-nephew relationship for their leaders.

Why is it significant for Muslim "great men" to have been orphaned or at least separated from their biological parents? What makes the uncle so important? The key to the riddle lies in the prophet's family story. Indeed, Muhammad was orphaned in his infancy and brought up by his uncle. And in the Muslim world, the prophet is offered as a supreme saintly model. Since childhood, every believer has learned the details of the prophet's life. As a result, the notions of "orphan" and "uncle's custody" conjure up the memory of the prophet and provoke immediate sympathy and affection. Moreover, in the Middle East, any coincidence or parallel with legendary or real heroes is considered a heavenly sign and interpreted as a good omen.

It often happens that some kids, more sensitive and impressionable than others, who are living with their uncles come to believe that they are predestined to accomplish great deeds. Khomeini is almost a perfect example of this syndrome: His father was killed in a brawl when the son was six months old. In the superstitious environment of the small town of Khomein, he was considered "ill-omened," having "caused" his father's death (concomitance equated with causality). His mother, who was only twenty-four years old, remarried after giving the infant to her sister. It is most probable that the future ayatollah, aware of his embarrassing start in life, overcompensated for his situation as an unloved orphan by highlighting his early experience as "resembling" the prophet's beginnings. At any rate, very early in his youth, a sense of mission emerged in him.[2] Consciously or not, he gradually identified with the "Hidden Imam."[3] The symptoms of the uncle syndrome accompanied him during his whole life.

I have coined the phrase "uncle syndrome" to explain, at least partially, the mechanism of the rise of charismatic militant fundamentalist leaders and the deep devotion of their followers.

Navab Safavi was also a casualty (or a victim) of the syndrome. In his mid-twenties he seriously thought that he was endowed with the mission to restore Islam's total rule in Iran. After a few years at Tehran's German Technical School, he served a stint at the Anglo-Iranian Oil Company in Abadan. He then followed his family to Najaf, a Shiite holy "oasis-city" in the Iraqi desert, where Reza Shah's interdiction of turbans and women's veils did not apply. Navab immediately donned the seyeds' green belt and black turban. He began religious studies but soon abandoned them to concentrate on "action."

According to some of his biographers, in the late 1930s Navab traveled to Cairo where he met with Hassan al-Banna, the supreme guide of the Muslim Brotherhood. It is said that he proposed the mass conversion of al-

Banna's followers to Shiism. Navab returned to Najaf, convinced that Islam needed a group of devoted fighters prepared to kill and be killed. One of his biographers attributes to him the following advice: "Throw away your worry beads [chaplets] and buy a gun, for worry beads keep you silent, while guns silence the enemies of Allah."[4]

Like al-Banna and others, Navab often referred to the following Koranic verse: "The unbelievers follow falsehood while the believers follow the Truth. Thus Allah coineth their similitudes for mankind. Now when you meet the unbelievers, then strike off their heads and when you have routed them, bind them firmly" (Surat XLVII, verses 3 and 4). But unlike al-Banna, Navab did not favor bombing public places where innocent people, together with the unbelievers, might be hurt. He pinpointed the most obvious "enemies of God," those who are *mahdur-o-dam* (those whose blood is worthless and must be shed). Moreover, contrary to the Muslim Brotherhood, Navab preferred small groups of dedicated and determined people. He opened a "school" for training terrorists. High-ranking clerics passing through Najaf visited him. Khomeini, a young mullah, is said to have been impressed by his activism and dedication.

At the start of World War II, Navab tried to organize a campaign to assassinate British officers in Iraq. Having failed, he contacted Ayatollah Abdul Qassem Kashani who advocated the seizure of power by the clergy. An oral agreement was concluded between them. Navab, as a very young activist, needed the sponsorship of a recognized cleric. Kashani, for his part, welcomed the addition of an armed unit to his political movement. Developments caused by war gave both the opportunity to act inside Iran.[5]

IRAN IN THE LATE 1940s

The military occupation of the country triggered two trends in its social fabric. On the one hand, most of Reza Shah's modernizing reforms were stopped. On the other, traditional political forces, including clergy and bazaar merchants, reemerged. The presence of the allies, especially of the Americans, encouraged the display of limited democracy, at least in the capital. The young Muhammad Reza Pahlavi, lacking the decisiveness of his father, was no match for the clerics and the older generation of politicians. For the first time since the constitutional revolution of 1906, free elections took place. In the countryside, clerics and feudal landowners naturally triumphed. But in the large cities, nationalists (grouped behind Dr. Mossadegh, who advocated the nationalization of the oil industry) and communists (members of the Tudeh party) obtained a respectable number of seats in the parliament. The militant fundamentalists (under the thumb of Ayatollah Kashani) and even fascists (in the guise of "pan-Iranism") were also represented.

Egregious poverty, if not famine, gripped the lower strata of the population. Landowners almost starved their peasants in order to sell at huge profits most of the agricultural output to foreign troops. Graft and corruption had become a way of life. Malady was rampant, and the economy was in shambles. Secessionist drives menaced several provinces (Azerbaijan, Kurdistan, Baluchistan, and others). The only thing that kept Iranians alive and united was their immense hatred of foreigners in general and the British in particular. Since the last decades of the nineteenth century, the British were considered, at every level of Iranian society, the devil incarnate, agents of Ahriman (the devil in Zoroastrianism and ancient Iranian mythology).[6] In the eyes of the masses, they used supernatural devices to afflict and distress Iranians. Even droughts and locust plagues were attributed to their evil designs. They played the star role in Iranian conspiracy fantasies (with Khomeini in the 1980s, the part was assigned to the Americans). To explain such an exaggerated reaction on the part of Iranians, it must be said that the British Oil Company cynically interfered in Iranian politics, bribed politicians and tribal chiefs, and unashamedly exploited the riches of the country. (Between 1945 and 1950, for instance, the company registered more than 250 million pounds of profit, paying Iran less than 90 million.)

In the meantime, the murder of the writer Kasravi brought instant notoriety to the Fedayin-e-Islam. The actual killer was arrested, tried, and condemned to death but was later pardoned under pressure from the clergy. This impunity encouraged the Fedayin to proceed with their murderous programs. Navab drew up a blacklist. One of his hirelings even shot at the shah, but missed him. The authorities took advantage of the incident to crack down on both the Fedayin and the communists. Ayatollah Kashani was exiled once again.

Until the 1950s, the British, who were worried by the expansion of the pro-Soviet Tudeh party, helped the religious fundamentalists. But by 1950 Ayatollah Kashani and other fundamentalist militants struck an alliance with Dr. Muhammad Mossadegh's National Front. The nationalization of the Anglo-Iranian Oil Company (AIOC) constituted the central piece of Mossadegh's program. That year, in Tehran's elections, the National Front managed to win a number of seats, despite electoral fraud. Among the fundamentalists, Kashani was also elected and therefore was able to return from exile. Manipulated by him, the Fedayin, now a tightly knit clandestine organization, assassinated the pro-British prime minister, General Razmara, thus opening the way for a government presided over by Dr. Mossadegh. In the parliament, taking advantage of the confusion created by the Fedayin and the Tudeh party (which also had a few representatives), Kashani introduced a bill that quashed the death sentence issued against Razmara's murderer.

A FRAGILE ALLIANCE WITH FUNDAMENTALISTS

As for Mossadegh, nicknamed "Old Mossy" by the Americans, his first act was to propose the nationalization of Iran's oil industry. A skinny, bald man with sly eyes, he was an aristocrat from the former Kajar dynasty and was one of the richest feudal landowners. Yet he donned the mantle of a reformer and a progressive politician. He received a doctorate in law from Paris and Geneva universities and was active, as a young intellectual, in the 1906 constitutional revolution. In the 1920s he helped bring about the rise of Reza Shah and held a number of ministerial posts, but he was cast aside because of his opposition to the new monarch's moves toward dictatorship. Mossadegh attributed his misfortune to the British and brooded about their role during the quarter century that he was confined to private life. As a result, his anti-British feelings turned into an obsession. After Reza Shah's forced abdication, Old Mossy reappeared on the political stage, surrounded by the aura of his long, "silent" opposition to the monarch. His personal style of mixing theatrics and politics (he received Iranians as well as foreigners in pajamas in his bedroom) gained him instant celebrity throughout the world. He outwitted everybody: leftists, fundamentalists, foreign diplomats, and members of his cabinet. But because of his rhetoric and his difficult alliance with Ayatollah Kashani and other fundamentalists, he was caught in a vise and was unable to reach a compromise on major issues.

Neither Mossadegh nor Kashani took any step toward enforcing the sharia. Navab Safavi and his friends grew impatient. They expected that the former, as prime minister, and the latter, as speaker of the parliament, would fulfill their promises. Instead, they dragged their feet, arguing that first they had to solve the "oil problem." Indeed, the government needed the backing of all political groups in order to implement the nationalization of the oil industry. The secular elements in the parliament opposed any "Islamization" of the civil laws, and the militant fundamentalists became more and more vocal. By mid-1951, the "unwritten" trilateral alliance among Kashani, Mossadegh, and the Fedayin withered away. With Kashani's approval, the police cracked down on the militants. Navab managed to escape and hide in Tehran, but he was finally arrested en route to a secret meeting even though he was disguised as a veiled woman. A rift broke out inside the fundamentalist organization between the members who supported Kashani and Mossadegh and those who opposed them.[7]

At the same time, Mossadegh tried shrewdly to exploit the differences between the British and the Americans. All in all, the Truman administration was not unsympathetic to the Iranian's plight. The President himself considered the AIOC officials as "typical nineteenth-century colonial exploiters."[8] The Americans understood that the prime minister was constrained by the need to contain those who were more nationalist, more fundamentalist, and more anti-British than he.

A YANKEE VISITS AN AYATOLLAH

As the oil crisis lingered and tension grew in the Persian Gulf, the United States decided to play the part of an "honest broker." President Truman sent Averell Harriman to Tehran. For days, former President Roosevelt's special envoy discussed the situation with the bedridden Old Mossy. It seemed to him that the pajama-clad prime minister feared particularly the Muslim fundamentalists who opposed any arrangement with the West. Harriman therefore decided to call on Ayatollah Kashani, the fundamentalist speaker of the parliament.

Like Old Mossy, the ayatollah began the discussion by explaining that the British were the "most evil people" on Earth. Then he proceeded to tell the fictitious story of an American wildcatter involved in the oil business who had been shot in a Tehran street and then butchered on an operating table in a hospital. Harriman dismissed the "disguised" threat conveyed by the cleric, "I do not frighten easily." The mullah responded laughingly, "There was no harm in trying." Kashani accused Mossadegh of harboring pro-British feelings: "He will be killed if he yields to their demands." Obviously, the ayatollah was opposed to any deal. On the other hand, Mossadegh did in no way seek better financial terms. He wanted to put an end to the British company's presence in Iran. He expected the backing of Truman, but that was not possible, for the Americans could not help oust an ally.

Harriman understood all this too well. He attributed Kashani's attitude to his hatred of all foreigners, especially the British. But one point escaped him: Iranians in general and Mossadegh and Kashani in particular did not trust him. At that time, their mistrust did not extend to all U.S. officials, as it did later with the Eisenhower administration. It had to do with the person of Harriman or, rather, with his name. *Harriman*, in Farsi, sounded like

Ahriman, the devil of the Iranian multimillenary ethos. The West had sent Satan to them!

Be that as it may, Harriman's mission failed. In 1952 Churchill and the Tories returned to Downing Street, and Eisenhower and the Republicans entered the White House. Soon a rift developed between Mossadegh and Kashani. The latter, while still officially backing the prime minister's nationalization policy, conducted secret meetings with the shah and other opponents. Old Mossy was aware of Kashani's double game. By the end of 1952, they openly split. The parliament was dissolved and pending new elections, Mossadegh concentrated all powers in his own hands. Kashani, behind the curtain, conducted a policy favorable to the shah and to those who tried to forge a compromise concerning the oil "impasse." Curiously enough, Navab Safavi, who had been released from prison, met with the ayatollah, in spite of their previous wranglings. By now, modernizers, nationalists, and some liberals were dominant in Mossadegh's entourage. The Tudeh party was infiltrating the bureaucracy and the army. Americans were worried about a possible communist coup.

In August 1953, a CIA-engineered coup ousted Mossadegh and replaced him with a government favorable to the shah and supportive of a compromise on the oil question. Navab, who had criticized Mossadegh during the last two years of his government, enjoyed freedom of action. He was authorized to travel to Jerusalem (then part of the Hashemite Kingdom of Jordan) in order to participate in the Conference on the Future of Palestine. He also went to Cairo where he met the new leadership of the Muslim Brotherhood, including the radical seyed Qutb.

On his return, he tried to reactivate the Fedayin-e-Islam and resume political assassinations. Once again his relations with the authorities deteriorated. In 1955, he was implicated in a scheme to kill the shah. He was arrested with several other high-ranking members of his organization, tried, condemned to death, and executed. The organization faded away. From time to time some of its former members committed terrorist acts on their own or on behalf of some religious authority. Thus in 1965, one of them shot to death Prime Minister Hassan Ali Mansour on Khomeini's suggestion.

A LOOSE ORGANIZATION

Compared to the Muslim Brotherhood's elaborate pyramidal structure that contained a separate military arm, the Fedayin's organization seemed rather amateurish. It consisted of a limited number of horizontally connected cells. Navab, though a devoted Muslim, did not possess a deep religious education and therefore could not play the part of an *imam* (supreme guide). That is why he always tried to find a sponsor among the upper crust of the clergy.

New members were tested by older ones who first indoctrinated them and assigned them some elementary tasks such as admonishing transgressors of Islamic law and designating for boycott shops belonging to non-Muslims. Moreover, as already indicated, Navab preferred to keep the organization as small as possible so that he could control it. If, after several months, a new member seemed ready to sacrifice his own life for the cause, he would be instructed to kill targeted officials. In the meantime, all members had to attend many religious ceremonies and project the public image of a true and exemplary Muslim. They also had to participate in charitable activities, helping, for instance, vulnerable members of society.

Navab did not believe in the usefulness of proselytism. Instead, he advised his colleagues and followers to "work" with Muslims who "did not know how to live as good Muslims."[9] A group of his friends who believed in the necessity of converting non-Muslims separated from his organization after the 1953 coup against Mossadegh's government and formed the Hojatieh Society, which today devotes most of its energy to converting Bahais.[10]

5

Some Precursors

As one can infer from the foregoing narrative, militant Islamic fundamentalism is not new. It existed and operated in the early decades of the twentieth century as well as in the 1950s and 1960s, before Ayatollah Khomeini put it back in the news in the 1980s. Scholars trace its roots even further in the past. They have related, for instance, President Sadat's murder to the killings of three of the first four caliphs in the seventh century. They also have equated the Muslim Brotherhood and the Fedayin-e-Islam with the so-called hashashins (assassins) of the eleventh century. When he visited the Sudan recently, a journalist noted many similarities with the Mahdya movement of the nineteenth century.[1] In fact, Islam's history bears witness to many fundamentalist sects that conducted terrorist activities and sometimes founded their own theocracies.

MUSLIM SECTS

According to a *hadith* (saying of the prophet), Muhammad once stated, "The Israelites were divided into 71 or 72 sects. The Christians also. My community shall be divided into 73."[2]

The two largest sects are the Sunnites and the Shiites, representing respectively about 80 percent and 20 percent of all Muslims. They both consider Muhammad the "last" prophet and the Koran God's "last message." Therefore, both consider that Islam supersedes all other revealed religions. Consequently, humanity should convert to Islam or at least live under Muslim rule.

In the view of Sunnites, nobody stands between the Koran and the faithful. But the Shiites affirm that under Allah's orders, Muhammad entrusted his son-in-law, Ali, the fourth caliph, and his direct descendants with the "hidden" meanings of the Koran that were to be revealed gradually to believers. Thus Ali and his descendants are the guides (*imams*) who, unlike the Sunni caliphs, inherited not only Muhammad's temporal powers but also the prerogative of interpreting the Koran in depth.

The twelfth imam disappeared in his early childhood and entered into "occultation." As announced in one of the prophet's hadiths, he will return in due time as the mahdi (messianic leader) to restore "true" Islam and impose it on the entire planet before the "end of the world." Therefore, the Shiites consider that they have been entrusted with "the Truth." Conversely, they are regarded as heresiarchs by the Sunnites. Only recently has a kind of modus vivendi been established between the two sects.

In Iran, "twelver" Shiism, acknowledging twelve imams, became the official religion in 1502 under the Safavid dynasty. Shiism proved a fertile crucible for a host of fundamentalist groups and sects. Thus the Ismailis (led in present days by the Agha Khan who resides in Europe) acknowledge only seven imams and are therefore called "seveners." In the ninth century, they set up an elaborate secret organization, including a political-religious body and an activist arm. They sent disguised missionaries everywhere to enlist and initiate devoted followers into the secrets of their sect. They eventually succeeded in founding the Fatimid caliphate in Tunisia and Egypt in the tenth century (which was overthrown by Saladin in the twelfth century).

The essence of the Ismailiya doctrine, called Batini (inner, esoteric) by mainstream ulemas, is that the "Truth" is hidden in the outer form of the Koran verses and should be revealed to the uninitiated by those who know under an oath of secrecy. Before the end of the ninth century, one of the converts, an Iraqi peasant named Qarmat, founded a Batini sect of his own and recruited followers from the poorest classes of society. His successors established their own Qarmatic state—based on a communistic system—on the western shore of the Persian Gulf; conquered Oman; and pushed as far as Mecca, where they carried off the sacred black stone. Theirs was a strict and repressive regime that eventually fell in the early decades of the tenth century. But the secret Batini doctrine survived in the Fatimid dynasty and the sects that developed later such as the Druze (whose followers, dispersed in Syria, Lebanon, and Israel, fought fiercely against the Christian Maronites in the nineteenth and early twentieth centuries). The group called Nussayris is another offshoot of the Batinis. Its members consider Ali, the son-in-law of the prophet, the incarnation of deity. Because of that belief they are also called Alawites. Their descendants live as a minority in northern Syria. Like the Druze, they clothe their doctrine in a veil of secrecy. Syria's President Assad is a member of that community.[3]

The most famous Ismailiya offshoot is the sect of The New Convocation, which came to be known by the name Assassins. I shall describe it a little more extensively because many specialists consider it the model of modern militant fundamentalist groups that practice terrorism as a means of overthrowing governments in order to replace them with theocratic regimes. This, as I will show, is a mistake.

THE ASSASSINS

The founder of this organization, Hassan Sabbah, was born in the holy city of Qum (Iran) to a Shiite family. He studied in Koranic schools and seminars in Ray (the Raghes of the Bible) and Neyshapur (Iran), where he met and befriended the poet Omar Khayyam and the future grand vizir of Malakshah, the Seljuk sultan Nizam-ul-Mulk. (Later he opposed the latter and had him murdered by one of his "assassins.") After a near fatal illness, he chose the Ismailiya branch of Shiism and followed an initiation course. He was then sent as a *Da'i* (propagandist) to Egypt where the Ismailiya Fatimids reigned (in the year 1078). He did not agree with them and prudently fled the country by sea. Caught in a tempest, he was saved by a merchant boat en route to Syria. He returned to Iran where he exercised his propaganda skills in the north. At the same time, he developed his own doctrine called the New Convocation. Hassan Sabbah chose the region of Dailam, a section of the Elburz Mountains harboring powerful fortresses surrounded by orchards and pine forests. One of them, Alamut, near the village of Rudbar, drew his attention. His erudition and charisma impressed the villagers who converted and helped him occupy the fortress and expel the Seljuk governor. He sent the governor back to Bagdad with a defiant message to the sultan. His followers occupied other westward fortresses, including Jabal Bahra in Syria. These bases served as springboards for sending messages to members living in enemy territory and for dispatching assassins.

Like all fundamentalists, Hassan Sabbah continuously reaffirmed his goal of rebuilding the world according to "Allah's will and commands." His was a secretive politico-religious credo that professed the necessity of seizing power and ruling with an iron rod. He kept his final aims to himself, often citing a hadith according to which the prophet had said, "He who keeps secrets shall soon attain his objectives." His followers also kept secret their affiliations with the sect, which was not difficult, for all Shiites living in a Sunnite environment hostile to them applied the principle of "dissimulation" (*taqiyah* or *ketman*), dispensing them from the requirements of religion when facing danger.[4]

Hassan Sabbah, who presented himself to the people as one directly guided by God, bore the title of grand master. Under him stood deputies in charge of different districts: propagandists and *Fedayin* (literally: those prepared to sacrifice their lives and to kill for Allah; it was from the time of Sabbah that the term *Fedai*, the singular of *Fedayin*, became a permanent word in the vocabulary of militant Islamic groups).

The Fedayin were subjected to long periods of training that included doctrinal initiation and "glimpses of paradise" (through the use of narcotics, especially hashish that grew in that part of Iran and whose properties were known to Sabbah; thus the Fedayin were surnamed *hashashins* (literally: users of hashish). Western travelers transcribed it "assassin," which became a synonym for murderer in European languages.

THE GATES OF PARADISE

The paradise of the assassins was composed of beautiful gardens that Marco Polo, who traveled in the vicinity in 1271 (long after the death of the grand master), described in these terms:

> He [the grand master] would introduce them [the Fedayin] in his garden, some four or six or ten at a time, having first made them drink a certain potion which cast them into a deep sleep and then caused them to be lifted and carried in. So when they awoke and found themselves in the garden, they deemed that it was paradise in very truth. And the ladies and damsels dallied with them to their heart's content. . . . So when the old man[5] would have any prince slain, he would say to such a youth: "Go thou and slay so and so; and when thou returnest my Angels shall bear thee into paradise. And shouldst thou die, natheless even so will I send my angels to carry thee back into paradise."[6]

Nizam-ul-Mulk's skill in using propaganda against the enemies of the state enabled the Seljuk dynasty to contain the danger represented by Hassan Sabbah. In his book *Siassat Nameh* (The Art of Politics), often compared to Machiavelli's *The Prince*, the grand vizir noted:

> The example of austerity is far more effective than that of corruption. The heretic [i.e., Hassan Sabbah] knows all too well where he is heading. His long experience, his deep knowledge of men, and his profound study of politics and history have taught him that impiety and corruption might, at times, bring about the fall of a dynasty but could never serve as a basis for founding a new one. He knows that he must make himself respected and that the mass [of the people] cannot be controlled without order. He also knows that religion and ethics are the only [effective means] of guaranteeing the obedience of the people.[7]

As one can see, Nizam-ul-Mulk knew well the psychology of his fellow Muslims. Although Sabbah attacked only high officials, the grand vizir succeeded in provoking awe among the people and having all orthodox mullahs declare Hassan Sabbah to be an "enemy of God" and an infidel hiding behind an Islamic facade. (He was eventually killed by a Fedai.) The sultan sent troops, but the soldiers failed in their assault against the fortress of Alamut. Years later, the Mongols, in their drive across the Muslim world, overwhelmed it and destroyed the sect's records. Since then all available information about Sabbah has come mainly from hostile sources. It is not therefore astonishing that many historians qualify Sabbah and his followers as terrorists and present them as precursors of modern militant Islamic fundamentalists.

This is nonsense. In fact, basic differences separate Sabbah's Fedayin from the Muslim Brotherhood, the Hezbollah, and similar contemporary groups. Sabbah resorted to assassinations not to frighten people but as part of a larger plan intended to impair the Seljuk grip on power. His actions were based on coherent political and military thinking concerning the "science" of warfare rather than methods of terrorism. Hassan Sabbah's aim was to reform Islamic theology and society and to reopen the "gates of progress." His goals contradict those of today's militant fundamentalists who call for a return to the remote past. It is true that contemporary militants hail him as a "hero of Islam" because of his fight against the Crusaders, but they carefully avoid the subject of his religious beliefs and social ideas.[8]

A BERBER "MESSIAH"

The intrusion of Western Crusaders in the eleventh century served as a clarion call to all fundamentalists, especially the orthodox Sunni ulemas.

How was it possible that infidels could invade Muslim lands and create a Christian kingdom in the heart of one of the most sacred sites of Islam? Taking advantage of the commotion that shook the masses of believers, the orthodox clergy denounced reformers as well as Shiite fundamentalists. Later, in the thirteenth century, the Mongol invasion compounded the dangers facing Islam and thus further nurtured fundamentalism. Hassan Sabbah's "new" or "reformed" Ismailism fizzled out. But other forms of fundamentalism, turned toward the past, flourished.

Thus in the Maghreb (present-day Morocco) of the early decades of the twelfth century, Muhammad Ibn Tumart (1078–1130), a member of a Berber tribe, proclaimed himself the Mahdi who, according to a hadith, would restore Islam to its purity and original orthodoxy. His doctrine preached the "unity" of God, *tawhid* in Arabic. His followers were called *al-mowahaddin*, *almohades* in Latin. Physically, he was small and misshapen. Son of a mosque lamplighter, Ibn Tumart in his early childhood knew the Koran by heart. He lived the life of an ascetic and scolded those who did not follow Islamic law to the letter. In his youth, he stoned women who ventured out unveiled. In his zeal, he once assaulted the sister of the sultan in a Fez street. He was in favor of banning music, songs, and dance as anti-Islamic practices. The number of his followers swelled rapidly, and after his death, his closest aide and general succeeded him as caliph, conquered the whole of North Africa and Andalusia, and founded the Al Mowahaddin dynasty. The first and second Almohad sultans showed some degree of liberalism toward intellectuals and artists. But soon the strictest orthodoxy triumphed. Fundamentalist clerics condemned philosophers and scientists. The great Córdoba library was expurged, and many valuable manuscripts were destroyed. Averroës was imprisoned in the sultan's palace. Jews and Christians were offered a choice between exile or conversion to Islam.

In many respects, Ibn Tumart reminds one of Ayatollah Khomeini. Indeed, his was a fundamentalist politico-religious movement that succeeded in overthrowing the Almoravid sultans and replacing their regime with a fundamentalist theocracy. But one should remain wary of hasty comparisons: Basic differences separate today's militant fundamentalists from their precursors. For one thing, Ibn Tumart, and others like him, operated in an environment of relative openness and freedom of thought, whereas contemporary militants act in a Muslim world dominated by fundamentalist readings of the Koran. They are, as it were, *super*fundamentalists. As a matter of fact, the so-called precursors contributed to a turning point in the history of the Muslim world.

6

The Turning Point

In October 1996 a symposium on international terrorism was convened in
New York under the joint auspices of the American Council on Germany
and the Jewish Community Relations Council[1] A German deputy minister
of the interior and an ambassador from the State Department attended.
The discussions centered on Islamic terrorism. Because it seemed that all
the participants were blaming Muslim fundamentalists, at one point the
State Department representative reminded the audience that a clear line
should be drawn between the extremists, who are only a tiny minority, and
the majority of Muslims who condemn violence and killings. He recalled
that Islam is one of the three Abrahamic monotheisms that has more than a
billion followers throughout the world. I agree with the necessity of making
a distinction between militant Islamic fundamentalism and mainstream Islam. But while listening to the ambassador, I felt somehow ill at ease. What
he was saying was true. Yet it was not all the truth. Something was missing.
My thoughts wandered into the realm of history. I tried to assess the situation of the Muslim world at the end of the second millennium and on the
threshold of the twenty-first century.

THE MARTIAN VISITOR

A gloomy picture cast a pall over my thoughts: All Muslim nations are steeped in underdevelopment and backwardness. Arab or non-Arab, rich or poor, they are lingering far behind the West and even some rapidly developing Asian and Latin American countries that possess no oil. From the Atlantic to the Indian oceans and from Africa to Central Asia, millions of the faithful live in the throes of hunger, malady, and ignorance. In many places men and women are stoned to death; thieves' hands are chopped off; drunkards are flogged. Everywhere, more or less, authoritarian governments rule with rods of iron, trampling all human rights. Censorship and repression stifle any attempt at free expression.

Yet at the beginning of the same millennium, in the year 1001, the Muslim world was the most advanced and prosperous part of the planet. Its numerous achievements induced the envy of others. Western academics flocked to its boundaries, in Spain, to acquire manuscripts and to study Muslim science. Backward Europe admired the spirit of tolerance of the Muslim world and its advances and superiority in all fields. Indeed, a refined culture scintillated in the "East"; ideas bloomed, progress seemed unremitting.

All of a sudden this great civilization came to naught, and after the twelfth century, the Muslim world went into decline. In the following eight centuries, it never regained its splendor. There were, to be sure, some fits of accomplishments: In the fourteenth century the great historian Ibn Khaldun laid down the foundations of modern sociology, and in the fifteenth, the mathematician Ibn Massud made striking advances in calculus. As the scholar Marshall Hodgson once noted, a Martian arriving on Earth in the sixteenth century would have concluded that the world was on the verge of becoming Muslim. Indeed, three Islamic empires were shining: the Mogul (India), the Safavid (Iran), and the Ottoman. But the Turks, in spite of their victories in Eastern Europe, did not produce any intellectual achievements comparable to those of their predecessors. The glory of the Moguls and Safavids was short-lived.

One can therefore consider the twelfth century as a turning point in the history of the Muslim world. What happened then that provoked such a complete reversal of fortune? It is not easy to clarify the conundrum, especially when, on the surface, Muslims seemed to be moving toward more successes. The Mowahaddins (Almohads), for instance, defeated the Christians who had been menacing Andalusia. Ibn Rushd (Averroës) was producing the bulk of his scientific and philosophical works that would soon become the basis of study in Western universities. It was also toward the end of the twelfth century that Salah-ad-Din (Saladin) expelled the Crusaders from Jerusalem.

Yet the virus of decadence was at work. In order to locate it, one must first understand how and why in the four previous centuries Islam was able to conquer a vast empire and create a fabulous civilization. A bird's-eye view of early Islamic history will help us develop some insight at this juncture.

ISLAM ON THE MOVE

The rapidity of the Arab conquests is probably unique in the ancient world. In less than half a century, approximately 40,000 horsemen from the Arabian Desert tribes defeated powerful armies and built an empire extending from India to Spain.

How did all this happen? Muslims attributed their victories to the will of God, which is a way of avoiding serious explanation. In fact, the Arabs had good generals and were highly motivated. One of their commanders specialized in blitzkriegs (in which camels prefigured tanks). A brilliant tactician and a natural leader, he received the title "Sword of Islam" from the prophet himself. His name was Khalid ibn Walid.[2] After the fall of Damascus, he was fighting against a Byzantine army near the river Jordan when an emissary arrived and notified him that the new caliph, Umar, had demoted him. He continued to pursue the enemy. "Didn't you hear me?" asked the emissary. "O, Yes," Khalid retorted. "But I am not fighting for Umar's sake but for the triumph of Islam!"

Such was the mind-set of Muslim warriors: Faith increased their ardor. There also was the incentive of booty, a part of which was distributed to the soldiers and their officers. After his dismissal, Khalid retired, a rich man. One can add that native people received the Arabs as "liberators" from tyranny. Indeed, the two great empires of that time, Byzantium and Persia, in continual wars with each other, were exhausted and reduced to a shadow of their former selves. Their rulers and clergy exploited the people mercilessly and imposed heavy taxes, censorship, and other forms of repression. City dwellers as well as peasants had little reason to defend their leaders. Moreover, the Arab invaders did not impose conversion or any other constraints. The Damascus surrender document that served as a model in later conquests read as follows: "[Khalid ibn Walid] promises to give the inhabitants security for their lives, property and churches. . . . So long as they pay the poll tax, nothing but good shall befall them."[3]

Lacking governmental tradition and skill, the Arab Beduins adopted local institutions and administrative rules. They did not introduce changes in the way of life. Theirs was a very liberal attitude for the time. Compared to Persian and Byzantine rule, Arab rule was tantamount to liberation. This atmosphere of relative freedom encouraged people to resume their activities. Science and philosophy, which had suffered badly under previous censorship, flourished anew. The Arabs opened themselves to the alien cultures they encountered. Their elites adopted Greek philosophy, Persian thinking, Indian knowledge, and so on. In its first two centuries, Islam was characterized by a great openness. A chronicle of the eighth century recounts the story of an intellectual whose wife was complaining about the time he devoted to reading; one day she scolded him: "By Allah! Your books are worse rivals to me than three additional wives!"[4] Several philosophical and religious schools existed, and their members discoursed freely with one another. One of these schools, called Mutazalite, introduced "rationalism" into Islam, while another one, founded by the theologian Ash'ari, rejected science and professed a blind submission to "God's will."

It was as if the Muslim world was being advanced by a groundswell. A whirl of creativity and progress was churning the whole new empire. Intellectually and materially, Muslims were on the move. This effervescence lasted for almost four centuries. Then, toward the end of the eleventh century, it came to a stop in the eastern part of the empire. By the end of the twelfth century, a similar fate hit the western reaches of the Muslim world. Many reasons, including economic, political, social, and cultural, account for this major interruption. Because their consideration is beyond the subject matter of this book, I shall focus on their "common denominator," which, in my view, is the triumph of fundamentalist interpretations of the Koran.

THE SIN OF ORTHODOXY

This fundamentalist trend was directly linked to the social and political evolution of the empire. As already mentioned, the Arabs represented only a tiny minority of the population of the conquered territories. Almost all important duties in government as well as in the private sector were performed by non-Arabs. Yet the highest positions were concentrated in the hands of the Arabs who as conquerors and "original" Muslims constituted a kind of aristocracy. The non-Arabs, who were the vast majority, suffered from this discriminatory situation and coveted positions of power. But how could they compete with the Arabs and skirt the established tradition? Arabs boasted that Allah had revealed the Koran to them. Therefore, the only way for non-Arabs to get ahead was to present themselves as "more

Muslim" than the Arabs. The ambitious Turks, Persians, and Berbers, for example, espoused fundamentalist doctrines and accused the Arabs of laxity in the religious field. The Seljuk dynasty is a case in point.

Its sultans needed to legitimize their rule, especially because their conquered empire comprised Mesopotamia and Bagdad where the Abbassid caliph resided. They favored Ash'ari's fundamentalist views. In 1085 their Persian Grand Vizir Nizam-ul-Mulk founded an Islamic university in Bagdad and appointed as rector a young compatriot of his, Abu Hamid Ghazali,5 who launched a scathing attack on philosophers and scientists. He wrote several treatises in which he expounded and developed Ash'ari's fundamentalism. It can be said that Ash'ari and his disciple, Ghazali, were instrumental in closing the Muslim world. Although both were Sunnites, they influenced other sects, including Shiites.

Ash'ari's thesis can be summed up as follows: Natural phenomena reflect an "order" instituted by God who, in his might, can change it according to His will at any moment; it is therefore sacrilegious and useless to devote oneself to the study of the "laws" of nature that are "instant" manifestations of God's will; nobody can question His will. Among the consequences of Ash'ari's doctrine is the denial of any link between causes and effects because God continually recreates the web and texture of events.

To Ash'ari and Ghazali, life on Earth is a provisional "station" imposed by God as a test; the aim of life is, in fact, the hereafter. To the students who often wrote to him for guidance, Ghazali recommended that they concentrate on studies that would be useful in the hereafter—theology, sharia, and the like—avoid poetry (literature), physics, chemistry, and so on. One can imagine the negative impact of such a master on the cultural life of a nation.6 If American university presidents gave the same advice to their students, scientific and technological creativity would immediately dry up, and the United States would turn into a poor, underdeveloped, and backward nation in a matter of decades. This is exactly what happened to the Muslims in the twelfth century.

In 1990, in an illuminating article written eleven years after his journey through a number of Muslim countries, V. S. Naipaul, trying to understand what had driven them to their fundamentalist "rage," pondered his experience. He thought he would see people like his own, Trinidad Indians (Hindus and Muslims), sharing the same community and colonial history, having experienced "many stages of knowledge." As Naipaul remarked, "I had been granted the idea of inquiry and the tools of scholarship. I could carry 4, 5, or 6 different cultural ideas in my head. Now, traveling . . . [in Muslim countries] I found myself among a colonized people who had been stripped by their faith of all that expanding cultural and historical knowledge of the world that I had been growing into on the other side of the world."[7]

During the peak of the Abbassid caliphate (ninth and tenth centuries), Muslim intellectuals—animated by a sense of curiosity, inquiry, and discovery—enlarged their knowledge by absorbing, without hesitation or shame, the progress that had been made by Indians, Iranians, Greeks, and others. Their studies did not create a feeling of guilt or of encroaching on God's forbidden domain. The surge of fundamentalism in the twelfth century sealed off the search for scientific knowledge.

Ghazali, in a way, reminds one of Jdanov who, under Joseph Stalin, was in charge of enforcing the "doctrinal correction" of intellectuals. One can say that he was a kind of Marxist fundamentalist who defended an orthodox interpretation of Karl Marx's views. He literally killed independent thought and research in the Soviet Union. To a large extent he destroyed Soviet science, especially in agronomy.[8] But unlike the influence of the communist censor, Ghazali's ideas continue to dominate the Muslim world. Half a century after Ghazali's death, Ibn Rushd (Averroës) confuted his cultural *diktats* but to no avail. He was branded a heretic by the fundamentalist clerics of Andalusia. His work, rejected by the Muslims, was welcomed in the West and helped the backward Europeans to extricate themselves from their decadence. The Italian historian Geoffredo Quadri asserts that the Renaissance became possible because of Averroës's ideas.[9]

In the twelfth century Ibn Tumart in North Africa spread his own fundamentalist interpretations, and Saladin in Egypt and Palestine resorted to similar concepts in order to galvanize Muslims in their war against the Crusaders. Thus in about half a century the whole Muslim world turned fundamentalist.

In each instance, what really contributed to the decline of Islamic culture was the alliance between the rulers and the fundamentalist clerics. Orthodoxy and science can in no way coexist. Since the end of the eleventh century, autos-da-fé (book burnings) and other forms of book destruction became common practice in the Muslim world. Often the ulemas, like Goebbels in Nazi Germany, presided over book burnings. Under the fallacious pretext of submitting to God's will, Muslims, abetted by their religious and civilian leaders, started to reject and then destroy the knowledge amassed by their scholars during the previous centuries.

What happened in the twelfth century was tantamount to a collective cultural suicide triggered mainly by the use of fundamentalism as an instrument of "legitimacy" in the political race for power. The antiscientific zeal of Muslim theologians of that time reminds one of the ardor of the Christian church of the third and fifteenth centuries in destroying whatever they considered contrary to the Bible and the Gospels. To the Christian clerics of those days, only the scriptures—not reason—could save men. All truth was contained in the revelations. They burned books, including the writings of the ancient Greeks. In the fourth century, Emperor Theodosius authorized the patriarch to set fire to the library of Serapeion. The only difference from the Muslims of the twelfth century is that the Christians destroyed the books of others, whereas the Muslims burned their own science.[10]

7

Fundamentalism Forever

Fundamentalists always try hard to bring entire societies to a standstill under their laws. But human nature has its weaknesses. After a more or less
long period, people tire of the strict and uncompromising rule of fundamentalism. Without challenging the authorities, they become lax in carrying
out the commandments, which, in turn, gives rise to new waves of fundamentalism and stirs up ambitions.

Thus in the second half of the thirteenth century, in Damascus, a theologian by the name of Ibn Taymiya (1263–1328) raised his voice against innovation, the worship of saints, vows, and pilgrimages to shrines.

THE ENEMY OF INNOVATION

Ibn Taymiya was the son of a professor of Hanbali law,[1] the strictest interpretation of Islamic law. At his father's death in 1282, he succeeded to his
position and proved even more conservative. His intransigence and hide-
bound opinions displeased many clerics who accused him of deviation from
"true" Islam and roused the public against him. After being dismissed in
1299 from his teaching position, he offered to lecture on the necessity of a
jihad against the Mongols who were menacing Syria and Egypt. He went to

Cairo in 1300 and participated in the battles that stopped the Mongol drive.

His unbounded hatred of heretics compelled him to fight all sects in Syria: Ismailis, Nusayris, Shiites, and others. Bitter enemy of "innovation," Ibn Taymiya condemned all attempts by the authorities to soften the sharia. He interpreted literally all verses of the Koran. Believing that Islam was the last message of Allah, he attacked Jews and Christians and campaigned in favor of forbidding the construction of churches and synagogues.

Based on the dissemination of ideas contained in his writings, he eventually found followers in several parts of the Muslim world. But he was not a successful leader. He never succeeded in mustering a sizable group of disciples, and he displeased many believers in Syria and Mesopotamia because he incited people to destroy shrines.

Ibn Taymiya scathingly criticized Ash'ari's Sunnism and proposed its reform on the basis of a literal interpretation of the Koran and the prophet's hadiths. His books influenced many fundamentalists. Even today some militants such as Algeria's Benhaj refer to his theological positions. In the eighteenth century, Ibn Taymiya's ideas profoundly impressed a fundamentalist from the eastern part of the Muslim world.[2]

WAHHABISM AND THE SAUDS

His name was Muhamad ibn-Abdal Wahhab (died in 1792), and his doctrine is the official theology of Saudi Arabia. He belonged to a tribe (Najd) of Central Arabia. After his Koranic studies, he traveled extensively to Hejaz, Iraq, and Syria, which were provinces of the Ottoman Empire. He was appalled by the practice of Islam that he witnessed in the cities he visited. The displays of worship at the tombs of Ali and Hussein as well as at the mausoleum of Saladin dismayed him. Such practices, in his opinion, reflected a return to paganism. The more he roamed in these Muslim regions, the more he became convinced of the necessity to apply Hanbal's interpretation of the sharia strictly and to stick to the letter of the revelations, as taught by Ibn Taymiya. His public speeches in the cities he visited amounted to a call to overthrow local authorities installed by the Ottomans. He was expelled from Iraq and went back to Arabia. He stopped in the province of Hasa (the site of the oil wells and the modern port of Dahran). He used the pulpits of the mosques to cultivate his propaganda in favor of a fundamentalist reform of current Islamic theology. His eloquence and zeal provoked turmoil among the local people. Once more, he was expelled and found refuge among the Sauds, a noble Bedouin family of the Najd. The tribe's chief, Muhamad ibn Saud (died in 1765), adopted his doctrine and married his daughter. He was elected the *imam*[3] of the tribe and encouraged his son-in-law to conquer the neighboring territories in order to create a theocratic state. The heirs of Muhamad ibn Saud invaded Mesopotamia (Iraq) and leveled Shiite shrines.

In the first years of the nineteenth century, the Sauds turned against the Hashemites who reigned in Mecca (Hejaz). The Ottomans asked Mohammed Ali, viceroy of Egypt, to reestablish order in Arabia. Mohammed Ali's troops eventually defeated the Sauds and their first Wahhabi state. The Sauds fled and found refuge among al-Sabahs' tribe in what is now Kuwait. (The second Wahhabi state was founded in the 1920s by King Abdul Aziz ibn Saud and was later named Saudi Arabia.)

The first Wahhabi state (like the second) was a fundamentalist theocracy that imposed a complete ban on music, tobacco, jewelry, and many other things considered manifestations of luxury.[4]

THE MAHDI OF SUDAN

In 1881 in the Sudan, the son of a poor boat builder named Muhammad Ahmad (1845–1885) proclaimed himself the Mahdi, whose coming is awaited by Sunni Muslims and who is supposed to restore "true" Islam and expel the infidels.[5] At that time a British force commanded by Charles Gordon occupied Sudan. The self-proclaimed Mahdi ordered a jihad that was enthusiastically accepted by the local tribes. Notwithstanding his lack of arms and trained soldiers, the Mahdi defeated the British, stormed their headquarters in Khartoum, and slaughtered Gordon. He established a harsh theocracy and banned singing, dancing, swearing, drinking, and using jewelry and other ornamental trinkets. Members of different tribes adored him, and he was able to unite for the first time the whole area under his despotic rule.[6]

Carried away by his own success and power, Muhammad Ahmad gave in to unconstrained sensuality and many other excesses. He grew so fat that he had to be transported by several followers to Friday prayers at the mosque. After his death in 1885, his closest aide, Abdullahi, reigned, having assumed the title of caliph. He expanded the limits of his domain but was finally swept away by the British Army in 1898–1899.

Muhammad Ahmad's adventure is remarkable not only because he succeeded in routing the British with his unshod and unarmed followers but also because he made the people believe that he was the "expected one." Those who had triumphed before him were educated Muslims or even religious scholars such as Ibn Tumart who established the Mowahaddin (Almohads) dynasty in the twelfth century. The Sudanese Mahdi had no special title or knowledge. He shrewdly used one of his physical defects: He had the same V-shaped gap between his front teeth as the prophet.[7] He also benefited from the fact that mainstream Islam had been "fundamentalized" since the twelfth century. Muhammad Ahmad's appeals struck a responsive chord among his countrymen.

FUNDAMENTALISM AND MAINSTREAM ISLAM

Indeed, fundamentalist readings of the Koran continue to dominate the Muslim world. The basic difference between mainstream religious leaders and militant fundamentalists concerns the claim by the latter to exercise political power. Otherwise, they share many beliefs. To cite an example, Sheikh Salah Abu Ismail, an Egyptian leader and scholar from the nonmilitant fundamentalist university al-Azhar, declared "lawful" the assassination of President Sadat,[8] as did the militant fundamentalist Sheikh Omar Abdal Rahman, who was convicted in New York in 1995. In 1993, almost ten years after Abu Ismail's declaration, another sheikh linked to al-Azhar, a paragon of mainstream scholarship who was given ample time to laud the "merciful virtues of Islam" on TV, testified in a criminal court that "a secularist represents a danger to society and the nation and must therefore be eliminated." He added, "It is the duty of the government to kill him."[9] The same sheikh, al-Ghozali, teamed up with other al-Azhar clerics to brand any argument in favor of the separation of state and religion as an act of "apostasy," a crime punishable by death under Islamic law. Both mainstream clerics and militant fundamentalists adhere to the orthodox versions of the religion that triumphed after the twelfth century.

Coming back to the symposium on international terrorism mentioned at the beginning of the previous chapter, I reaffirm that the State Department's participant was right to draw a line between the militant fundamentalists and the vast majority of Muslims. Indeed, in general, Muslims oppose violence and assassinations. On the other hand, the American ambassador did not reflect the "whole" reality. He probably was not aware of the basically fundamentalist character of today's mainstream Islam. It seems that many experts are more or less confused about the issue of Islamic fundamentalism. I have the impression that when it comes to Islam, most of those concerned do not quite know what to believe and do not quite believe what they know. The fundamentalist ingredient of mainstream Islam is an indisputable fact that often blurs discussions about militant fundamentalist activities. That is probably why so many law-abiding Muslims, even those holding American passports, hesitate to condemn terrorist acts.

Instead, they speak of grievances and other excuses while voicing their opposition to assassinations and bombings.

CONFUSION ABOUT ISLAM

Many Muslim intellectuals react with outrage to the phrase "Islamic terrorism," often used by journalists. Thus on January 23, 1996, *The New York Times* published a letter by a Muslim woman named Yasmine Salaam from Cambridge, Massachusetts, in which she asserted that "The presentation of Islam as the archenemy has continued since the 1979 Iranian revolution. The West's biggest threat has proved to be its own right-wing factions. Oklahoma City, Waco, Texas, and the deaths in France, . . . associated with an apparent cult-rite, attest to this. . . . It is time for the West to recognize that the malignancy lies within itself." Such reactions on the part of American Muslims are numerous. Even a less emotional one by Doctor Fazlur Rahman, an American citizen of Bangladeshi origin, practicing in Texas, illustrates the point. In an article published in 1988 (August 3) by *The Wall Street Journal*, he stated:

> Daily newspaper and TV coverage fosters the impression that the followers of Islam are a violent lot, a band of fanatics and terrorists who incite holy wars and are ruled by reckless men. I also sense pervasive bias against Islam from scholars and institutions of learning. Since Islamic studies departments as a rule are combined with Middle Eastern studies, political beliefs taint the way academics and students interpret the faith. But in the Islamic world, politics and religion are not usually synonymous. . . . Americans sometimes lose sight of the fact that Moslems, like everyone else, can be poor or rich, tolerant or intolerant . . . . The vast majority are busy running their daily lives. . . . They detest injustice and extremism just as others do.

Dr. Rahman then enumerated the positive contributions of Islam to the world. He wrote, "Between the ninth and the eleventh centuries Moslems established great universities. Thousand-year-old al-Azhar University in Cairo is the world's oldest still-functioning university. Twelfth-century philosopher Averroës (Ibn Rushd) immensely influenced Jewish and Christian thought."

The commentaries underline realities. But like the case of the American participant in the symposium on international terrorism, what they convey represents only one part of the reality. It cannot be denied that Muslims consider their faith predestined to animate the entire planet. Neither can it be denied that jihad propelled the birth of the Muslim empire. Moreover, many fundamentalist activists call for a renewal of jihad both inside and outside the Muslim world. Sheikh Hassan al-Banna, the founder and the first supreme guide of the Muslim Brotherhood, wrote, "It is the nature of Islam to dominate, not to be dominated, to impose its law in all nations and to extend its power to the entire planet."[10]

It is true that Muslim scholars have contributed to the advancement of the West. But it is equally true that most of them, including Averroës and Avicenna, have been condemned (and continue to be condemned) by ulemas who have branded them as heretics. In fact, both Muslims and non-Muslims sow confusion about Islam. That is one of the reasons I propose making a clear-cut distinction between militant Islamic fundamentalism and mainstream Islam (or Islams). Indeed, there is not one Islam. Traveling from country to country, one encounters different ways of expressing the religion and practicing it.

Be that as it may, the basic fundamentalist character of today's Islams explains how charismatic leaders such as nineteenth-century Sudan's Mahdi or twentieth-century Iran's Khomeini stirred the masses. It also helps clarify the violent reactions against writers such as Salman Rushdie and Nasrin Taslima on the part of their fellow Muslims.

In order to assess the recent waves of militant Islamic fundamentalism, one should keep in mind this characteristic of the Muslim world. The Muslim "power seekers" know it all too well and use it often with shrewdness and talent. The slogan "Islam is in danger," pronounced by Khomeini in Iran and by others elsewhere in the Muslim world, is a clarion call for provoking a jihad against local authorities or foreign powers. The slogan has been used by militant Islamic fundamentalists of the past. The Sudanese Mahdi, for one, used it successfully in order to create his "Islamic" state. But neither he nor his successor, Abdullahi, bothered to institutionalize their rule. Theirs was a vaguely "caliphal" government based on no principle other than the implementation of their own interpretations of the sharia and the Koran. They were not interested in elaborating a doctrinal precedent. It is curious to note that all militant fundamentalists of the twentieth century, including Khomeini, neglected to describe the "Islamic" government they advocated. The one exception was the Iranian Navab Safavi, founder of the Fedayin-e-Islam, who produced a detailed blueprint while he was in prison.

8

The Islamic State

Exhaustive in their criticism of the present regimes, militant fundamental-ists and their leaders are cryptic about the nature of the Islamic state they dream about. In their opinion, the Koran and the *hadiths* (the prophet's say-ings) contain all the necessary guidelines. But they prudently refrain from citing pertinent passages. As Khomeini did, most of them affirm that a "true" Islamic government existed only under the prophet himself and the first four caliphs. In fact, neither the Koran nor the hadiths contain clear indications of the nature and the structure of an Islamic state or govern-ment. Nevertheless, the question has been discussed by Muslim scholars, both in the past and in modern times. The great tenth-century scientist and philosopher al-Farabi (Alpharabius of Middle Age Latinists) devoted three major works to the problem.[1]

THE PHILOSOPHER-KING

Al-Farabi was born in 870 in Wasidj (Turkestan) to an Iranian family and died in Damascus in 950. He applied a philosophical approach to the study of political and religious phenomena and developed a theory of the state that combines Plato's and Aristotle's ideas with Islamic concepts. His works inspired men like Avicenna, Averroës, and Maimonides. The central theme of his theory is what he calls the "virtuous regime" in which men associate and cooperate with the aim of becoming virtuous, performing noble deeds, and attending happiness. This is a nonhereditary monarchical or aristocratic regime in which only the best rule. The rest of the citizens are associated in groups that are ruled and in turn rule those who are under them until one comes to the lowest group that is ruled but does not rule. The sole criterion for the rank of a citizen is the virtue he shows. The supreme ruler in al-Farabi's system is a prophet or a philosopher. "The rule of this man," al-Farabi says, "is the supreme rule; all other human rulerships are inferior to it and are derived from it."[2] He has the power to confirm, abrogate, or replace previous laws. The ruler-prophet receives directions from God, whereas the ruler-philosopher relies mostly on the wisdom of philosophy and on his rational faculties. Thus he must assess carefully the necessity of change; once he sees that it is necessary, he should take all precautions to minimize the danger of change to the well-being of the regime and its citizens. "[The successor] may change a great deal of what his predecessor had legislated . . . when he knows this to be best in his own time; not because his predecessor committed a mistake but because his predecessor decided on it according to what was best in his own time. Had his predecessor observed [the new conditions], he would have changed [his own law] also."[3]

The supreme ruler is the link between the divine and the citizens. He is the teacher and the guide. He must possess knowledge, comprehend everything that must be done, have the ability to make citizens perform the functions for which they are fit, and so on. He is the source of all knowledge and power. He is an "absolute" ruler. This notion of the absolutist nature of government pervades the thinking of all Muslim political thinkers and actors. It can be found, for instance, in the ideas of a nineteenth-century Muslim cleric of Iranian origin who undertook reformist action: Jamal-ud-Din Assadabadi, known in the Sunnite world as al-Afghani.

A DISGUISED AFGHAN

Born in Assadabad, a village west of Tehran, probably in 1828, he studied in a Koranic school. He adopted the surname Afghani in order to hide his Shiite origin when he traveled to Mecca, Istanbul, and Cairo. (Shiites were considered heretics by Sunnis.) After a stint at the celebrated al-Azhar University of Cairo, he went to Paris where he came to be known as Sheikh Afghani. In 1883 he met the French historian and philosopher Ernest Renan who used to attribute the decline of the Muslim world to the basic incompatibility between Islam and modern science. Al-Afghani, for his part, believed that the decline could be attributed to the fact that Muslim scholars and leaders not only rejected science and technology but also adopted some Western political and cultural values that represented a departure from authentic Koranic principles. He advocated a return to Islamic sources and the adoption of modern scientific values. He was thus at the same time a fundamentalist and a modern reformist.

A *seyed* (a descendant of the prophet in Iran), he avoided wearing the black turban and the green belt lest he be identified as a Shiite. According to some sources, he was admitted to a Masonic lodge and became a founder of Freemasonry in the Muslim world, which did not prevent Khomeini from hailing him as a "saint" of fundamentalism. In Paris he met a young Egyptian student named Muhammad Abdoh, the future al-Azhar "reformist" theologian who espoused most of his ideas. Together they edited an Arabic paper in Paris and maintained that there was no conflict whatsoever between Islam and modern science. But whereas al-Afghani advocated political change, Abdoh espoused religious "awakening" among Muslims. They both followed the thirteenth-century fundamentalist theologian Ibn Taymiya in condemning superstitions and the worship of saints that, they believed, contaminated the faith. But instead of advocating a return to the remote past, they prescribed the intellectual and political revivification of religion together with the unification of the Muslim world under one "supreme" leader.

Al-Afghani developed his political views in his writings and lectures in Egypt, where some freedom of expression was tolerated by the local authorities. In one of his essays entitled "Despotic Government," published in the weekly paper *MISR* (Egypt) on February 15, 1879,[4] one can see that his political ideas, in spite of some modern references, were deeply steeped in medieval Islamic conceptions. He extolled the forms of republican and constitutional government that existed in the West, but he concluded that they were not applicable, at least for the time being, to Muslim countries for several reasons.

First, "the long time in which the people of the East have spent under the arbitrary rule of despots . . . has entailed the alteration of their instincts . . . to the extent that they can hardly distinguish good from evil and the harmful from the useful." Second, "the prolongation of the period of their wallowing in superstitions which destroy perception and impose a complete obliteration [of insight] . . . and bring about a descent to the animal level." Third, the opposition to the "true sciences": "They endeavor to destroy books, to obliterate every trace of them, and to substitute for them that which has plunged them into abysmal darkness, out of which they might never find their way."

"All of these reasons," al-Afghani concluded, "prevent an Easterner from putting pen to paper in Eastern countries to mention republican government and to reveal its true nature, its merits, the happiness of those who have achieved it, and the fact that those governed by it enjoy a higher and loftier position than the other members of the human race. . . . The same reasons also restrain him from setting down on paper an exposition of the nature of constitutional government which would set forth its beneficial results and show how those governed by it . . . have cast off the burdens which despotic government lays upon them."

THE JUST DESPOT

Under the circumstances, al-Afghani considers that the best that Muslims can hope for is a benevolent, enlightened, paternalistic despotism that will introduce the new scientific and technological knowledge of the West and a more humane form of government. He compared this kind of despotic government to two others: "The first is the cruel government of which the members [the prince or sultan, ministers, and administrative and security officials] . . . resemble highway robbers . . . [who leave the subjects] in the wilderness or desert barefoot, naked, and hungry, cut off from all resources. . . . Examples of this class are the Jenghizid [Mongol], Timurid, and other Tatar and barbarian governments witnessed by history." Al-Afghani mentioned the "oppressive government" whose leaders are comparable to "the vile lovers of luxury who unjustly and unlawfully enslave people born free [and force them] to perform hard and onerous labor . . . [leaving for them] only that which will sustain their lowly life. . . . To this category belong most of the Eastern governments of bygone eras and the present as well; likewise, most of the Western governments in times past and also the British government of India."

Among the "compassionate" despots, al-Afghani mentioned the "ignorant" ones who wish the good of their people but fail to found and build useful institutions that can ameliorate their lot. Into this category falls also the "informed government" that creates the necessary elements but whose leaders are weak minded and allow disorder to take over. According to al-Afghani, "[i]t would seem that the governments of [the caliph] al-Mamun and some of the Saljuqs of Iran were examples of this type of government."

Al-Afghani also endeavored to describe "enlightened" or "just" despotism: "Its leaders are like the provident and discerning father who continually exerts himself in preparing the conditions which will ensure the happiness of his children." These "just" despots understand the importance of agriculture, industry, and commerce. They create schools and furnish agricultural implements and industrial machinery. They promote policies based on justice and equity. "They are aware that the fulfillment of the nation's happiness and the safeguarding of its independence will come about only through its political relations and commercial ties with other countries. They know too that this will not be realized save through the agency of expert, shrewd, discerning patriotic men." Such a "just" despot is never remiss in according his subjects their rights. Al-Afghani also gave a detailed account of the ways in which the "supreme" leader supervises all domains of human activity and ensures that justice and equity are respected in each of them.

At the end of his essay, al-Afghani addressed the leaders: "Perhaps you have been misled by the glorification of flatterers, the adulation of sycophants, and the eulogy of fawners. Woe to you! If only you knew your standing in people's hearts and your measure with the discerning and intelligent, you would have bid farewell to this vile world which has diverted you." To the people al-Afghani has this to say: "I shall certainly neither address myself to you nor remind you of your duties, for you have grown used to subservience and have resigned yourselves to a lowly life. You have substituted regrets and longing for strength and become like old women, unable to defend yourselves, to dare, to acquire, to repel, to restrain, or to remove. Verily we belong to God and to Him we shall return."

A few months after the publication of this article, al-Afghani, in a speech delivered in Alexandria, attacked despotism along with religious sectarianism as the main causes of the decadence of the Muslim world. But like his disciple Muhammad Abdoh, he continued to call for a just despot who would be able to save Muslims from their predicament.

In a way, al-Afghani's "just despot" is nothing more than a variation of the expected Sunnite "Mahdi" or the awaited Shiite "hidden imam" swathed in secular garb. Indeed, his profound knowledge of what is good for the people and his constant supervision of the smooth operation of government cannot be found in any "human" leader. Nevertheless, the rather oxymoronic concept of a just despot has stolen popular imagination in every corner of the Muslim world. The masses call for such a person who would restore the old glory of the Muslim world.

A study conducted by American sociologists in several Muslim countries in the mid- and late 1950s confirmed the inclination of the masses as well as the lower and upper middle classes toward some sort of just despotism. Asked what each would do as the head of the government, a lawyer answered: "The only way I can do something is to become a dictator"; a retired government official said: "All the bad things will be corrected by a dictator"; a schoolteacher stated: "I believe in dictatorship"; a student, a member of the Muslim Brotherhood, declared: "I would have a sword and kill all those in the big chairs in the government. . . . Once I have done that I could set up a dictatorship and strike with an iron hand all that dare move"; a young housewife remarked: "It is necessary to have a strong hand here, . . . a hand of iron to redress people and make them fulfill their duties."[5]

Confusion between the just despot and the Mahdi is evident on the part of many leaders. Thus it is alleged that in certain moments of mystical "hallucination," Qaddafi proclaimed himself to be the awaited Mahdi.[6] In the first years of his rule, many mullahs and plain believers considered Khomeini the twelfth imam who had returned from "occultation."

At any rate, in militant fundamentalism the supreme leader is not a political or even a religious leader in the ordinary sense of the term. He literally represents Allah's will on earth. He is above everybody and everything. He is not bound by normal political and state procedures. He does not have to convey his orders through any administrative hierarchy. An interview, a radio broadcast, or a TV appearance is enough. He will be immediately obeyed by all who read the interview, listened to the radio broadcast, or watched him on television. For example, Khomeini did not issue a fatwa in the case of the writer Kasravi. He mentioned Kasravi in one of his books, and Navab Safavi took it as an order to kill (which Khomeini did not refute).

The concept of a "just despot" is not the preserve of militant Islamic fundamentalists. It is respected by all Muslims. It helps illuminate some paradoxes in the conduct of Muslims, as, for instance, the mass demonstrations in favor of Saddam Hussein during the 1990 Persian Gulf crisis. All Muslim leaders, clerics, or "seculars" play the role of the just despot. But at least until now, instead of a "just and equitable" society, they have created tyrannical despotism that has devoured everybody, including their supporters and sometimes themselves.

9

Fundamentalist Agendas

The idea of a religious guide or a just despot looms large in the concept of Islamic government in all militant fundamentalist agendas. The leaders of the militant groups consider themselves "God's vicars" on Earth, a combination of the classical caliph and the awaited Mahdi. Hassan al-Banna, the Supreme Guide of the Muslim Brotherhood, expected blind obedience from his members, exactly as Hassan Sabbah expected from his "assassins" about eight centuries earlier. Hassan al-Banna was extremely vague about the Islamic state he wished to create. He said only that the Koran would be its "constitution" and the sharia would be its basic law.

The concept of the just despot also pervades the theory of the Islamic state developed by the Iranian fundamentalist Ali Shariaty. Indeed, Shariaty affirmed that the supreme leader could only be an imam, a religious high-ranking guide. The people would choose him from among the "most just and virtuous" ayatollahs; once elected, everybody would "submit" to him and execute his commandments without discussion.[1] But like almost all other theorists, Shariaty remained silent about the details of his ideal Islamic state.

In contrast, another Iranian fundamentalist (less educated than Shariaty) drew up a long blueprint of an Islamic government. He was Navab Safavi, the founder of the Fedayin-e-Islam, whom I mentioned in earlier chapters.

AN ELABORATE AGENDA

While in prison in the late 1940s, Navab wrote a pamphlet entitled *Handbook of All Truths.*[2] First published in 1950, it contained an elaborate program of government.

Navab affirmed that the Koran "contains answers to all the social, political, economic, moral, philosophical, and *scientific* problems confronting . . . men." In the present world, humans are prey to materialistic and satanic passions. A thorough implementation of the tenets and principles of Islam constitutes the only way to save them from social, economic, and moral misery. As for the Muslim world, the danger stems from the import of goods, ideas, and fashions from the West. Muslims should therefore reject the "corrupt and degrading" culture spread by the "decadent" West through such demonic devices as cinema, theater, novels, and music. Moral depravity is everywhere. Sexuality is breaking loose. Alcoholic beverages and drugs, including tobacco, are poisoning civilization. Prostitution is destroying the moral and physical health of the Iranian people. Usury, condemned by Islam, is spreading through so-called modern banking systems imported from Europe.

After defining the problem confronting Muslims in general and Iranians in particular, Navab listed remedial measures that should be carried out under the supervision of the clergy. In order to perform such a duty, the clergy should purge itself of all "imperfect" elements and undergo a program of "high educational" training. Mullahs would thus become a real "source of imitation" for the believers. They should try to keep everybody in Allah's "Right Path," as specified in the holy Koran. Senior clerics (ayatollahs) must control parliamentary and governmental decisions in order to ensure their consonance with Islamic tenets and laws. In short, society as well as individual citizens should follow the clergy's "guidance."

Navab reviewed each governmental department and suggested detailed measures. Because his views foreshadow those of fundamentalist groups that have emerged most recently, it seems useful to summarize some of them here. In the field of education and culture, he proposed separating boys and girls in schools and public institutions. Mandatory religious studies and daily prayers should take place in schools and universities. The government and parents should not send students abroad. Radio and other media, including the press, should promote the principles of Islam. Entertainment programs should be reduced in favor of religious ones. Newspapers should publish only what is in the interest of the commonweal and what glorifies Islam. Censorship should be exercised by the government under religious guidance. Films should tell Islamic and other morally enlightening stories. Space should be earmarked in theaters for prayers.

Public prayers together with daily salutes to the Islamic green flag should take place in all public and private offices. Women should be veiled, and men should reject the European hat, a symbol of dependence on the West. The Ministry of the Interior will enforce all the laws and see to it that the "external" signs of Islam are respected (women's garb and veil, men's hats, the strict separation of women and men, the interdiction of the use of opium and other drugs, including cigarettes).

The Ministry of Justice should introduce the Islamic penal code in all its harshness and choose judges from among upright and honest clerics. Trials should not last more than a few hours or days. "Temporary marriages" should be encouraged as a means to fight prostitution.

The Ministry of Finance should accomplish the following tasks: curtail importations and encourage national industries, especially cottage industries; give free loans to the needy in order to suppress poverty; convince the rich to help the poor; establish salaries based on the needs of the workers.

THE GROCER MODEL

In dealing with the national economy and the subject of thrift and savings, Navab, curiously enough, proposed organizing that part of the ministry on the model of a grocery shop. This was a serious proposal; fundamentalism does not admit humor. Navab maintained that the bazaar grocer or druggist avoids waste and patiently increases his fortune. He does not ordinarily buy the products he sells. He adjusts his stock based on his estimate of the average number of customers. He lives modestly and charges his buyers equitably. In contrast, Western-type financiers steal and squander the nation's wealth. Therefore, the national economy should be managed like a grocery or a drug store.

The Ministry of Finance[3] should strive to lower the cost of living and introduce justice and equity in the calculation of taxes. Once people see that their taxes are used for the commonweal, they will pay them wholeheartedly and even contribute more than their due. The extra money donated would primarily compensate for the "loss" of income arising from the interdiction of alcohol and prostitution.

The Ministry of Health should implement Islamic commandments in the domain of medicine. Indeed, the interdiction of alcohol, pork, and "bloody" meat, of intercourse with women who are menstruating, and of contact with dogs would improve general health. These commandments, Navab affirmed, were not discovered by the prophet in a laboratory. They were revealed by God himself.

Navab's pamphlet contains detailed prescriptions for organizing the Ministries of Defense, Post, Transport, Agriculture, Labor, and so on that are of the same nature as those enumerated for the Ministries of Finance and Health. His remarks on the Islamic parliament are noteworthy. God alone possesses legislative power, and He has revealed to the prophet all the necessary laws through which Muslims can organize a just society; the main responsibility of the parliament is to concentrate on developing the economy according to Islamic principles. Members of the clergy should supervise debates to ensure that they conform with the tenets of Islamic morality.

In Navab's blueprint there is no mention of human rights. Men have duties only. They must obey God's commandments as transmitted by their religious leaders. They must be ready to die for Islam. They must recognize that whereas wars result from ignorance, jihad is ordered by God for the salvation of humanity.

In short, Navab's conception of an Islamic state is a society in which the clergy controls every aspect of the life of its citizens. His is a paternalistic society that favors men over women, poor over rich, Muslims over infidels, and clerics over everybody else. Such an Islamic state, Navab concluded, would transform Iran into "paradise on Earth." His blueprint seems to be a mixture of populist, fascist, and naive ingredients, and many of his remedies sound like quackery.

In contrast, others such as Mawlana Abul Ala Mawdudi— a Sunni Pakistani thinker, pamphleteer, and politician—have produced more sophisticated plans and concepts. Mawdudi's abundant works continue to influence young activists around the Muslim world. His vision of the ideal society is more important than those of others, including Khomeini, because he addressed the issues that modernity poses to Islam.

A SELF-TAUGHT THEOLOGIAN

Mawdudi was born in 1903 to a very religious family. His father, an austere and devout Muslim, educated his children at home in order to protect them from the language of the English "masters," modern science, and the social customs of the West that were invading Indian society. He was sixteen years old when Gandhi started his nationalist campaign for "home rule." He cooperated with the Hindus for independence for some time but eventually separated himself from the cause. He devoted his time to studying the Koran and to developing his ideas on an Islamic society apart from India. His writings indicated how to stem the flood of Western influences, chanting the superiority of Islam over non-Islamic ideas.

In the mid-1930s, when the Muslim League of India started to propagate its idea that the Muslims of India constituted a separate and distinct nation, Mawdudi was incensed: He feared that Muslims would stray from Islam toward nationalism. Nationalism, in his view, was a Western idea that rested on non-Islamic concepts. In 1941, he created his own fundamentalist group, the Jamiati Islami (the Islamic Association). In his view, the best way to transform society was to create a small group of dedicated followers in order to capture political leadership. He cited the Fascists in Italy and the Nazis in Germany as examples. His intention was to restructure the whole of Indian society on an Islamic pattern.

After the creation of Pakistan in 1947, Mawdudi sent preachers to the villages of the new state. Very soon the number of his supporters swelled, and the Jamiati Islami emerged as a genuine political party. The government jailed Mawdudi and two of his lieutenants. But the organization continued to develop and to strengthen. Released from prison in 1950, Mawdudi became a kind of hero. After riots in Lahore, he was arrested and condemned to death by a military tribunal; but as a result of public outcry, his sentence was commuted, and he was subsequently released from prison. Meanwhile, the Jamiati Islami lost its popularity. Moreover, it fell under the general ban on political parties imposed by the leaders of a military coup in 1958. The ban was lifted in 1962, and Mawdudi became active once more. But Jamiati Islami's attacks on the government prompted its dissolution and the imprisonment of its leaders, including Mawdudi. Eventually, the Supreme Court ruled the ban unconstitutional.

On his release, Mawdudi resumed his activities. Despite the fact that his association had lost its political clout, his ideas gained wide popularity in fundamentalist circles both in Pakistan and in the Muslim world at large. His concept of an Islamic state was used in 1978 by General Zia to justify his coup against the elected government of Zulfiqar Ali Bhutto. The general declared that he was a "soldier of Islam" dedicated to creating in Pakistan an Islamic state based on Mawdudi's ideas. Although the leader of the Jamiati Islami was not there to give his opinion (he died in 1972), his supporters denounced Zia as a usurper. Despite the fact that the Jamiati Islami lost its importance as a fundamentalist group, the writings of Mawdudi, especially his concept of an Islamic state, have penetrated every corner of the Muslim world.

THE STATE AS A CARRIAGE

The basic proposition in Mawdudi's theory is God's exclusive "possession" of sovereignty. According to him,

It covers all aspects of political and legal sovereignty also, and in these too no one other than God has any share. . . . [N]o monarch, no royal family, no elite class, no leader of any religious group, no democracy vested in the sovereignty of the people can participate in God's sovereignty. Whoever claims such a position is a rebel. . . . Similarly, any institution or individual attempting to assume political and legal sovereignty and seeking thereby to restrict the jurisdiction of God to spheres of personal law or religious duties is a usurper and a rebel. The truth is that no one can claim to be a lawgiver save under the dispensation of God; no one can challenge the supreme authority of God almighty in any sphere.[4]

Mawdudi considered the decadence of the time to flow from the fact that people have accepted sovereigns other than God, namely, the will of the people, the law of rulers, the nation-state, custom, personal preference, and so on. Islam, which means "total submission to God," represents a whole civilization, a complete culture, and a comprehensive world order. The prophet and his companions developed and established a complete model of Islam on this Earth for mankind to follow.[5]

The Islamic state is ruled by a single man "whose tenure of power and of office are limited only by his faithfulness to Islam." He is elected without having put forward his candidacy. The people choose him because of his wisdom, ability, and conduct. He is assisted by a legislative council composed of men whose knowledge of the Koran and the Hadith has been ascertained. The council's opinions are not binding on the ruler. There will be no political parties, for Islam constitutes the only ideology of the state.

Non-Muslims can live in the Islamic state as *dhimmis* (persons protected by the state). They can practice their own religions but not propagate them. Human society, explained Mawdudi, is like a carriage. It goes where the driver takes it. It is therefore essential that the right people, holding the right ideas, occupy the upper posts.

In sum, the Islamic state is a monolithic institution that upholds one ideology, which is Islam, and uses all its enforcement agencies to ensure that Islamic principles are respected by everybody in all walks of life. The absolute authority of the state cannot be questioned. The Islamic state is therefore a kind of totalitarian state. But because its only purpose is to implement God's will and commands, there is no cause for concern: God is just and benevolent.

Mawdudi's conception of an Islamic state rejects any Western model. In his view, everything about Western civilization is wrong and harmful because it is not God-given but elaborated by political leaders on the basis of false beliefs. The West long ago denied the sovereignty of God. Therefore, all the things its people have constructed are unacceptable. It is probable that the Iranian writer Jalal Ale-Ahmad (and Khomeini himself) knew the works of Mawdudi at least partly. Indeed, Ale-Ahmad's notion of "Westoxication" is reminiscent of the Pakistani thinker's criticism of the West.

The works of Mawdudi were translated into Arabic as well as other languages as early as 1940. Sayed Qutb, the Egyptian fundamentalist executed by Colonel Nasser, read them and quoted extensively from them. They exerted a profound influence on the Muslim Brotherhood both in Egypt and in other Muslim countries. According to many specialists, they helped shape contemporary militant fundamentalist movements.

In a way, Mawdudi was an "innovator of a fairly radical type."[6] Indeed, he addressed the problems confronting Muslim communities of the twentieth century as they faced the advance of Western modernity. Another reason for his appeal to young Muslim militants is the "resemblance he bears to the modernists in spirit, method, and content of thought." Contrary to a Navab or a Khomeini, he used the language of the day and wrote simply and clearly. That is probably why some Muslim intellectuals of the subcontinent call him "ignorant and superficial."[7]

Be that as it may, Mawlana Abul Ala Mawdudi, although not a classical Muslim cleric and scholar, played a key role in the spread of militant Islamic fundamentalism. As early as 1926, when he was a journalist in India, he wrote that "Islam was a *revolutionary ideology*" aimed at "destroying the social order of the world totally and rebuilding it from scratch." At the same time, he wrote that jihad was a "revolutionary struggle" and that the "pristine struggle between good and evil had evolved into a conflict between Islam and un-Islam."[8] His ideas epitomize the views of today's militant fundamentalists who belive that contemporary Muslim societies have returned to *jahilya* (the state of ignorance and unbelief that preceded the revelation of Islam). They also consider that only "political force" can return Muslims to the "right path."[9]

It took Mawdudi almost three decades to become a politico-religious figure among his fellow Indian Muslims and to be recognized as a revolutionary "scholar" in the Muslim world.

In contrast, Khomeini gained instant fame when he was expelled from Najaf by Saddam Hussein in September 1978 at the demand of the shah. Five months later he returned in triumph to Iran and established the Islamic Republic.

10

Enter Khomeini

With television cameras from all over the world focused on Iran, Khomeini's victory fired up imaginations in Muslim countries. Opponents of local regimes as well as militant fundamentalists looked with envy at the ayatollah and tried to follow in his footsteps. His adherence to the Shiite theology did not deter Sunnite admiration, for his success meant that it was possible to overthrow powerful rulers in the name of Islam. Groups that had gone underground reemerged, and other extremist organizations were founded. Riots and terrorist activities began to shake up the entire Middle East. Suicide attacks and hostage takings became typical, especially after the seizure of the U.S. embassy in Tehran by "students following the imam's line."

Yet the revolution was not entirely Islamic, at least at its beginning: numerous secular liberals, middle-class members, and workers participated in it. Moreover, Khomeini's views departed from mainstream Shiism. But before developing and analyzing these points, a short biographical sketch may help to place Khomeini's ideology in perspective.

A PREDESTINED CHILD

Ruhollah (literally, "spirit of Allah") Khomeini was born in 1900 in Khomein, a very small town practically lost in the midst of large agricultural estates. His grandfather, a poor *seyed*, settled there in the 1840s as a mullah serving the local feudal lord. Ruhollah's father died only a few months after his birth, in a row with the bailiff. In the superstition-ridden atmosphere of the Iranian countryside, people linked the two events and branded the infant *badghadam* (ill-omened).

To stave off bad luck, his mother gave the baby to her sister when she remarried a few months later. At the age of four he attended the local Koranic school, where he learned about the prophet—who was an orphan brought up by his uncle—and most likely recognized the similarities in their backgrounds. Undoubtedly what I call the "uncle syndrome" played some role in his case.[1] He probably thought that God had chosen him to accomplish some religious feat. Later his followers went so far as to contend that his rather uncommon name, Ruhollah, had been dictated to his father by an angel of God.

At the age of sixteen he went to Arak, near Tehran, to pursue theological studies under a conservative cleric opposed to the 1906 constitutional revolution that created a parliamentary system. Although the majority of the clergy approved the new constitution, a minority rejected it on the grounds that sovereignty belonged only to God. The leader of the latter group, Sheikh Fazlollah Nuri, was condemned by his peers and hanged. Khomeini leaned toward the doctrines of his conservative teacher.

In those days there were only two ways for people to move upward outside the upper crusts of society: the mosque or the army. Khomeini was determined to become a full-time mullah. While he was contemplating a trip to the saint-city of Qum to perfect his religious foundation, Reza Shah, the modernizer, started his reign by banning the garb and the turban of the mullahs. Even though Qum remained untouched by the reforms, the young Ruhollah rapidly became disillusioned: The clerics did not approve of any action against the government's decision, even after the 1935 sacrilegious incident in Mashad, another saint-city (the site of the shrine of Imam Reza). There a group of mullahs and bazaar merchants protesting against the shah's reforms took refuge inside the shrine. The shah sent an army brigade with heavy artillery, demolished the walls, and dislodged them.[2] An earthquake in the region of the holy city was immediately construed as a warning from God. The people, hopeful that the shah's reforms would improve their lot, did not follow calls for demonstrations, especially because the ayatollahs advised restraint.

Frustrated, Khomeini, by now a young mullah, decided to accomplish the prescribed *haj*. On his way back from Mecca, he spent some time in the Iraqi holy city of Najaf where he met, among others, Navab Safavi, some representatives of the Muslim Brotherhood, and friends of Rashid Ali Gaylani (who briefly toppled Iraq's monarchy with Nazi help in 1941).

Back in Qum in 1938, he and his brother founded a company that prospered during World War II. He rejoiced at the abdication and exile of Reza Shah, a "punishment imposed by God." The majority of the clergy was neutral or sympathetic toward the new shah who was religious to the point of superstition. (He believed that Imam Reza had saved him in his childhood and later, in a dream, ordered him to fight communist heretics.)

DOUBLE DEALINGS

Ambitious as he was, Khomeini courted an emerging grand ayatollah, Boroujerdi, whom the shah was discreetly promoting. He became one of his secretaries-advisers. At the same time, he established relations with Ayatollah Kashani, the fundamentalist cleric who had been exiled by the British because of his pro-Nazi links[3] and who continued to advocate for a political role for the clergy.

In 1945, the anticlerical writer Kasravi was assassinated by a member of the Fedayin-e-Islam.[4] Although he was one of the instigators (through his writings), Khomeini, on Ayatollah Boroujerdi's advice, set out for Tehran with a delegation of clerics to obtain pardon for the murderer. He met with the shah and obtained the pardon. According to witnesses, the two men took an instant dislike to each other.

A year later, Khomeini was sent again to the shah by Boroujerdi, this time to ask for financial support for the construction of a mosque. But before long Boroujerdi received reports about his young assistant's relations with Kashani, whose political ideas he disapproved of. The grand ayatollah dismissed Khomeini, who joined forces with Kashani when the latter, after the nationalization of the oil industry, became speaker of the parliament.[5]

In the meantime, Khomeini had gained the reputation of being an able Islamic law teacher and had already published several books based on his lectures, including *Towzih-ol-Massayel* (Explanation of the Problems). The number of his students and followers swelled (many of them were to become high-ranking officials of the Islamic Republic). His collaboration with Kashani did not last long. Disagreeing with both the ayatollah and Prime Minister Mossadegh, he decided to steer clear of politics for the time being and to concentrate on three personal aims: demolishing Boroujerdi's reputation; establishing his own credentials as an ayatollah; and expanding his own estate and fortune. He succeeded in achieving the latter two goals; as for the Grand Ayatollah Boroujerdi, he died of natural causes.

In the early 1960s, Khomeini undertook a one-month "mystical retreat" from which he emerged more convinced than ever that God wanted him to perform major duties, including the "elimination of corruption from the surface of Earth." (His followers were convinced that during his retreat he had contacts with the twelfth hidden imam and God himself and that he had received specific instructions from the Almighty.) To visitors who saw him after the retreat he appeared cold and distant: "His deep black eyes looked like two wild ravens struggling to break out of an iron cage. His bushy eyebrows added a further note of harshness to a face already harsh enough. And his beard, now uniting the conflicting extremes of white and black, denoted a passionately anarchistic owner. . . ."[6]

CONFRONTING THE SHAH

In the early 1960s, under pressure from the Kennedy administration, the shah started his own program of modernization known as the white revolution. Khomeini, by now a full-fledged ayatollah, did not remain passive. In disagreement with the bulk of the clergy, he vehemently criticized the program and encouraged among his followers an all-out attack on the monarch. But for some time he remained on the sidelines; he wanted to allow all opposition elements to use their own forces before he officially stepped in and presented his clerics as the only effective alternative to the regime.

In 1963, for the first time, he tried to foment a revolt. He failed to mobilize the masses, was imprisoned, and was later exiled first to Turkey and then to Najaf in Iraq. To the initial slogan "Islam Is in Danger," he added two others that reflected anti-Semitism and xenophobia, which were (and still are) powerful themes in all Muslim countries. But his isolation and lack of financial means impaired his influence. Nevertheless, his former students kept the flame alight and taking advantage of some of the reforms that challenged deep-seated beliefs (as, for instance, equality for women), rekindled the slogan "Islam Is in Danger." They were able to collect contributions from bazaar merchants, whose range of profits had been endangered since the creation of modern banks and a stock market.

Some of Khomeini's former pupils revived the Fedayin-e-Islam and issued a "death sentence" against the shah's new prime minister, Hassan Ali Mansour, who was eventually assassinated in January 1965. This daring act rekindled some enthusiasm for militant Islamic fundamentalism in younger generations and many mullahs. But improving economic conditions, on the one hand, and the opposition of a majority of ayatollahs to the use of violence and interference in politics, on the other hand, impaired

Khomeini's influence at least temporarily. In response, Khomeini hastily formulated his theory of *Velayat-e-Faghih* (the regency or custodianship of the theologian), which became a book entitled *Islamic Government*. In it Khomeini repeated what other fundamentalists (such as Hassan al-Banna and Mawdudi) had proclaimed before him: He affirmed that sovereignty and government are God's "properties" and that concepts such as nationalism and the separation of religion and state are heretical and sacrilegious. God sends prophets whose mission is to rule over men according to divine law (set once and for all in the Koran). Because Muhammad was the "last prophet," power should be wielded after him by those who know the divine law best, that is, the top-ranking clerics. Khomeini's theory of the cleric-ruler is not in line with the opinion of the majority of Shiite theologians.

THE MULLAH AND THE PRINCE

A story my mother used to tell me in my childhood can help explicate the rift between Khomeini and other ayatollahs about government. In the nineteenth century, a high-ranking and devout cleric was forced to pay a visit to the then shah (a Kajar) in the royal palace. He refused the chair he was offered, lifted the carpet with his cane, and sat down on the ground. That was not a mystic's act of self-mortification. Nor was it meant to offend the monarch. Indeed, for "twelver" Shiites, the government belongs to the imams and therefore remains the "property" of the twelfth who disappeared and is due to return. The palaces and everything inside them are owned by the absent imam. Whoever uses them is in the position of a robber committing a sinful act. The high-ranking mullah in my mother's story was avoiding a sinful act. The shahs, before the Pahlavis, used to pay a kind of "rent" to the mosque in order to justify their presence in the palaces.

No ruler, in the absence of the twelfth imam, can be legitimized. He can only be tolerated because society needs a "keeper" in order to avoid anarchy. Once the ruler is "provisionally" accepted, it is the duty of the clergy to exercise control in order to make sure that the ruler's edicts are in consonance with religious law.

On the basis of this theory, Iranian clerics steered clear of government. They accepted the constitution of 1906 only after a provision was included to create a Council of Religious Experts to evaluate and oversee laws adopted by parliament. According to this conception of government, the Islamic Republic lacks legitimacy. The clergy, in the absence of the twelfth imam, should play the part of watchdog in order to keep the faith and save it from destruction. It cannot be the ruler and the overseeing judge at the same time.

Most of the grand ayatollahs of the 1950s and 1960s were resolutely opposed to the mullahs' involvement in politics. In 1967, the defeat of the Arabs in the Six Day War sent shock waves throughout the Muslim world. An Iraqi Shiite cleric, Muhammad-Baqer Sadr, started a campaign to put senior members of the clergy in charge of government. He argued that Israel had won the war because Arab leaders were corrupt and had strayed from Allah's commandments. He drew up plans for the creation of an organization to be called *al-Da'wa* (The Call) to prepare the ground for a universal Islamic state led by clerics. He visited all the top mullahs residing in Najaf in order to obtain their backing. Khomeini encouraged him, but others were reticent and followed Grand Ayatollah Hakim, who was against religious authorities' involvement in government. After Hakim died in 1968, the question of Islamic government was taken up in most of Najaf's seminars. Ayatollah Khoi, who was the most senior cleric after Hakim, gave a series of lectures in which he upheld the traditional view that mullahs should remain above secular society and play the part of watchdogs. Khomeini criticized Khoi (without mentioning him by name) in his own lessons, which were published in book form under the title of *Velayat-e-Faghih* (The Custodianship of the Jurisconsult or Theologian) and later in *Islamic Government.*

There have always been some high-ranking Shiite theologians who defend the thesis of direct rule by mullahs. Khomeini quoted them at length in his book. Allah, he wrote, sent about 124,000 prophets, the first of whom was Adam. Some of them were not only "messengers" but also *nabis* (vicars of God on Earth) who could rule: Moses, Solomon, David, Jesus, and Muhammad. According to Khomeini, Jesus was not given an opportunity to form a government: "He would have used the sword like any other nabi. Those who say he was the type who would always offer his other cheek only degrade him."[7] Khomeini also enlisted the support of Plato, asserting that the Greek philosopher meant the clergy when he spoke of government by "wise men."

Khomeini's was a minority view, but the success of his revolution tipped the balance in his favor. The senior ayatollahs remained silent after he seized power. It is only now, years after his death, that they have begun to criticize him. And their criticism is rather low key.

It has always been a tradition among top clerics to maintain a degree of respect and consideration for one another. Iran's religious history offers only a few exceptions to this unwritten law.

11

Theologian and Tactician

Khomeini was not an ordinary ayatollah. From a purely religious viewpoint, he could not hold a candle to some of the top grand ayatollahs, but he was more vocal and practical than most of them. Moreover, he firmly believed that he was endowed with a messianic mission. Since childhood he was obsessed by the notion that because his early life paralled the early life of the prophet of Islam, so too would his later life. In addition, he was a descendant of Muhammad and the saint-imams. He was a *seyed*, authorized to wear the black turban and the green belt. He felt that he was predestined to accomplish great feats. In his early adolescence he understood the necessity of carrying out his responsibilities.

His first theology teacher in Arak opened his eyes to the "un-Islamic" character of the 1906 constitutional revolution. On top of that, Reza Shah, like his friend Mustafa Kemal in neighboring Turkey, imposed "un-Islamic" secular reforms. Elsewhere infidel colonialists and imperialists were ruling over Muslims. After World War II, the new shah, instead of heeding the religious establishment, followed in his father's footsteps. Newly independent Muslim countries were also pursuing an un-Islamic course of modernization. Because the creation of Israel stripped Muslims of their legitimate lands in Palestine and established a Western foothold inside *Dar-al-Islam* (the "House of Islam"), Khomeini had to step in and save Islam first in Iran and then in the rest of the Muslim world before imposing its rule on the entire planet.

THE VIRTUE OF PATIENCE

To accomplish these tasks Khomeini had to accede to power in Iran. Both Muhammad and his son-in-law Ali, the first Shiite imam, accumulated in their hands religious, political, and military duties. Ruhollah Khomeini, their descendant and heir, having reached the rank of ayatollah, had to follow suit and fight against those who had strayed from Islam.

Like his holy ancestors, Khomeini cultivated the virtue of patience. The prophet succeeded in imposing Islam on Meccans and Arabian Peninsula tribes only two years before his death. And had not Ali waited twenty-four years to become caliph? Thus Khomeini bided his time. After years of teaching, he published "Rule of the Jurisprudent or Theologian" (*Velayat-e-Faghih*). He then concentrated on tactical considerations and devised a careful plan. In the first phase, his former students, by now full mullahs, would spread his ideas about an Islamic government among members of the clergy. Indeed, the ayatollah knew all too well that his only constituency inside Iran was the corps of 200,000 mullahs serving the numerous mosques across Iran. Some of his former pupils who had already reached the ranks of the higher clergy (Montazeri, Rafsanjani, Khamenei, et al.) started a systematic campaign among the religious establishment and the wealthy bazaar merchants.

The bulk of the mullahs depended for their living on senior ayatollahs (privately funded by rich believers' donations) or on government subsidies. To enlist them Khomeini needed large amounts of money. How could his pupils convince bazaar merchants to fund him instead of the grand ayatollahs inside Iran? He was not yet well known and had only a limited audience, even in Najaf where he lived. Two unexpected events came to his rescue.

The first concerned new technologies: Thanks to the "chip" revolution, small and relatively inexpensive recorders reached Najaf's stores. Although Muslim theologians do not welcome innovation, Khomeini's pupils immediately understood the potentialities of this new Western invention. They finally convinced the ayatollah to use the device. Soon tapes of Khomeini's lectures were smuggled into Iran and widely distributed throughout the country. Played in mosques and private homes, they contributed to enlarging the ayatollah's audience in no time at all. Even liberals, notwithstanding their anti-clerical positions, listened to them because Khomeini vehemently criticized the regime and the shah.

The second unexpected event was the visit of a young cleric named Musa Sadr. On his way to Beirut, he decided to undertake a pilgrimage to the holy cities of Karbela and Najaf and at the same time to pay his respects to the ayatollahs living there.

A BLUE-EYED MULLAH

Encouraged by the Iranian authorities, Musa Sadr decided to try his chances in the large Lebanese Shiite community whose leaders always looked toward Iran. The blue-eyed cleric actually had historic ties to Lebanon: His ancestors had been brought to Persia four centuries earlier, when the Safavid dynasty decided to proclaim Shiism the state religion and badly needed trained clerics to enforce its decision. The shah sent funds to Sadr through the Iranian embassy in Beirut. But Sadr's relations with Iran soured, and he turned toward other sponsors. Libya's Colonel Qaddafi, who wanted to gain a foothold in Lebanon, helped Sadr most generously.

Sadr, who was a charismatic orator, in short order imposed himself as the leader of the Shiite community. Unlike other clerics, who courted the rich landowners, he organized the bulk of the peasants into an active, fanaticized group. In Beirut, he established a Supreme Shiite Council and created a populist movement called *Amal* (in Arabic, "Hope"). He also set up the Organization of the Disinherited (*Mostazafin*), which Khomeini adopted later in Iran. Soon Sadr became an important religious and political leader on the Lebanese stage. He allied himself with the Syrians after Hafiz Assad's coup (Assad's community, called Alawite, is in fact an offshoot of Shiism). Because the PLO (Palestinian Liberation Organization) had training camps near Tyre, a predominantly Shiite port in southern Lebanon, Sadr established close cooperation with Arafat who agreed to train Shiite fighters for the recently created military arm of Amal. Among the trainees were many Iranians who joined Khomeini in 1978.

Hani al-Hassan, a member of the PLO's High Command, boasted in 1979 that his organization had trained more than 10,000 anti-shah guerrillas.[1] Be that as it may, Sadr, who was a fundamentalist, helped Khomeini in more ways than one. First, he opened Lebanon to the ayatollah's influence. He arranged with the PLO to train Iranians as militiamen for the coming Islamic revolution. He also was instrumental in building an alliance between the ayatollah and Syria's Assad. The latter and Arafat helped the nascent Khomeini movement prepare cadres for its revolutionary activities both inside and outside of Iran. They also arranged arms smuggling and organized anti-shah Iranian-student movements in Europe and the United States.[2]

With the funds he received from Libya, Musa Sadr also helped Khomeini. But like his previous relations with the shah, his relations with Qaddafi soured. In late August 1978, he vanished during a visit to Tripoli. It was learned later that he and his companions had been assassinated on the Libyan dictator's order.[3] Many Lebanese Shiites believe that he is alive and that he went into hiding like the twelfth imam. At any rate, he left a profound imprint on Lebanese Shiites by giving them dignity and strength in face of the Sunnite and Christian communities. Like Khomeini, he was a fundamentalist cleric who was more inclined toward politics and action than theology. After the revolution in Iran, some of his close aides formed the Lebanese Hezbollah with financial and military help provided by Iran.

A SHORT-LIVED ALLIANCE WITH "LIBERALS"

Khomeini despised liberals and so-called politicians. In his view, they were all tainted by alien Western ideas. Moreover, they did not represent a real force, for the masses remained attached to the mosques and the mullahs. But as a shrewd player on the political scene, he deemed it prudent to enlist them even though it was known that they would not support a theocratic government. The ayatollah resorted to *ketman*, the Shiite-recommended "dissimulation." He hid his real objectives behind most soothing speeches. He spoke of a "democratic" Islamic Republic. Their hatred of the shah led liberals and leftists to suspend any capacity for rational assessment.

A host of reasons pushed Khomeini to seek an alliance with liberals and even leftists. First, he feared that the shah might appoint one of them as prime minister. Such a move would have convinced people who were predisposed to wait and see what advantage the new government would offer them. The Islamic revolution would have been postponed, as happened in the early 1960s when the shah named a cabinet of young "technocrats" to carry out his "white revolution." The majority of the people in 1963 did not respond to Khomeini's call for an uprising against the shah and his reforms.

The liberals could also help Khomeini alleviate Western concerns and fears. American Democratic congressmen and senators had a liking for the former members of Mossadegh's National Front—human rights activists and politicians educated in American universities. By recruiting as many of these people as possible, Khomeini thought he would appease the West and prompt it to suspend its support for the shah. He still dreaded the "Great Satan": He remembered the outcome of Mossadegh's overthrow in a CIA-engineered coup in 1953. Therefore, during the four months that he spent in France, he surrounded himself with aides in Western garb. No mullahs were visible. In his interviews, he used democratic language. In fact, he never intended to share power with liberals; nor did he intend to play the part of a Kerenski.[4]

Even a religiously prone "liberal" like Mehdi Bazargan—who was the prime minister for a few months—believed that once the revolution was victorious, Khomeini and his mullahs would return to their mosques and seminars, leaving the conduct of government business to civilians. The liberals transmitted their belief to the Americans and other Westerners. Foreign press and media delivered a message that played into the hands of the ayatollah: Iranian clergy would rid Iran of the hated shah and replace him with a democratic system. In retrospect, Khomeini appears a sly master in the art of deception.

To be sure, the alliance with the liberals and other civilians did not last long. Almost as soon as he returned to Iran, Khomeini unsheathed his sword. He addressed Bazargan as "Mister" to show his disapproval of the prime minister's European appearance and Western "language." He completely altered his declarations and dropped once and for all the word *democracy* from his speeches, stressing the duty of all Iranians to obey the orders of the mullahs.

During the preparatory stage of the revolution, Khomeini succeeded in creating a broad international base for his fundamentalist movement. In the late 1960s and early 1970s, he appointed personal representatives in many countries where Shiite minorities lived: Turkey, India, Pakistan, Kuwait, Bahrain, Qatar, the United Arab Emirates, and others. He also named representatives in Europe and in the United States in order to set up or bolster existing anti-shah organizations and Muslim associations. These representatives spread propaganda and undertook fund-raising activities. In Muslim and third-world countries, they helped facilitate the rise of fundamentalist groups. In the West, they succeeded in forging working arrangements between Islamic groups and leftist associations to such an extent that by 1977 a powerful network was in place in Washington as well as in other Western capitals. This network acted as a lobby group against the shah.

HOW THE AMERICANS HELPED KHOMEINI

In one of his first interviews in 1979, Bazargan, the Islamic Republic's first prime minister, affirmed that without the United States the revolution could not have triumphed. This assertion is true in several respects. First, Jimmy Carter's election to the presidency in November 1976 gave an involuntary boost to Khomeini's campaign against the shah. The entourage of the president-elect did not hide their contempt for the monarch, who was mainly supported by the Republicans. Iranian liberals who were in contact with the Democrats had prepared the terrain. Moreover, in the fall of 1976, after the election, Carter's staff failed to answer the shah's congratulatory cable for twenty-seven days. In a country like Iran, where people attribute symbolic significance to the most trivial incident, this delay was construed as the harbinger of a shift in American foreign policy vis-à-vis the monarch. Rumor mills overflowed. At every level of society, people became convinced that the Americans were abandoning the shah. Many liberal opponents broke their self-imposed silence and began to publish protest letters asking for the implementation of freedom of speech and other political rights.

It is true that the regime's human rights record was not good. But the opponents exaggerated their claims. Indeed, the representative of the International Commission of Jurists who investigated human rights conditions in Iran in 1976 said in his report, "The shah was way down the list of tyrants. He would not even make the A List."[5]

But the dice were cast. The leftists, the liberals, the students' associations, and even the religious groups, both inside and outside the country, used the subject to level unremitting attacks against the monarch, who was lost in his dream of transforming Iran into a world power and was not paying attention. On the contrary, he was alienating the West by emphasizing its "character flaws." Since the dramatic rise in oil prices, he had given many interviews in which he issued solemn declarations that provoked reactions on the part of the media. Thus Iran's human rights problems became the subject of more reports than those highlighting the worse records of other countries. On top of that, in early 1977 the shah sparked the discontent of the whole clergy, including the mullahs opposed to fundamentalism and to Khomeini, when he replaced the Islamic calendar with an "imperial" one starting with Cyrus's proclamation of the ancient Persian Empire.

Curiously enough, the urban guerrilla groups suddenly stopped their terrorist operations in response to an order given by Khomeini through his representatives. Indeed, Khomeini thought that if the guerrillas continued to kill American military personnel, the killings would reinforce the pro-shah lobby in Washington. The success of the Islamic revolution would be jeopardized if the United States actively opposed it.

The shah and his opponents were carefully monitoring every move made by Carter and his aides. Each speech, comment, interview, or foreign policy decision was analyzed and assessed as if it specially concerned Iran. For instance, when the President, in a speech, affirmed: "We are now free of that inordinate fear of communism which once led us to embrace any dictator who joined us in that fear,"[6] Iranians thought that he had the shah in mind. The new American administration was unaware of the convoluted ways in which the Iranian mind-set functioned.

At this juncture, the shah brought grist to Khomeini's mill by appointing a prime minister who was obsessed with inflation and decided to cut off all government subsidies to the mullahs. That was an unexpected gift to Khomeini: The clerics who had refused to join him because they received financial support from the government turned their mantles, as it were, and flocked around him. The shah and his prime minister wanted to please the new American administration that insisted on "morality and ethics" in politics; they thought that "bribing" the mullahs was unethical.

Be that as it may, Carter's aides did not hide their revulsion for the shah's rule, "which they viewed as heavily dependent on the stick of often indiscriminate brutality wielded by security forces like Savak and the carrot of vast sums of money."[7] To them the shah was "the problem," and his survival was not desired. Their objective was an "orderly transition."[8]

In sum, Iranians inferred negative messages from everything emanating from Washington because they attributed to Americans their own ways of thinking and acting. In their view, American messages never meant what their words denoted; they contained hidden meanings that had to be deciphered by Iranians. On the other hand, Americans, unaware of the Iranian propensity to decode uncoded messages, ascribed to Iranians the capacity to infer the intent of their policies. In fact, each misunderstood the other. As a result, the shah became demoralized and depressed while his opponents became elated and encouraged. Khomeini and his clerics gloated. The ayatollah understood that the time for action had come at last. The pace of the revolution would have to be stepped up before any change of "signals" could be emitted by Washington.

12

The Kindling of the Revolution

Khomeini used to tell his pupils that God endowed "great" prophets (*nabis*) with political power. He often referred to Jesus Christ as a first-rate leader and tactician. Curiously enough, the American essayist Jay Haley shares this opinion.[1] In a relatively recent study, Haley demonstrated that Jesus used the poorest elements of society to spread his teachings. He enticed them by calling them the most deserving, the salt of the Earth, and the light of the universe. He showed how one could bypass the regimes in power. Khomeini and, after him, other militant Islamic fundamentalists turned toward the "disinherited" and promoted social programs in their favor. Jesus' only mistake, in Haley's view, was to let the authorities arrest him: He should have gone underground. In contrast, the ayatollah was quick to seize the opportunities that the Carter administration's indecisiveness offered him. In contrast, the shah did not respond to the mounting uproar against his regime because he was preoccupied with his health. He kept secret his terminal illness, and after pondering the situation, he concluded that it was time to transform Iran into a "real" constitutional monarchy (which it was nominally). Indeed, the monarch had no confidence in the abilities of his son and thought that the best way to ensure the survival of his dynasty was to transfer authority to a freely elected parliament. In November 1977 he launched a "liberalization" program under which many political prisoners were released; a certain degree of freedom of the press was allowed and a committee was created to study how to conduct free elections with the participation of all political parties in the summer of 1979.[2] Obviously, the liberalization program would have strengthened secular society and jeopardized Khomeini's plans. Indeed, if implemented, the shah's plan would have stolen a march on the militant fundamentalists. In any event, it is almost certain that the shah's move had a bearing on the ayatollah's decision to issue his edict.

THE EDICT

In early December 1977, Khomeini issued a religious edict (*fatwa*) "deposing" the shah and "abrogating" the constitution. For the first time, he used in his signature the title of imam, which in the "twelver" Shiite tradition is reserved to Ali and his direct descendants.[3] Referring to his "religious authority," he ordered the "faithful" not to pay taxes and not to obey "laws promulgated by the usurper." He also called on students not to attend classes except to utter their hatred of the "dethroned" monarch and his "Western corrupt" policies.

Following the secret distribution of the edict, the clandestine "cells" created by the ayatollah's followers came out in the open to encourage people to implement the instructions given by the imam. At the same time, the liberals, heartened by Carter's insistence on human rights, started their own campaign for political freedom. The criticism of the regime also gained momentum in the Western media.

Incensed by Khomeini's insolence, the shah responded with a personal attack on him. He had a "letter" prepared and published in one of the large-circulation dailies of the capital. In it Khomeini was described as a mad "poet" of Indian origin who had homosexual tendencies and was a retainer of the British Intelligence Service. The letter appeared on January 7, 1978, and immediately provoked the anger of all clerics, even those opposed to Khomeini. Incited by Khomeini's followers, the bazaar in Qum went on strike on January 9, while young activist mullahs rampaged through the streets and attacked all the symbols of the modernizing policies of the regime such as banks, government offices, girls' schools, restaurants, and other sites. The police fired on the crowd, killing several demonstrators. The army had to be called in to restore order.

Khomeini's men in Iran took advantage of this first outburst. They set in motion the rumor mills of the mosques and bazaars to smear the shah and his family. The most fantastic news circulated: The shah was a Jew, his sisters were "cross-worshipers," his brothers and nephews were drug addicts, and so on. On top of that, Khomeini, in Najaf, declared the shah *mahdur-o-dam* (literally: "blood worthless"), meaning that any Muslim could kill him without retribution. The pro-Khomeini mullahs argued that the presence in Iran of more than 40,000 American military and civilian advisers constituted the first step of a conspiracy aimed at eradicating Islam in the country.

At about the same time, the American embassy widely distributed the text of a speech by Cyrus Vance (secretary of state) that was critical of the shah's human rights record. This was construed as a message announcing the abandonment of the shah by Washington. Both the liberals and the fundamentalists stepped up their campaign against the regime, and Khomeini's taped attacks were widely distributed in Tehran and other major cities. An atmosphere signaling the "end of an era" shrouded the capital.

According to Shiite tradition, mourning ceremonies were held forty days after the riots in Qum in memory of the martyred demonstrators. In some cities, the mourners marched in the streets, confronting police forces. Again, people were killed and wounded.

THE "CHAIN OF MARTYRDOM"

Thus was started what Amir Taheri aptly called the chain of martyrdom.[4] The guerrilla forces of the "Mujaheddin-e-Khalgh," who had stopped their terrorist activities, joined forces with the mourners. The shah, however, still felt confident that he would succeed in crushing the "unholy" alliance of the "red and black reactionaries" (as he liked to call the guerrillas and the militant fundamentalist mullahs). Repression of the critics of the regime did not stop the relentless cycle of mourning protests. On the contrary, it served only to swell the ranks of the marchers, for "secular" opposition to the shah (liberals, leftists, communists, intellectuals, and others) joined the demonstrations.

In addition to the "mourning," peaceful demonstrations were organized in Tehran and other cities by secular protesters and students. Very soon the mullahs and their clients joined the marchers from whom they stole the leadership. In some cases, Khomeini's agents resorted to violence to accelerate the "Islamic revolution." Thus the torching of a cinema in Abadan claimed more than 200 lives and was attributed to Savak (the shah's secret police), whereas it was actually the work of a militant Islamic fundamentalist.

By the summer of 1978, Khomeini had consolidated his leadership of the movement. He issued a declaration in which he affirmed, among other things, that "This holy movement . . . was founded by the powerful hand of the clergy with the support of the great Iranian nation. It is being led by the clergy without the interference of any party, front, or personality. Our movement, which is fifteen years old, is purely Islamic and shall continue under the leadership of the clergy without the slightest participation of anyone else."[5]

The Persian service of London's BBC began to broadcast Khomeini's communiqués regularly. The shah's supporters (and, indeed, the monarch himself) construed this as a British government decision to support their "own agent," Khomeini. The public at large construed it as a further sign of the abandonment of the shah by the West. In fact, some of Khomeini's sympathizers had joined the BBC. Moreover, the truth is that many organizations, including the communist Tudeh party, the Mujahiddin, the guerrillas trained by the PLO, journalists' associations, the National Front (of Mossadegh), and others, helped the ayatollah.

In September 1978 a bloody demonstration, which constituted a turning point, occurred in Tehran. The government began to collapse, but the shah refused to suppress the demonstrators. Instead, he continued to pursue his liberalization course. He seemed more and more distant and unable to understand the gravity of the situation. In fact, he was terminally ill and receiving heavy chemotherapy. Saddam Hussein dispatched the chief of his secret police to Tehran with a proposal to suppress the ayatollah. The shah, instead, asked that Khomeini be expelled to France, where the ayatollah began to enjoy unexpected access to the world media. According to numerous visitors to Neauphle-le-Chateau, near Paris, the old man firmly believed that he was in "direct communication" with God and the twelfth imam.

December 1978 coincided with Ashura, the month of mourning for Imam Hussein's assassination. Khomeini ordered demonstrations against the shah: "This would be a month of vengeance." Strikes were waged throughout the country, paralyzing the economy. In January the shah named a member of the National Front as prime minister and, accepting the advice of Americans, left the country. Immediately Khomeini named his own prime minister, Mehdi Bazargan, to head a provisional Islamic government. In February, the ayatollah and his retinue landed in Tehran airport aboard a Boeing 777. He was acclaimed by almost one million well-wishers. The Islamic Republic of Iran was born.

THE IMPORTANCE OF KHOMEINI'S REVOLUTION

I have described the rise of Khomeini in some detail because, as Bernard Lewis said, the Iranian Islamic revolution constitutes "by far the most powerful and significant movement within the Islamic world for more than a century."[6] It certainly marks a turning point in the history of twentieth-century Islamic fundamentalism and in the history of many Muslim countries.

Indeed, while sitting on his carpet in a modest room, a frail, old, bearded man wearing a black turban dethroned a forceful shah who controlled the sixth most powerful army of the world. At the same time, he ended 2,500 years of Iranian monarchy.

The elderly cleric not only succeeded in deposing a lofty monarch but also put an end to a whole era characterized by strong "modernizers" such as Atatürk (Turkey), Bourguiba (Tunisia), Boumedienne (Algeria), Nasser (Egypt), and Reza Shah (Iran). He killed, as it were, reformist movements among Muslim clerics—at least for some time.

Moreover, he triggered in the Muslim world a new kind of aggressive militant Islamic fundamentalism and revived the idea of waging a *jihad* against the infidels. Islamic terrorist movements, which mushroomed after him, unleashed a wave of killings, hostage takings, and suicide bombings both inside and outside the Muslim world.

The Iranian revolution has also become a model for all the "power seek-ers" of Muslim countries. Indeed, it presents a model for minority groups to use to win over the majority. It is, in a way, an Islamic version of the manner in which the Fascists in Italy, the Nazis in Germany, and the Bolsheviks in Russia came to power in the first decades of the twentieth century. It shows how the use of Islam (or a certain reading of the religious texts) can become more efficacious than any other approach to mobilizing the masses.

Finally, the Iranian revolution is also a lesson for extant governments: Fundamentalism will win if it is not stopped. It seems that the Algerian militias have carefully studied the events of 1977–79 in Iran.

The shah could have followed a confrontational course with the mili-tant fundamentalists, especially since many top ayatollahs did not approve of Khomeini. But he looked toward the United States rather than toward the holy city of Qum. Illuminating in that regard is an analysis made by two American experts a year after the birth of the Islamic Republic:

It may be argued that there were two possible lines of action for the American government. The first was to speed up the shah's departure and attempt to get a reformist government in power as quickly as pos-sible in order to block the revolution short of total takeover. The second was to encourage the use of the iron fist. . . . The Carter ad-ministration did neither; it hoped for the best and got the worse. . . . In the absence of any clear go-ahead from the White House a man [the shah] with a reputation for increasing indecisiveness and intensifying medical problems—with the psychological effects of both the cancer and the treatment—could hardly be expected to play a hero's role.[7]

THE PAPER TIGER

Khomeini's revolution had a number of consequences for the world. For one thing, it disturbed, at least to some degree, the international order inasmuch as it imperiled the governments of some of the major Middle East oil producers and provoked disagreements between the United States and its Western allies. But perhaps one of its most significant consequences is that it changed the way in which the United States was perceived by the Third World.

Ledeen and Lewis wrote in this respect as early as April 1980:

When it was finally realized that the Carter administration had not ever really formulated a policy, established objectives, or designed tactics to deal with the Iranian crisis, leaders and students of international affairs were forced to reevaluate their view of the effective power of the American government. If the Americans would not act in the Iranian crisis, under what circumstances could they be expected to move? If the Carter administration did not judge Iran to be a vital interest of the United States, what ally could consider itself truly supported by American expressions of loyalty?[8]

Once in power, Khomeini had ample opportunity to reflect on events. For one thing, he and his close aides were sure that God and the hidden imam had guided them. But beyond the hand of Allah, how come the Americans and "their" shah did not use the immense forces at their disposal? Khomeini probably concluded that Mao was right: America was, after all, a "paper tiger." It had accepted a cease-fire in Korea; it had been defeated in Viet Nam; and now in Iran it had lost the shah. Hence the ayatollah's many declarations to the effect that Muslims in general and Iranians in particular should not dread the United States. The fiasco of the rescue operation of 1979 and the absence of any move in the hostage crisis for more than a year proved the impotence of the United States, which could not be attributed exclusively to the indecisiveness of Carter and his administration. Under Reagan it was more of the same. The ayatollah was hesitant about the Beirut operation but when the Americans decided to leave Lebanon after the suicide bombing of the marine barracks, no doubt could survive in Khomeini's mind. Indeed, the United States was a paper tiger—a message that has been transmitted to all Muslim militant fundamentalists. They can put aside all their fears and prepare for the final jihad.

13

The Party of God

One of the most immediate consequences of the Iranian revolution was the emergence of a new breed of terrorist. Until the late 1970s, hijackings, abductions, assassinations, and bombings were carried out by groups of handsomely paid and well-disciplined "professionals" or extensively trained mercenaries. Since Khomeini, terrorists have become bands of "believers" who devote their entire lives to the advancement of a cause. Such terrorists do not fear death: They have been taught that the sacrifice of their earthly existence will open for them the "gates of paradise." They work for no pay or very low pay and consider terror a powerful and legitimate weapon in their struggle against the "enemies of God." Their training is limited and often superficial. Their promoters do not spend much on them, and in the case of suicide bombings, they serve only once. Moreover, their leaders value commitment ahead of competence. They keep them in small, loose, and unstructured groups that have no direct links with one another. The religiously bent political groups that proliferated after the Iranian revolution make extensive use of the "new" terrorists. In this respect, the Hezbollah (Party of God) is a case in point.

EVERYWHERE AND NOWHERE . . .

Under this appellation (taken from a verse of the Koran), a young mullah by the name of Hadi Ghaffary, acting at Khomeini's behest, joined to-

gether several small Islamic organizations that had long records of violence.
The Hezbollah was initially designated to help the newly created Revolu-
tionary Guards fight active opponents who demonstrated in the streets.
The name was used as early as 1973 by Hadi's father, Ayatollah Mahmood
Ghaffary. It was resurrected in 1978 in one of the revolution's slogans: "Our
Party Is the Party of Allah and Our Leader Is Ruh Allah."

The so-called party consisted of a thousand young thugs who infested
Tehran's poor neighborhoods. For a modest monthly allowance, they
waged street battles against members of more sophisticated political groups.
In contrast to its beginning, the "party" today boasts a membership of more
than one million adherents in Iran alone. Its offshoots in Muslim countries,
Europe, and America act as operatives and as a vanguard for the Islamic Republic of Iran. In Lebanon, the party also has a powerful military wing that
has bombed Israel and given assistance to militant groups like Hamas in the
Gaza Strip.

As noted by the journalist and writer Amir Taheri,[1] it is not a political
organization in the classical sense but a semisecret fraternity without a central committee, executive direction, and annual congresses. Hadi Ghaffary
used to say: "Hezbollah is an ethereal organization. It is everywhere and yet
nowhere. It is everywhere because it is nowhere! All I need to do is to pick
up the phone and in no time half a million people will gather in the streets."
Curiously enough, this language recalls that used by the mystery writers Sax
Rohmer and Alain-Sylvestre to describe their evil heroes Fu-Manchu and
Fantomas.

Hezbollah's ideology is as simple as the organization is "ethereal." The
members are taught that humans form two groups: the partisans of Allah
(Muslims) and the followers of Satan (infidels) who should be suppressed so
that Allah's rule will extend to the whole planet. Satan, they have been
told, manifests himself in all sorts of disguises: a woman's lock showing from
under her veil (chador); the bare leg of an adolescent boy; women and men
mixing in public places (cinemas, cafés, restaurants); the Israeli occupation
of Palestine; and so on. The struggle against Satan is a full-time job for party
members; the party's manifesto clearly states: "Our religion is not a mere
part-time hobby like cross-worshipers who go to church on Sunday to bribe
their God."[2]

The party recruits "volunteers for martyrdom," trains them, and sends
them on missions. In October 1983, such volunteers carried out the suicide
bombing of the American marines and French commandos in Beirut.
Other members prowl the streets, throwing acid on women's unveiled
faces, beating opponents, setting fire to newspaper offices, and so on. The

party also broadcasts courses on radio and TV on how to use various fire-arms, techniques of guerrilla warfare, kidnappings, assassinations of "ene-mies of God," and other deeds.

The bulk of the membership is composed of teenagers and even children. During the eight-year war with Iraq, "children martyrs" were regularly sent to the mine fields to clear the way for tanks. A senior member of the party explained that children could be replaced at less cost than the tanks. Khomeini's justification was obviously less cynical: Those under twenty have not yet been contaminated by satanic Western culture.[3]

In its first months, the Islamic Republic used Syrian and Palestinian ter-rorists to carry out assassinations of opponents in foreign countries. In 1980, Khomeini ordered the creation of an Iranian force capable of striking anywhere in the world. Hojatol-Islam Fazlollah Mahalati, with the assis-tance of Hadi Ghaffary and Chamran, a pro-Khomeini revolutionary who lived in Lebanon (who had both been trained in PLO camps in the early 1970s), was assigned to the task. By 1981 the hit squads started their inter-national operations.

THE LEBANESE HEZBOLLAH

With help from Iran, the Lebanese Hezbollah was established in 1982 by two members of the local Shiite political organization Amal: Abbas Mus-savi and Sheikh Subhi Tufayl. A senior local cleric, Sheikh Muhammad Hussein Fadlallah, was named its "spiritual" leader. With the consent of Syria, Khomeini also sent about one thousand Revolutionary Guards to Baalbek, in the Bekaa Valley, to train the party's members.

Like many other militant Islamic fundamentalist organizations, the Lebanese Hezbollah was able to penetrate the lower layers of the Shiite community through a vast social welfare system. (As noted by Professor R. Scott Appleby, fundamentalist welfare programs provide a way to recruit members, build sympathy in the larger community, and fight secular re-gimes.)[4] It brought relief and work to the most neglected parts of Lebanon. Using money donated by Iran, the party created a network of medical clin-ics, hospitals, schools, and job opportunities. As a result of the visible Ira-nian presence, Baalbek was dubbed Little Iran. Later the name was also applied to some southern Beirut suburbs because of the thousands of por-traits of Khomeini that were plastered on the street walls.

Hezbollah has also developed a full-fledged military wing in southern Lebanon from which it conducts its operations against Israel. It is said that Iran funds the party by providing an annual budget of from $60 million to

$100 million. Like its Iranian namesake, the Lebanese Hezbollah encompasses many small groups. It also operates the Martyrs' Foundation and two radio stations. Local councils supervise the action that the party takes in the three major areas of Shiite concentration: Beirut, the Bekaa Valley, and southern Lebanon. The overall decision-making body, the "Showra" (consultative council), is at the apex of the party. It consists of twelve leaders, the majority of whom are clerics. As in Iran, the party keeps secret the names of most of its leaders.

Hezbollah's manifesto repeats many of the Iranian credos. It states, "We are headed for confronting evil at its roots, and the roots are in America, the Great Satan." In an interview after its publication, Sheikh Fadlallah, the spiritual leader, declared, "We want to see Islam prevail throughout the world."[5] The manifesto pledges the party's obedience to Khomeini and his "divinely inspired ideas" in the following manner:

> We are the sons of the Nation of Hezbollah, whose vanguard God made victorious in Iran and who reestablished the nucleus of a central Islamic state in the world. We abide by the orders of the sole wise and just command represented by the Supreme Jurisconsult who meets the necessary qualifications and who is presently incarnate in the imam and guide, the great ayatollah . . . Khomeini, . . . enabler of the revolution of the Muslims and harbinger of their glorious renaissance.

The Lebanese party espouses Khomeini's radical theology and jurisprudence in its totality. Because compromise with non-Muslims is not allowed, the manifesto calls on Lebanese Christians to convert: "O Christians, we call on you to join Islam. In Islam you will find your safety, your happiness, the rewards of this life and of the Hereafter."

The Hezbollah has established close ties to all Palestinian radical groups,[6] including Hamas, whose leaders often visit Iran. Over the years Iran has come to use the Hezbollah as a kind of cover for its own operations. Indeed, since 1980 Hezbollah has maintained an international section called the Special Security Apparatus. Both Iran and the Hezbollah regularly deny any involvement in terrorist activities. In fact, they use aliases that vary according to the regions where their operatives strike: Islamic Resistance; Revolutionary Justice Organization; Islamic Jihad; Organization of the Oppressed on Earth, and others. In addition, party members insist that the sum of $60 million (plus) from Iran is used for welfare programs.[7]

AN ASSESSMENT

Recently a growing number of observers in Lebanon have begun to assert that the group's days as an active militant force are numbered.[8] They contend that the Hezbollah represents a minority among Lebanese Shiites. Its trained fighters are probably under one thousand. Moreover, it depends heavily on Iranian support. Since participating in the last parliamentary elections, the Hezbollah has gained representation both in the legislative body and in the government. Finally, the very existence of the party hinges on Syria's approval. Indeed, with its 35,000 troops in Lebanon, Syria has a decisive say in Lebanese affairs. Damascus has pledged to keep the peace after Israel's withdrawal from a strip in southern Lebanon, and Hezbollah's leaders have issued multiple declarations to the effect that they will continue their guerrilla operations as long as a "single" Israeli soldier remains on the soil of Lebanon. Under the leadership of Sheikh Hassan Nasrallah, who replaced Sheikh Tufayl, the Lebanese party has adopted a moderate outlook. But many commentators take issue with the view that the Hezbollah will fade away as a fighting unit after a political solution to the Syrian–Israeli conflict becomes effective.

The success of Khomeini in Iran has also encouraged Sunnite fundamentalists to reactivate old organizations or to create new ones. Thus one hears new or old names: Islamic Unification, Makassed, the Federation of the Ulemas, Islamic Liberation, and others. Some of these organizations receive financial assistance from Libya or Saudi Arabia. But none has the scope or the clout of Hezbollah.

The Iranian revolution has also encouraged former members of the Muslim Brotherhood in Egypt and Palestine to reactivate their units or to create other ones. Some of them have become very active: Hamas in the Gaza Strip, FIS[9] in Algeria, and Turabi's National Islamic Front in Sudan.

FROM STONES TO BULLETS

Hamas, an offshoot of the Muslim Brotherhood, began its operations by throwing stones at Israeli soldiers (incidents that came to be known as the *intifada*) in the Gaza Strip. It very rapidly grew into a large and efficient organization. Its name is the acronym of its Arabic title: *Harakat al-Muqawama al-Islamya* (Islamic Fighting Movement). The word also means "fieriness." The organization was founded in 1988 by Sheikh Ahmad Yassin, a paralyzed cleric from Gaza and a former member of the Muslim Brotherhood, who is currently in an Israeli prison. He is known for having lived modestly in one room and for having presented the following assessment to his foreign visitors: "The PLO is like a weak man. It has chosen to yield, to recognize the Jewish state, to accept compromises. . . . Two states, one Palestinian and one Israeli, cannot coexist." Even in prison, Yassin remains the spiritual guide of the movement.

Parallel to Hamas, another militant group emerged under the name of the Islamic Jihad Movement of Palestine. Directly inspired by the Iranian revolution, its duty is the eradication of all Western influence from the entire Muslim world. Its attacks against Israel are said to be only a tiny part of its global strategy.

With funds provided mainly by Saudi Arabia, Hamas, like the Muslim Brotherhood in Egypt and Hezbollah in Lebanon, has set up a network of welfare activities providing for the communal needs of fellow Palestinians. It has also formed a military arm containing the name of a prewar martyr, Iz-zadin Qassam Battalions.[10] After Arafat signed an accord with the Israelis, Hamas took the initiative and succeeded in forming a "Front of Ten" with the PLO factions opposed to the "peace process."[11]

Since 1992, Hamas has been represented in Tehran, a status that enables it to enjoy diplomatic privileges. It also has representatives in the United States who use front organizations for their activities.[12]

In 1993, the arrest of two American Palestinians in Israel drew attention to Hamas's activities in the United States. The two men had in their possession large sums of money.[13] According to several sources, one of the organizations that promotes Hamas's views in the United States is the Islamic Association for Palestine in North America, based in Dallas, Texas. It publishes the bimonthly *Palestine Monitor*. It also distributes English translations of Hamas literature. Another organization is called the Islamic Committee for Palestine. In December 1990, during the Persian Gulf crisis provoked by Iraq's invasion of Kuwait, it sponsored an international conference of major Islamic militant fundamentalists from the Middle East. Among the invited speakers were representatives of the Muslim Brotherhood, Islamic Jihad, Hamas, and the leader of Sudan's National Islamic Front, Hassan al-Turabi.

THE AYATOLLAH OF KHARTOUM

By all accounts, al-Turabi is the mastermind of the coup that brought theocracy to Sudan in 1989. But, unlike to Iranian militant fundamentalists, al-Turabi dons Western-style clothing when he travels outside his country. With foreigners he always uses moderate language and tries to distance himself from Iran's theocracy. He studied law and philosophy in Paris and London before he joined the Muslim Brotherhood and later created the National Islamic Front. His appearance and manners are a far cry from those of anti-Western activists. In 1994, he told an American reporter that he respected Western culture and denounced sectarianism.[14] As the journalist noted: "Mr. Turabi's conciliatory tone has come to epitomize the new and more flexible leadership in the region's Islamist movements. . . . Many argue that Turabi has become adept at telling Western audiences what they want to hear rather than what he actually believes." Like Shiite clerics, he uses dissimulation.[15] Hence the title of ayatollah bestowed on him by many observers.

The Reagan administration and Saudi Arabia wholeheartedly supported al-Turabi because of his anticommunism, especially during the Afghan revolt against Soviet occupation.[16] He was given a visa to the United States even after Sudan supported Iraq in the Persian Gulf War. The Bush administration did not put Sudan on the list of terrorist-sponsoring states before it was proved that Sudanese diplomats were not involved in the Trade Center bombing plot.

After the Gulf War, al-Turabi founded another organization called the Popular Islamic and Arab Conference. According to Egyptians, al-Turabi uses it the way the Soviet communists used the Comintern. An Egyptian intelligence officer went so far as to call it Khomeinintern.[17] Al-Turabi maintains contacts with almost all the leaders of militant Islamic fundamentalist groups both inside and outside Muslim countries. One of his most committed supporters is Rashid al-Ghannushi of Tunisia, who created the al-Nahda group and now lives in exile in London. Like al-Turabi, al-Ghannushi holds high degrees from London and Paris. He too presents to his visitors a democratic outlook and speaks of reform and pluralism. So do the Algerian leaders of the FIS. So did Khomeini during his short-lived exile in Neauphle-le-Chateau near Paris. But once back in Iran the ayatollah established an intolerant theocracy.

Al-Turabi, most candidly, told a visiting journalist that "Revolution would be the fundamentalist's only resort if other means of coming to power were denied to him or otherwise blocked."[18]

In another context, he spoke even more openly. He said that ultimately it mattered little whether Islam came to power through the ballot box or the barricades. "What matters," he added, "is that history be permitted to take its course. Islam," he declared, "is the future."[19]

Despite all the subtleties of *ketman* (dissimulation or misinformation), fundamentalists do not always hide their final aims. After recent talks with Lebanese Hezbollah spokesmen, some observers seemed convinced that the party had changed "into a different creature, equally ferocious but shrewdly planning for a role as a mainstream political party in a rebuilt Lebanon. Hezbollah is no longer demanding an Islamic revolution throughout the region. . . . The transformation of Hezbollah merely reflects the changes in Tehran. After Khomeini's death . . . power passed to younger and more tolerant religious leadership. Yet Hezbollah's tenacity has remained."[20]

Judging by its activities and the help it provides to its "aliases" or other militant organizations like Hamas, one is prompted to think: "Once a militant fundamentalist, always a militant fundamentalist."

14

The Stretching Shadow

In the Ottoman Empire, the citizens considered their sultan to be "God's shadow" on Earth. In Iran, guests are still greeted with the following words: "May your shadow never diminish." With the success of his revolution, Khomeini's shadow extended over the Muslim world.

THE SECOND MOST POPULAR MAN

Traditionally, Indonesia's Islam has been very different from that of the Middle East. It has been called the Islam of the Tropics in contract to the Islam of the Deserts. The sharia (Islamic law) is much more lenient and tolerant than it is in Saudi Arabia or Iran. Women do not wear the Islamic veil; alcoholic beverages are sold in public places; the Islamic penal code is ignored. Its population reached 165 million in the mid-1980s, and it is one of the greatest Muslim countries, although its two presidents since independence in 1946 have resisted all pressures aimed at declaring an Islamic state. Instead, they have promoted a state philosophy named Pancasila, which recognizes one God and prescribes social justice. It is neither attached to one religion, nor is it secular. The government has concluded that this doctrine has avoided violent clashes among Buddhists, Hindus, Christians,

Muslims, and others who have plagued and continue to plague Sri Lanka, the subcontinent, and other places.[1]

Yet in 1979, many portraits of Khomeini appeared on the walls of all major Indonesian cities, prompting a respected local Muslim scholar to say, "The ayatollah is the most popular man after President Suharto."[2] Since the Iranian revolution, young radical preachers have emerged in mosques, and some incidents, including attacks against precincts, took place in several cities in the early 1980s. The army and the people clashed in one of the poorest districts of Jakarta, the capital. The government reacted by forbidding the mixing of politics and religion and launching a campaign against *all* forms of extremism. In 1983, a young Muslim militant accused of participating in a violent action was condemned to death and executed. Four ex-communist leaders met the same fate two years later.

But if Indonesia succeeded in stemming the groundswell of militant fundamentalism triggered by Khomeini's rise to power in Iran, other Muslim countries, especially in the Middle East, were less lucky. Thus Egypt is still battling the fundamentalists who were once concentrated in the Muslim Brotherhood but have since created a host of smaller militant groups. One of the most active is the *Gameat-al-Islamia* (Islamic Association), inspired and led by the now famous Sheikh Omar Abdal Rahman who was sentenced to life imprisonment by a New York court.

In previous chapters, I have recounted the difficult relationship between the Muslim Brotherhood and Egyptian authorities: Nasser dissolved it and executed its leader, Sayed Qutb, in the early 1960s; Sadat revived it in order to fight his leftist opposition; Mubarak, while cracking down on militant fundamentalists, courts mainstream clerics of al-Azhar Islamic University who are no less doctrinally fundamentalist than the Brotherhood.

BLIND SHEIKHS

Sadat's assassination brought to light the Gameat-al-Islamia and its leader, Sheikh Omar Abdal Rahman, who had "blessed" many murders, including those of President Sadat in 1981 and the writer Faraj Foda in 1994. The latter mocked another blind cleric, Sheikh Kishk, who in his sermons promised "good" Muslims a lot in paradise together with "eternal erection" and the company of "adolescents of both sexes." In a debate, the al-Azhar sheikhs agreed on "frequent" erections but doubted their perpetuity. Foda, who wrote a column in a large circulation daily, riled all the sheikhs by asking: "Is that what preoccupies Muslim scholars at the end of the twentieth century?" The al-Azhar clerics advised the government to forbid him to continue writing. Sheikh Omar proved most adamant. Emulating Khomeini, he issued a death sentence, which was eventually carried out by an activist of the Gameat-al-Islamia.

Sheikh Omar's case sheds light on the way a militant Islamic group operates. A long-time member of the Brotherhood, his fiery sermons attracted a number of followers. He urged students and teachers not to sing the national anthem: They should not identify themselves as Egyptians but as Muslims, members of the *umma* (community of Muslims). He taught his audiences that it was permissible to rob Christians in order to buy weapons for "Islamic" operations and promoted the killing of Copts.[3] Arrested in connection with Sadat's murder, Sheikh Omar was released and flew to Sudan where he met with al-Turabi. He then went to Pakistan and Afghanistan where, with American encouragement, he preached jihad against the Soviets. He obtained a tourist visa for the United States and took up residence in New Jersey as imam of a local mosque. He was a suspect in the murder of the Jewish militant fundamentalist Rabbi Kahane (1990) and the slaying of an American Egyptian fund-raiser in Brooklyn (1992). Egyptian security accused him of having inspired the murders of Egyptian writers and journalists as well as several attacks on tourists and other non-Muslims.[4] He was finally arrested in connection with a terrorist scheme in the United States.

The prosecution at his trial presented a complete "theory of militant Islamic activity" in the United States.[5] Sheikh Omar was at the center of a plot to blow up New York City landmarks, having led thirteen other codefendants in a mission aimed at "punishing the United States for its perceived status as the leader of the 'infidel' order to be toppled." He called on his followers to sacrifice themselves in jihad against the enemies of Islam. Among the actions of the conspiracy were plans to assassinate President Mubarak of Egypt, to bomb United Nations headquarters, to bomb the federal building in New York City, and to destroy Hudson River bridges and tunnels. His jihad organization carried out paramilitary training at remote spots in New York State and Connecticut. Along with five other militants, Sheikh Omar was convicted and sentenced to life in prison.

Before his trial, Sheikh Omar gave an interview in which he condemned all Arab governments, except the Sudanese, and called for their overthrow. He also extolled Khomeini and attacked the "fanatic" West and its "dishonest" and "racist" media.[6] In September 1996, he sent a recorded message from prison to a conference convened in London by Muslim fundamentalists. Several Arab governments, among them Egypt and Algeria, protested and accused the British of helping militant fundamentalism and allowing in their country "the paymasters, ideologists, financiers, and zealots of international terrorism."[7]

KHOMEINI IN THE CASBAH

The leaders of the Algerian Islamic Salvation Front, more widely known as FIS (the acronym of its name in French), claim Iran as their model. Indeed, they use the same methods and tactics as Khomeini's followers did. It is certain that they have studied Iran's revolution with care and most probable that they have been in contact with the ayatollah's entourage.

The organization is presided over by a soft-spoken sheikh, Abbassi Madani, who, like Sudan's al-Turabi, holds a doctorate in philosophy from the Sorbonne. Among its younger leaders, Ali Benhaj, a young, charismatic preacher, should be mentioned. Since its foundation, FIS has recruited members among shopkeepers and young, unemployed residents of poorer neighborhoods. Like its Iranian model, FIS organized peaceful demonstrations until the militias seized power in 1994, after the annulment of the elections, which the fundamentalists were winning.

Madani was born in 1931 in a small town. His father, a devout Muslim, sent him to a Koranic school before allowing him to study in French institutions. He cooperated with the nationalists during the war for liberation but became rapidly disenchanted because of their secular policies that aped the former French colonialists. Khomeini's success in Iran prompted him and his friends to create their own party. The principal objective of the FIS is to establish an Islamic state in Algeria "not necessarily like Khomeini's," Madani says. He recognizes that basic differences exist between sharia and democracy but considers the two to be "compatible" on some points. In his words, "Our aim is to improve society. We are Muslims, and it is not our intention to convert or impose something. We want to convince in practice without fanaticism."[8]

Ali-Benhaj, the "theorist" of the movement, uses much more radical language and calls for violence against infidels. Born in 1956 in a refugee camp in Tunisia, he was orphaned when he was a child and was reared by his uncle. Like Khomeini, he drew parallels to his situation when he read the prophet's biography. In his teens, he considered himself predestined. His knowledge of Arabic allowed him to become a teacher. He also preached in a mosque where the faithful soon chose him as their imam. In an interview, Ali Benhaj said, "My father and those of his 'generation' expelled the French colonialists from our country. It is up to me and my brothers to uproot all French intellectual influence. . . . In so doing our aim is to help Algeria become predominant once again in the Mediterranean." Asked about Palestine, he declared, "With the Jews our only relation is war . . . jihad." On democracy, "It has nothing to do with God's commandments and should therefore be rejected."[9]

Yet the FIS, dominated by Madani's "soft" tactics, entered the "democratic game" and participated in the 1991 legislative elections. In the first round, it won 188 seats compared to 15 for the government. It was obvious that in the second round it would obtain the two-thirds majority that would allow it to change the constitution and establish its Islamic state. The army overtook the government, banned the FIS, and arrested its leaders. The fundamentalists resorted to violence. In the kind of civil war that is going on, more than ten thousand people have already been killed. In addition to "officials," the fundamentalists have targeted intellectuals, journalists, women who do not wear the veil, and foreigners.

At present it seems that FIS leaders are no longer in control of their members. Radical splinter groups are directing the violence and alienating the majority of the people who are opposed to brute force—regardless of its origins. As Judith Miller noted in a recent book, Algerians are "trapped, anxiously waiting to see who will prove stronger in the savage scramble for power."[10] I would add that the outcome remains linked to the future of militant fundamentalism in other Muslim countries, principally in Iran and Sudan. At any rate, Algerian intellectuals tell the following pun: "ISF [Islamic Salvation Front] is, in fact, the acronym for Iran-Sudan Front."

A TUNISIAN CONNECTION

In 1987, Tunisia severed diplomatic relations with Tehran, accusing Khomeini's agents of plotting against it. Members of the Tunisian Islamic Tendency Movement, a fundamentalist organization created by al-Ghannushi, the leader of al-Nahda, were in cahoots with the Iranian embassy, preparing to overthrow the Tunisian regime and replace it with an Islamic government. The Iranian chargé d'affaires was an officer of the Revolutionary Guards who was actively helping the plotters.[11]

In fact, reactions against the secular policies of the Tunisian government began as early as 1976, when al-Ghannushi set up a group of about two hundred teachers and students under the name L'Action Islamique. The group changed its name several times. Beginning in 1981, it organized Koranic classes and offered lectures on the works of al-Banna, Mawdudi, Qutb, and Khomeini. Over the years, the more radical elements split and founded their own clandestine revolutionary cells under the guidance of Sheikh

Abdul-Fattah Mocnor, nicknamed the Tunisian Khomeini. In 1984 the militants, in collusion with Iranian-inspired elements, organized so-called bread riots against rising prices, which were tinged with Islamist overtones. In 1985, an underground "Tunisian Section of Islamic Jihad" proclaimed a jihad against the government. The "first phase" of its "armed struggle" consisted of acid attacks on unveiled women and petrol bombings of American businesses. The second phase, which occurred the following year, was focused on attacking banks and government offices.[12] Most of its leaders were arrested and tried. One leader defended his action by referring to the "duty of every Muslim to fight the infidels. . . . [We wanted to fight against a regime that has sold itself to American and French imperialism. . . . We wanted to create anarchy and a climate suitable for an Islamic revolution."[13]

Khomeini's shadow also extended to Morocco, where several militant fundamentalist groups, some of which openly advocated the overthrow of the monarchy, were formed. But in each case, they were rapidly dismantled, and the leaders who escaped established offices in European capitals. Given the tribal support enjoyed by the monarchy in Morocco, it does not seem that the militant fundamentalists have immediate chances of success. But with outside pressures and the new technologies of electronic information, the situation might change.

INSIDE ISRAEL

Undoubtedly Khomeini struck a deep chord with Muslims at large irrespective of their sects. His influence has even reached Israel. It is true that a surge of religious assiduity has been evident among Israeli Muslims since the Six Day War of 1967, but that trend suddenly swelled after Khomeini's victory over the shah.

In the occupied territories, long before the appearance of Hamas, militant fundamentalist groups became active in Gaza and the West Bank. The Muslim Brotherhood and *Tahrir* (Liberation) exhorted people to observe Islamic rules in their daily lives as a sign of protest against the Jewish state. Israeli authorities turned a blind eye on their activities because these fundamentalists fought the secular left as well as the PLO; it is said that they even helped Hamas when it was founded.

After 1979 Khomeini's influence compounded Islamist trends. Inside Israel, many young Arab Israelis who were members of leftist parties joined the Islamic groups. A clandestine organization known as the Family of Jihad carried out sabotage such as burning crops and uprooting trees. Another secret group called the Family of Religion spread fundamentalist propaganda. Although tight controls and severe repression limited the efficiency of these movements, religious fervor thrived. Numerous mosques were built in cities and villages. Muslims in Israel did not hide their admiration for Khomeini, and their approval of Iran inspired Hezbollah attacks against Israel.

Reporting from Umm al-Fahim in Israel, *New York Times* columnist Thomas Friedman noted in 1987 that Khomeini "appears to be totally discredited in the eyes of Muslim Israelis . . . because of the way they view the Iranian revolution as having devoured its own children and divided the Islamic world."[14] Be that as it may, the shadow that Khomeini cast over Israel triggered the Islamic fundamentalist revival inside Israel.

The Iranian revolution has also had visible effects in the other Muslim countries (Malaysia, Pakistan, Central Asian republics) as well as on Muslim minorities in India and Muslim immigrants in Europe and the Americas. Tehran obviously prods the surge of fundamentalism as much as it can. One of the most striking successes of militant fundamentalism after Iran and Sudan is the position of the Welfare party in Turkey and the nomination of its leader as prime minister. Aproximately seventy-two years after the emergence of a secular state, the fundamentalists came to power through the ballot box.

THE STRANGE CASE OF TURKEY

In 1979, a few months after the triumph of theocracy in Iran, a Turkish senator published an article entitled "Iran Would Never Be Able to Export Its Religious Revolution to Turkey."[15] He argued that his country was a "constitutional democracy" that had no "supreme leader" and that members of the clergy had been reduced to the level of government employees. On the other hand, the Turkish Army, contrary to Iran's, was institutionalized and not under the authority of one person (such as the shah in Iran). Turkey's problems, added the senator, were of an economic, not a religious, nature. He concluded, "Anything can happen in Turkey, except a political void."

While the senator was boasting of the solidity of Turkey's secular system, Islamic fundamentalists were on the move, like termites undermining the foundations of a house. One of their leaders, Necmettin Erbakan, founded the *Refah* (Welfare) party, which won more parliamentary seats than any of its two secular rivals in 1996. As usual, Western observers pointed their fingers at Turkey's economic ills. It is true that many Turks who voted for Refah are opposed to fundamentalism. Typical of this group is a young shopkeeper in Ankara who does not observe the sharia and whose girlfriend is Christian. He explains:

> I love traveling in Europe. At night I go to discos and drink alcohol.
> All of this means that I shouldn't like Refah. But I gave them my vote.
> I did it because 80 percent of the people in this country are poor and
> the leaders of other parties don't do anything for them. The corruption and bribery are just too much. I am not afraid of fundamentalists
> because the army will never allow them. My vote was not for Islam but
> for cleaner and better government.[16]

Indeed, the army considers itself the ultimate guarantor of secular rule and other reforms instituted by Atatürk.[17] Moreover, economic problems are piling up dangerously. But without Khomeini's victory in Iran, the success of his tactics, and the revival of Islamic discourse, no Islamic fundamentalist politician would have succeeded in Turkey or, for that matter, elsewhere.

Moreover, one should not forget that even though seventy years have elapsed since Atatürk's secular reforms became effective, the "religious question" remains unsolved and resurfaces regularly, sometimes violently. As Altan Gokalp, a Turkish scholar, emphasized in a recent study, militant fundamentalism was never disarmed in Turkey; instead, it adopted a low profile and went underground.[18] It is more than probable that Khomeini's rise in Iran gave fundamentalism in Turkey, as in other Muslim countries, a new lease on life.

According to an American reporter visiting Istanbul after the 1995 riots that arrayed radical Sunnites against the Alevis, a minority representing almost 20 percent of the Muslims, "many Turks believe that their country will have to find a middle path between secularism and Islamic fundamentalism."[19] The "Kemalists" have failed to produce a "moral code" to replace the old Muslim one.[20]

As David Pryce-Jones put it in his study of the region:

> Atatürk's resort to traditional despotic methods in order to compel his
> people to modernize without forms of voluntary associations was a
> very great paradox and likely to cause dislocation and lasting strains. . . .
> To a devout Muslim this was heresy. Whether it is feasible to decree
> into existence a supposedly modern and democratically conceived
> state did not concern Atatürk, and he certainly sought no systematic
> or philosophical reconciliation between such a state and Islam.[21]

The ground was being prepared for a revival of fundamentalism when Iranian activists began to cross the Turkish border.

EXPORTING THE REVOLUTION

At the beginning (February 1979) of their Islamic revolution, Khomeini and his closest allies (who continue to influence events) clearly stated their intention to encourage similar Islamic revolts throughout the Persian Gulf region and in the Muslim world beyond. In many cases, they did not have to intervene directly, for local activists preempted them. Thus the frustrated Muslims of Lucknow, the capital of the Indian state of Uttar Pradesh, did not wait for Iranian agents to encourage them to proclaim their "submission" to the ayatollah. The local Shiite community plastered pictures of Khomeini on the walls of the capital. Some people went so far as to claim that the imam was born there.[22]

The Iranian example also triggered a growing wave of fundamentalism in Malaysia, threatening the delicate balance between the Muslim Malays, who constitute 50 percent of the population, and the rest of the population—Chinese, Indian, and Southeast Asians who practice a variety of religions, including Buddhism, Taoism, Hinduism, and Sikh. The government launched a campaign to convince fundamentalists—many of them young people—that because Islam is "vital and adaptable," there is no need to reject progress and social liberalism.

With Iranian encouragement, a local Hezbollah was formed in Srinagar, Kashmir. Its members traveled clandestinely to Pakistan, where Afghan mujahiddins taught them guerrilla warfare.[23]

In Lebanon, Sheikh Fadlallah's bodyguards display buttons championing the Islamic Republic of Iran in Persian and English.[24] In Pakistan in 1988, the dictator Zia ul Haq instituted the sharia as the law of the country without consulting the voters. In Nigeria, Khomeini's example kindled a burst of Muslim fundamentalist fervor. In the northern heartland of the country, demands for Islamization grew loud. The resulting agitation continues to threaten the stability of the entire country.[25]

In 1981, Khomeini ordered the creation of an "army of 20 million, which . . . would fight to hoist the flag of Allah in every capital of the world."[26] The ayatollah's wish did not materialize, but almost a decade after his death, his shadow continues to obscure the skies over some Muslim countries.

15

The Causes of Militant Fundamentalism

By itself, Khomeini's rise to power in Iran could not have generated militant fundamentalism in other Muslim countries if the ground had not already been prepared and if conditions and circumstances had not been suitable. In previous chapters, I tackled the question of causes, which vary from one country to another according to the nature and intensity of local problems. But it seems possible to identify common denominators, which would help illuminate the phenomenon wherever it arises. Many experts highlight economic conditions as the main element in the propagation of militant fundamentalism.

THE "BREAD RIOTS"

In Jordan, the lifting of government subsidies for bread in mid-August 1996 sent prices up and provoked riots in the Dead Sea town of Kerak. Most observers attributed them to "deep frustrations among Jordan's poor over the lack of any tangible dividends from recent events: the introduction of limited democracy, the IMF austerity program, and, above all, the peace treaty signed with Israel." In the view of one *New York Times* reporter, "all this has given ready ammunition to the Islamic opposition which has opposed pro-Western and pro-Israel facets of the King's policies."[1]

In the opinion of most specialists, the failure of almost all economic development programs to improve the lot of the masses has stirred frustrations and disappointments. At the same time, the fundamentalists have set up their own welfare networks to help the needy. Moreover, the continuing population explosion has multiplied the number of jobless and erased the benefits of any economic progress. As an American observer wrote in 1993 about Egypt, "[The country] would face a fundamentalist threat even if Iran and Sudan did not exist. Home-grown poverty, overpopulation, poor housing, and rampant corruption would almost certainly stir radicalism and unrest without any agitation from outside."[2] Referring to the welfare networks that he called "Islamicization by the bottom" (as opposed to governmental promotion of Islamic values by providing help to the religious establishment), the French scholar Gilles Kepel has affirmed that this "economic action" explains the sweeping success of militant Islam in the Algerian electoral processes in 1990 and 1992.[3] I would say only partially. Indeed, the case of Saudi Arabia tends to prove the contrary. The regime, already fundamentalist and strictly implementing the Islamic code, has used part of its oil riches to transform the whole country into a kind of welfare state that is absolutely unique in the world. Yet militant fundamentalists are taking swipes at the Saudi rulers.

The economic causes of fundamentalism should not be exaggerated. The gap between rich and poor is certainly not the essential element in the fundamentalist surge. One should not forget that many *surats* (chapters) of the Koran forbid the faithful to question social inequalities.[4] Indeed, as a young Egyptian worker, "riding a low-grade train," confided to the American reporter Chris Hedges, "We know that God created different classes of people. Life is like riding on a train: There are first, second, and third class. So we were created to be in the third class. It is not for us to ask why."[5]

POLITICAL TYRANNY AND PETRO-DOLLARS

To economic causes, many observers add political repression as a reason for the spread of fundamentalism. Thus A. M. Rosenthal said in one of his weekly columns, "Their nature of government created the condition for revolt: tyranny and exploitation of the people. In the name of Islam, fundamentalists seized the opportunity for revolution."[6]

These observers tend to forget the proclivity of the Muslim masses for an "absolute" leader. They yearn for what the nineteenth-century theorist al-Afghani called the just despot (see chapter 8). If the Iranian masses revolted against the shah's absolutism, why did they submit to Khomeini's will immediately after the monarch's departure? Right after his return to Iran, the ayatollah decreed, "Obey God and those among you who represent divine authority. . . . The only government God accepts is one organized according to His laws and this is impossible without the complete control of the clergy."[7]

It is true that Muslims are often angry at their governments. On the train mentioned above, a passenger told Chris Hedges, "My brother has not had a job for over two years. It is not his fault. He can't have a normal life, so of course he goes to the mosques. He listens to what these militants say, though he has not joined them, because he is desperate and angry. Those who have enough do not understand how disoriented and desperate people become." Hedges adds: "Other passengers, while wary of the Islamic movement, praised what they see as the militants' courage and moral probity and their call for a more equitable society." It seems that today's Muslims are torn between two opposing tendencies: resignation and resentment against their governments.

Muslim governments often helped in the development of Islamic fundamentalism. Their double-edged policies, which simultaneously fight violent militant fundamentalism and court the so-called Muslim centrists, have, in fact, given a boost to the extremists. Mainstream Muslim clerics hold the same beliefs as the militants but use a less aggressive terminology. Moreover, in Egypt, for instance, Sadat legally reestablished the Muslim Brotherhood banned by his predecessor, Nasser, and used the militants to fight against his own leftist opposition. In Iran in the mid-1970s, the shah, while fighting against the militant Islamists, created, alongside the Literacy Corps, a Religious Corps composed of young mullahs who were sent across the country to teach strict Islamic principles to students and illiterate adults. A French scholar recently wrote:

In order to try to profit from this new source of legitimacy [religion], governments generally reinforce the position of institutional Islam [symbolized in Egypt by the al-Azhar University], which they manage to keep under control, and reinject great quantities of religious terms into their political rhetoric. The paradox of this trend is that it lends credibility to the very people it aims at driving from the political scene.[8]

Another case in point is Saudi Arabia, where the king used his sudden dollar surpluses to fund Islamic "charitable" organizations set up by local militants in order to attract members to their fundamentalist groups. It is instructive to recall that the "bombing manual" found in the possession of one of the "Trade Center" convicts was printed by the World Assembly of Muslim Youths, founded by Saudi Arabia.

As long ago as the 1950s, the Saudis considered the Egyptian Muslim Brotherhood with sympathy. They had not forgotten the role that Egypt played in the destruction of the first Saudi regime in the nineteenth century when Mohammed Ali's troops expelled them from Arabia. Moreover, Nasser opposed them.[9]

In the same manner, the United States bears great responsibility for the spread of fundamentalism both inside and outside the Muslim world. Indeed, the Americans dealt with the cold war by playing the "Islamic card" from the bottom of the deck. They encouraged Saudi Arabia's King Faisal to organize the Islamic Conference to oppose Arab nationalism, whose adherents were leaning toward the Soviets. They inspired the oil-enriched sheikhs to create the Islamic Development Bank, which gave generous loans to countries that agreed to implement the sharia.

The Americans went even further when the Soviets invaded Afghanistan. They poured billions of dollars into the coffers of Afghan chieftains, favoring the militant fundamentalists among them. The CIA trained their militants, who are now performing terrorist activities in both the Western and Muslim worlds.[10]

THE INFERIORITY COMPLEX

In my opinion, cultural factors are more important than economic and political ones. From this angle, one can say that three interacting factors are nurturing the present wave of militant Islamic fundamentalism. One is a complex reaction to the humiliations to which Muslims were subjected for more than a century. Another is related to the history of Muslims since the twelfth century. The third factor concerns what I would call a general malaise, which has pervaded the Muslim world since the mid-1950s.

For many centuries, Muslims have lived with a sense that their world is superior to the non-Muslim world. They believe that Islam is the "last" religion, the final message sent by God to humans. Since the twelfth century, they have been told by their highest religious authorities that the Koran contains all they need to know.

In the nineteenth century, when Muslims began to discover that the West had advanced ahead of them, both in technology and in military science, a feeling of humiliation stirred in them. They had lost their dominant place in the world to the advancing Christians. In their own countries, foreign ideas and ways of life confronted them. In many cases, foreign "rulers" imposed themselves and reduced Muslim countries to the status of colonial "foreign possessions." Finally, emancipated women and children began to challenge their authority inside their homes. The fabric of their social and private life was fizzling away. The feeling of humiliation reached its peak with the Arab defeat of 1967 by Israel's tiny army. Nationalism, which had soothed Muslims for some decades, lost its attraction.

At that point, militant fundamentalism came into the picture. Its activists stepped in and filled the void left by nationalists and modernizers: Only God could help Muslims in their adversity, and for that to happen they had to return to the strict implementation of the divine law. Militant fundamentalism helped Muslims restore their sense of superiority. The widespread admiration for Khomeini stemmed principally from the fact that he invoked Islam and withstood the mightiest superpower, the United States. The suicide bombings of the American marines and the French commandos in Beirut in 1983 and the ensuing withdrawal of Western forces elicited a burst of joy.

Fundamentalism has given Muslims confidence in their future. That is one of the reasons why they refuse to condemn terrorist acts in Israel and elsewhere even when they are basically opposed to violence. The slogans Islam Is the Solution, Everything Is in the Koran, Islam Is Superior to Other Religions, Let's Start a New Jihad, and so on have renewed the pride of Muslims. Hence support given by students and highly educated people to militant fundamentalists. (Indeed, engineers, doctors, lawyers, and professors in many countries cooperate closely with the militants.)

AMERICA CAN DO NOTHING!

Khomeini's victory in Iran helped Muslims throughout the world rid themselves of their inferiority complex. By calling the United States the Great Satan and confronting it, Khomeini offered Muslims an outlet for their explosive feelings stemming from vivid memories of Western colonial rule and imperialism, of humiliation suffered at the hands of Western infidels and their Israeli "pawns." He showed that it was possible for Muslims to envisage fighting a superpower. In the 1980s, the leader of the Lebanese Hezbollah used to boast, "The great achievement of Hezbollah in this period is that by way of two martyrdom operations against the U.S. Marines and French paratroopers, it evicted America and the multinational forces from Lebanon."[11]

Khomeini proved that "America can do nothing" when confronted with "true" Muslims. Indeed, not only can the faithful engage in a battle with the "evil" one, but it is his duty to do so. The photographs of the American embassy in Tehran, seized almost twenty years ago and still in the hands of Iranians, constitute a perfect reminder of U.S. impotence. Ironically, the embassy has been transformed into a school for the training of Revolutionary Guards. The enemies of the West are well and still in power.

Muslims are no longer afraid of the superiority of the American superpower. As an Arab writer noted, "The overthrow of the shah of Iran was the first sign of the power that the people of the Middle East realized they could muster in the face of superior force."[12]

At the same time, Muslims were able to overcome the obsessive fears that had been triggered by their old beliefs in conspiracy theories. The 1950s, when the CIA organized a successful coup d'état against Mossadegh, and the 1960s, when Israel attacked the Arabs and defeated them in less than a week, were definitely over. Qaddafi in Libya, Assad in Syria, the mullahs in Iran, and Saddam Hussein in Iraq were still in place, despite America's opposition to them.

Another factor that helped spread militant fundamentalism is the favorable ground on which it developed. The entire Muslim world turned fundamentalist around the twelfth century,[13] when ultraconservative interpretations of the Koran triumphed. Since that time, whenever Islamic ways of life have "softened," ultrafundamentalists have reacted against the laxity of leaders who failed to implement the sharia. Therefore, the ground was ready in Iran as well as elsewhere for the surge of militant Islamic movements.

THE GREAT MALAISE

The third factor that interacted with the two already mentioned and facilitated the spread of militancy is the general malaise that has gripped Muslim societies at almost every level for more than a century. It can be traced to the second half of the nineteenth century, when Muslims came into contact with a strong and aggressive Europe that was animated by ideas of modernization. In the twentieth century, programs were undertaken in many parts of the "House of Islam"—to the dismay of the Sunnite ulemas and Shiite ayatollahs. As one can imagine, the innovations clashed, sometimes violently, with the local traditional culture. In the second half of the twentieth century, this malaise was aggravated by the one that struck the Western world itself.

In earlier chapters, I touched on the effects of reforms introduced by such leaders as Atatürk in Turkey and Reza Shah in Iran. In 1928, for instance, Reza Shah introduced compulsory military service and a version of the European suit to be worn with a specially designated kepi. He thought that after living two years under one flag flown in different parts of the country, young men would lose their tribal and regional loyalties and become full citizens of the national state and use the Persian language instead of local dialects. Until 1928, a man's ethnic and tribal origin as well as his station in society was visible through his clothes and hat. The "uniform" costume and kepi, in Reza Shah's view, would blur tribal and class distinctions.

In a way, these sudden signs of change underlined the sweeping transformation that the country was undergoing and provoked a general malaise. The changes imposed great strains and stresses on the traditional society and cracked the structure of loyalties and the old system of values. Poorly understood and imperfectly implemented, the new institutions and values imported from the West failed to meet the needs and aspirations of the people. At the same time, the tribal chiefs and the mullahs understood that their existence as a privileged class was in danger.

For the first time in their lives, people had to line up to get "identity cards" containing chosen family names; decisions concerning justice, which had been almost instantaneously rendered in religious tribunals, now took months, forcing peasants and villagers to stay in town for the duration of trials; administrative and commercial paperwork obligated many illiterate citizens to resort to "middlemen" and other expensive kinds of intermediaries.

Indeed, modern societies impose excruciating personal choices and decisions on their members, whereas in a traditional environment, tribal chiefs, family members, and mullahs help people deal with their problems. The demads of modern life are complicated enough in advanced industrialized countries, but in emerging third-world societies, they could make life seem unbearable. Hence the appeal of fundamentalism in calling for a return to traditional ways of living. The slogan "Everything a Muslim Needs Has Been Laid Down by God in the Koran and the Sunna of the Prophet" contrasts sharply with the complexities of modern societies that require specialized knowledge and know-how at every level. The oversimplistic ratiocinations of fundamentalists please the uneducated masses and lure them into supporting the militants, at least before they seize power.

In the 1960s and 1970s, all Muslim countries introduced development plans inspired by what was going on in capitalist or socialist societies. In order to stave off objections by clerics, technocrats referred to the Koran's verses or culled some of the prophet's sayings to justify such reforms as monogamy, the distribution of land to the peasants, the collection of taxes, and so on. But for a host of reasons (incompetence, corruption, haste, religious resistance, and other hindrances), the programs did not live up to their expectations. Their failure helped militant fundamentalists attribute the fiasco to "straying from the sharia."

In the best case, modernization half succeeded and split Muslim societies into communities of two levels. The countries presented to the outside a facade of progress, while inside the traditional ways survived more or less intact. Thus, for example, almost all Muslim countries have elected parliaments, but governments resort to severe repression and censorship, and leaders cling to power by getting themselves reelected with more than 95 percent of the votes. As the late scholar G. E. Von Grunebaum remarked, "Even an educated citizen is forced to play two completely different parts: one traditional and one westernized."[14]

A CONVERSATION ABOUT "IDENTITY"

Von Grunebaum's remark reminds me of what Albert Hourani, a brilliant Lebanese-Christian scholar, once wrote:

> To be a Levantine is to live in two worlds or more at once, without belonging to either; to be able to go through the external forms which indicate the possession of a certain nationality, religion, culture without actually possessing it. It is no longer to have standard values of one's own, not to be able to create but only able to imitate. It is to belong to no community and to possess nothing of one's own. It reveals itself in lostness, pretentiousness, cynicism, and despair.[15]

It has become the wont of specialists to speak about "the identity crisis" of Muslims. In the 1970s, when I was an adviser to the Aspen Institute for Humanistic Studies, I met among the trustees a distinguished Indonesian professor who had been involved in the modernization programs of his country. We had many conversations on the subject. I concurred with him that the breakdown of traditional structures and customs was accompanied in our part of the world by a genuine difficulty to relate to the emerging new social structures. Professor Soedjatmoko contended that that reaction had left many in our traditional societies with great uncertainty and anxiety, leading in some cases to a "crisis of identity." In his opinion, the image of one's self, the answer to questions such as Who am I? and Who do I want to be? had become blurred. Questions such as To whom or to what should I be loyal? On whom should I model myself? and Which pattern of behavior should I adjust to? no longer elicited meaningful answers, and no new ones seemed to suggest themselves.

In those days, it was fashionable to speak of "roots" and "identity." Everybody was eager to find his or her roots. As I told Soedjatmoko, to me the problem in developing countries like ours was somehow different. People felt at sea in the process of modernization because our leaders had imported merely the "material" side of modernity and rejected the rest, ignoring the "democratic" debate without which "new" elements cannot be usefully absorbed. People did not understand the what and the why of the changes. They could not effectively discuss, complain, approve, or reject. They had to bow to the will of the authorities. I added, "Only vegetals have roots . . . and as for identity, it is mainly a matter of interest to the police and other repressive agencies." Soedjatmoko laughed. He too had been shaped by Western culture. But we agreed about the idea of "split personality or identity" referred to by Von Grunebaum and Hourani. . . . It is obvious that the idea of returning to the mores and habits of the past has a "soothing" effect on citizens whose way of life has been shattered by too many innovations. I remember how long it took my grandmother to get used to our "family name" when family names became compulsory in Iran in the mid-1920s.

At any rate, the malaise of Muslim semimodernized societies is compounded by the one that strikes the Western world, where disenchantment with progress is accelerating. Indeed, the fundamentalists ask (with a grin), Why should we import Western ways and methods when Westerners themselves criticize them and complain of their harmful consequences? In December 1979 a young Tunisian told a friend of mine, who was conducting an inquiry in Tunis, "The West is on the downgrade. . . . We don't want to regress with them. . . . When we see our youth aping your ways of life, we think it would be much better to create our own Islamic system. . . ."[16]

A METAPHYSICAL DILEMMA

The necessity of change has created a dilemma for the contemporary educated Muslim. I shall quote here two Arab intellectuals whose remarks open a window on the preoccupations of modern Muslims.

The first is an Algerian who spoke with a French reporter in 1956 (eight years before independence):

What distresses me and even fills me with unbearable anguish are all these pell-mell borrowings from the West which do not take into account the fact that Islam has once and for all issued laws concerning every aspect of our private and collective lives. These laws encompass everything from the family to the collective body of our nation. Christian religious texts are silent about all that. Islamic society is governed by divine law while other societies live under human-made ones.[17]

The second example concerns an English-educated Jordanian who in 1960 confided to a French journalist,

As I live within my time and have been educated in the West, it seems to me that progress can be achieved *only outside* of tradition. We are a number of friends in Jordan who think along this line. We try to imagine difficult, if not impossible, combinations of modernity and tradition. Ours is a *tragic dilemma*. Is it possible to avoid "killing" God when we try to isolate religion from our social system which is condemned by technical and scientific progress? In our Islam, society and religion are mingled together. They both exist by their union. Can we modernize without incurring *damnation?*[18]

The above two comments by highly educated Muslims shed light on the drama of modernization in the Muslim world. The problem is not only economic and social; it has a deep and troubling metaphysical dimension that militant fundamentalists often manipulate in order to fulfill their quest for power. Recently a Turkish intellectual summarized the dilemma in slightly different terms, "We have never learned a natural way to deal with religion. People feel they have to be either fundamentalist or atheist."[19]

Indeed, fundamentalism, which triumphed around the twelfth century, has stripped from Muslims all reasonable alternatives. An American Muslim from the subcontinent documented this sad situation in a recent essay: "The dogmatists had created a situation in which Muslim societies faced with the imperative need to educate their people for life in the modern world were forced to make a painful and self-defeating choice: Either abandon the Koran and Islam, or turn their back on the modern world."[20]

16

The Broken Crescent

Local sociopolitical circumstances might shape different versions of militant Islamic fundamentalism in different ways, but all of them share the same general goal: Seize power in order to implement divine law on Earth. All fundamentalists yearn for the establishment of Islamic governments in their respective countries pending the "reunification" of the "community of Muslims" under the rule of one leader (*caliph*) and the launching of the "final" jihad, which will bring the whole planet into the fold of Islam. They long for the "absolute" commander, the "philosopher-king" (Farabi, tenth century), the "just despot" (al-Afghani, nineteenth century), or the "ruler whose tenure of power and office is limited only by his fidelity to Islam" (Mawdudi, twentieth century) who would guide them on the "right path."[1] Awaiting the emergence of such a government, fundamentalists obey their "spiritual leaders": a sheikh (among Sunnites) or an ayatollah (among Shiites).

FROM WORDS TO DEEDS

To a large extent, Khomeini carried out his declared intentions. His book describing his theory of "Velayat-e-Faghih" (republished after the revolution under the title *Islamic Government*) contained the following lines: "What is the good of us [clergy] asking for the hand of a thieve [*sic*] to be severed or an adulteress to be stoned to death when all we can do is recommend such punishments, having no power to implement them?" In the ayatollah's view, Islam has strict rules for every aspect of life, and only mullahs who know Allah's will can enforce them. Therefore, the government should be in the hands of the clergy.

Although Khomeini gave no details of the government that he envisioned, he indicated that the "supreme leader" should know the sharia and be "just" and "free of sin." He refrained from advancing his own candidacy for the position of "supreme leader of all Muslims." (Indeed, he made clear that there could be only *one* Islamic universal state. The unification of all Muslims under one rule is actually the only part of his theory that he failed to realize.) The power of such a "guide" is limited only by God's authority.

In the Islamic Republic of Iran, the highest authority is not the president but the supreme spiritual guide (vicar-jurisprudent) who can unilaterally void any governmental or parliamentary decision. In Sudan, where theocracy was instituted via a 1989 military coup, the real power lies in the hands of Turabi who has no governmental rank. The concept of "supreme leader" is in line with Islamic tradition. Indeed, the four caliphs "elected" after Muhammad's death exerted absolute power, and their opponents could only resort to violence to unseat them. (The second, third, and fourth—Umar, Uthman, and Ali—were murdered; the fifth instituted a hereditary kingship that was bloodily suppressed in 750 by the Abbassids.)

Khomeini's Islamic government was not basically different from the early caliphates. He used the title of caliph as well as imam and faghih (jurisprudent) often in his book. He wrote, "It is up to the imams and faghihs to form the government and use it to implement the divine prescriptions and establish a just and equitable Islamic regime in the service of the people. This entails a lot of work and burdens for them. But what can they do? They have been endowed with this divine mission. . . ." In another part of his book, Khomeini emphasized that the Islamic government is a "constitutional one in the sense that the responsible authorities are bound by a set of conditions defined in the Koran and the prophet's Sunna."

A few weeks before his return to Iran, Khomeini declared, "We, the clergy, have no intention of governing. The religious leaders direct the people in order to clarify the objectives and the exigencies of Islam."[2] After his return, in a speech delivered on June 16, 1979, he affirmed, "We want to draft the constitution of the Islamic Republic. If it was an ordinary constitution or a democratic one, you, the westernized jurists and intellectuals, would be competent to advise. But for an Islamic republic you are not authorized to interfere because you don't know Islam. . . . The duty of the clergy is to supervise the affairs of the state."[3] In August 1979, when he addressed the Assembly of Experts in charge of drafting the constitution, Khomeini declared, "You are here in order to write a 100 percent Islamic constitution.... The religious leaders alone have the right to decide what is or is not in congruence with Islam. The other members should refrain from interfering.[4]

A CURIOUS COINCIDENCE

As I indicated earlier,[5] Jamal-ud-Din al-Afghani described his concept of the just despot in an article published in February 1879. Khomeini returned to Iran in February 1979, exactly one hundred years after his fellow Iranian mullah defined the "despotic" nature of the Islamic regime that he proposed. Whatever meaning one ascribes to this temporal coincidence, it is true that the constitution of Khomeini's Islamic Republic reflects many conceptions of the nineteenth-century mullah.

The Islamic Republic is conceived as a government literally under God, who has delegated his power on Earth to Muhammad. The latter, in turn, entrusted Ali and his direct descendants with the task of guiding the "community of believers." The twelfth imam entered the "grand occultation" in his childhood and is to return one day in order to establish justice on Earth. In his absence, the supreme guide acts as his vicar or representative in order to keep the faith and supervise the strict enforcement of the sharia. Thus, in a way, the supreme guide is in touch with the "unseen," with the twelfth imam and, therfore, God. He must therefore be obeyed blindly. He can annul any law adopted by the parliament or any decision taken by the government. All ministries and agencies are under the direct or indirect supervision of the supreme guide, who is the true head of state. The president of the republic is no more than a cog in the machinery. The concept of supreme guide as defined in the constitution is reminiscent of the absolute monarchs of the past who ruled in the "name of God." It conforms with the traditions of pre-Islamic Iran.

Aware of almost three thousand years of Iranian recorded history, Khomeini and his mullahs undertook the task of systematically rewriting history with a view to making it conform to their own Islamic conceptions.[6] Pre-Islamic Persia is hardly mentioned in the new textbooks. Deep-rooted Iranian festivals and traditions have been linked to Islamic ones. Facts have been distorted or ignored. The rewriting of past events to accommodate present rulers is not particular to Muslim clerics. It is a current practice in all dictatorships and is a common feature of all kinds of totalitarianism, particularly fascist and communist regimes.

The idea of the supreme guide is reminiscent of the führer (Hitler), the duce (Mussolini), or the "Great Helmsman" (Mao). At any rate, it seems that Muslims (even highly educated people such as al-Afghani) harbor dreams of an absolute leader who would propel them overnight out of backwardness and into the vanguard of the twenty-first century, who would restore their past "glory" without altering their traditions, mores, and superstitions.

The underlying objective that both Muslim intellectuals and Western observers miss in trying to explain the recent wave of fundamentalism by attributing it to causes ranging from poverty to humiliation to plundering by the West is the intention of militant Islamic fundamentalists to establish a more or less fascist regime, first in their countries and then in the whole world (which, according to their interpretation of jihad, exists only to be conquered by Allah's armies). When antishah demonstrations occured in late 1978 in Iran, the French orientalist Maxime Rodinson was the only one to warn about this tendency of militant fundamentalism. He said,

> There are those who wholeheartedly want power in order to enforce Islam and those who choose Islam as an instrument to conquer power. Such a distinction has no real importance in politics, for the result is often similar. Thus the vast underground movement of the Muslim Brotherhood harbors many branches, and it is difficult to discern their differences. But, to be sure, the major dominating tendency is a kind of "archaic fascism" which appears in their goal of establishing a totalitarian and authoritarian state whose "political police" would ferociously maintain social and moral order; it would at the same time impose conformity with traditional religious norms interpreted in the most conservative sense. Some of the activists consider essential such an artificially imposed renewal of faith, while others welcome it as an "anesthetic" for revolt against a reactionary social reform.[7]

MILITANT FUNDAMENTALISM AND FASCISM

In April 1990, a spokesman of al-Nahda, the Tunisian fundamentalist movement, described his model Islamic society as follows: laws made by clerics; the gradual suppression of tourism; banks giving loans without interest; women veiled; in short, "Islam over everything else [Islam uber alles]."[8]

Immediately after the collapse of the shah's regime and the seizure of power by the clerics, repressive measures and other suppressions of freedoms disquieted most of those who had supported the revolution. Khomeini multiplied his dreadful declarations, which often contradicted what he had said a few months earlier at his Paris suburban residence. Thus, for instance, he declared on November 1, 1978, "In the Islamic Republic of Iran all political parties and all newspapers will enjoy a total freedom of expression." On August 18, 1979, he warned, "The so-called liberals who form parties and publish newspapers in order to criticize us should stop their activities. We cannot give them the liberty to write what they want. We will stop their writings and destroy them." On October 22, he added, "I warn you for the last time: Stop your meetings, your 'prattle,' your 'tracts'; or I will break your teeth." Observers around the world witnessed with dismay the development of repression, the gross violations of human rights, the summary trials and executions. Responding to international criticism, the ayatollah said, "These people [the members of the previous regime] should have been killed the first day instead of being jailed. . . . They are not accused of crimes. They are criminals. They should not be tried but executed. I am sorry to see that westernism is still alive among us."[9]

The brutal enforcement of Islamic law by squads of bearded thugs, the attacks on newspaper offices and printing presses, the beatings of opponents, the assassinations of dissidents at home and abroad were reminiscent of the methods and tactics of intimidation used by the Nazis and Bolsheviks. A few months after Khomeini's return to Iran, Rowland Evans and Robert Novak said that the ayatollah was moving toward "religious fascism." The Italian journalist Oriana Fallaci incensed Khomeini by telling him that the Iranian crowds seemed to adore him in the same "fanatic" manner that many Italians had hailed Mussolini.

In July 1980, Fergus Bordewich, who had edited a Tehran English daily, did not hesitate to call the new Iranian regime fascist.[10] He used for his "demonstration" John Weiss's definition: Fascism is rather the effort of entrenched conservative groups to save their way of life, privileges, and class values from destruction by industrialization, urbanization, and socialist or liberal policies. Bordewich noted:

The movement that now rules Iran comprises the classical fascist constituencies. The spearhead of the movement, the mullahs, is at the same time a class of conservative intellectuals and a major landholding elite that was stripped of some 10,000 revenue-producing villages. . . . The bulk of the movement's rank and file is drawn from lower-middle-class property owners, shopkeepers, traditional merchants, and craftsmen—the groups that have been most threatened by industrialization and mass marketing. . . . Ayatollah Khomeini is not Hitler. Nor is the Muslim religion fascist. . . . But the version of Islam proclaimed by fundamentalist thinkers is simply an interpretation of faith. It serves to provide an ideological basis for intellectual, political, educational, and moral conformity under the pervasive supervision of the mullahs who have become in effect the Gauleiters of the revolution. . . . Religion and fascism can easily coexist or overlap.

Then Bordewich spoke of the xenophobia that the regime encouraged and compared it to anti-Semitism in Hitler's Germany. After that, he focused on some of the institutions and actions of the Islamic regime such as the establishment of an intellectual and "spiritual" rationale for political repression; the imprisonment or exile of liberals; the wrecking of independent newspapers by members of the Hezbollah; mandatory religious education; the dismissal of "Westernized" teachers, professors, and others. Bordewich concluded, "All this is not religion gone awry or an expression of unfathomable chaos. It is fascist politics."

Ten years after Bordewich's analysis, Michael Barry, a specialist on Middle East problems, in considering all militant Islamic movements, said, "The fundamentalist doctrine can be compared to the 1930s fascist movements in the West. You could find its members both among Catholics and Protestants. The rivalry between the Saudis and the Khomeinists is more political than doctrinal."[11]

FEATURES OF MILITANT FUNDAMENTALISM

Dedicated communists in the Soviet Union considered Marx's and Lenin's writings guidelines for the conduct of personal, social, and government affairs. In the mid-1940s, Jdanov, a protégé of Stalin, was entrusted with the task of determining whether literary or artistic works conformed to tenets. Fundamentalists of all creeds (Muslim, Christian, Jewish, and others) practice censorship. As Professor Scott Appleby remarked:

For the fundamentalist, the sacred text is a blueprint for sociopolitical action as well as a guide to spiritual life. . . . In fact, the supernatural character of revelation is particularly important to the fundamentalist sense of identity in that it connotes a way of knowing and a source of truth superior to those of the secular scientist or philosopher. Belief

in things unseen is considered unreliable in secular pursuits; fundamentalists make it the central tenet of their identity[12]: what is not in
line with the sacred books is sacrilegious.

Fundamentalists, either religious or secular, seek to remake the world by
strictly applying their beliefs. In this respect, Professors Martin Marty and
Scott Appleby noted that "such an endeavor often requires charismatic
and authoritarian leadership, depends on a disciplined inner core of adherents, and promotes a rigorous sociomoral code for all followers. Boundaries
are set, the enemy identified, converts sought, and institutions created and
sustained in pursuit of a comprehensive reconstruction of society."[13] Professor Appleby underlines in another book the central role played by authoritarian male leaders. He emphasized, "Fundamentalist movements are
highly dependent on their charismatic leader to break open the religious
tradition for his followers. . . . It is he who reads the signs, interprets the will
of God, and devises a general plan for action. The charismatic leader speaks
for an angry God who calls true believers to uncommon feats of devotion
and self-sacrifice in the battle against evil."[14]

Resemblances between militant fundamentalism and other forms of
authoritarianism abound. I shall indicate here only a few. The way in which
fascists and Soviet or Chinese communists enforced their official doctrines
is reminiscent of the "morality" police of Saudi Arabia, the agents of Iran's
Hezbollah, and the Revolutionary Guards. All kinds of militant fundamentalism nurture a vision of society entirely committed to the idea represented by its supreme leader, the idea that is supposed to be the key to and
the center of the movement: in communism, the "class struggle" and the
eventual disappearance of classes; in Nazism, the racial struggle and the
eventual triumph of the superior race; in religious fundamentalism, the religious struggle and its eventual victory over evil. Indeed, totalitarianism
needs to create an atmosphere of "final struggle," of "apocalyptic" war. Its
exponents need to identify "physically," as it were, one or several enemies:
for Hitler, the Jews and the communists; for Stalin, the capitalist world and
its agents; for today's European far rightists, immigrants; for Khomeini, the
United States and other smaller "satans."

Another feature of militant fundamentalism is what I call acute paternalism: submission to the will of the father; in other words, the identifica-
tion of the supreme leader as an all-powerful father. Actually, paternalism is
widespread in Middle Eastern societies. In his recent essay, Walter Laqueur
alerts readers to the fact that fascism could have a "second coming" that
would most likely look quite different from the first. He also expressed the

opinion that if fascism has a future, it would be in the Middle East, where the conjunction of "cultural and structural crisis" has been most dramatic.[15] (Laqueur recognizes that "religious fanaticism" is neither identical to fascism nor peculiar to the Middle East.)

Comparing militant fundamentalists to Hitler or Mao might offend some genuine believers. In fact, it should not, for the militants very often use the religion only to impose their own political agenda on the majority of the faithful. Moreover, as a general rule, they distort religious principles to serve their own interests. Some years ago the Egyptian judge al-Ashmawy published a book under the title of *Islamists Against Islam* in which he showed how militant fundamentalists had strayed from the tenets of Islam.[16] Be that as it may, societies in the grip of militant fundamentalism exhibit many traits of fascist or communist states. Totalitarianism and authoritarianism, although they differ from each other, share a number of features.

At any rate, the combination of transcendent moralism and politics constitutes a highly explosive mixture that is always conducive to tyranny. Indeed, in the name of an ethical ideal, such a mixture suppresses freedom of speech and of belief. When one looks at the militant Islamic fundamentalists in Iran, Sudan, and elsewhere and when one listens to their admirers, one has the impression that they have "broken" the crescent, as the Nazis "broke" the cross in the1930s.

17

The Case Against the West

In November 1979, Ayatollah Khomeini, the supreme guide of the Islamic Republic of Iran, received a special envoy of Pope John Paul II in connection with the takeover of the U.S. embassy by a group of radical students. In a long statement that was published as a full-page ad in *The New York Times*,[1] the ayatollah explained his position in vehement terms. His declaration amounted to an indictment of the United States.

THE "CRIMES" OF THE UNITED STATES

Khomeini began his indictment by condoning the action of the students because the documents they had seized convinced him "of a plot which was in the making against [Iran], . . . humanity, and Islamic countries . . . in that den of spies." After rejecting the pope's plea for the release of the hostages, the supreme guide presented his case against the United States:

> The 35 million [today more than 60 million] people of this country who have for many years suffered under the weight of American imperialism and more recently under the pressure by Carter, along with the millions of impoverished masses throughout the world, have long expected some form of consolation from the Pope. . . . We gave our

lives over a period of 50 years. Our people were massacred in masses. They imprisoned our people and tortured them in jails in a most inhumane manner. . . . It is therefore worth recalling that our people have been subjected to much torment by that person [the shah] who is now in the United States. He committed all sorts of treason for a period of 37 years. . . . In the face of this suffering our nation now demands the extradition of this criminal to Iran. If he is convicted, he should give back the property he has taken from us. Right now, the wealth he and his relatives have taken from this country is overflowing in banks in the United States and other Western countries.

The ayatollah continued his statement by indicting Reza Shah (the first Pahlavi king). Then he added,

The Allied powers imposed his criminal son (Muhammad Reza Shah) upon our nation. . . . As a result this man provided everything they demanded. . . . We would have liked to see personalities like the Pope . . . ask Carter why he is now playing host to a man whose crimes and treacheries of more than 30 years are quite evident. . . . We are not surprised by Carter's moves. . . . He commits any treachery to fulfill his personal interests under the illusion that he is serving his country. . . . We have only a fair demand. We say: You have taken our criminal and you are giving him refuge. We want you to surrender him to us . . . so that we may give him a fair trial. . . . Should it be proved that our claims are unfounded, then we will put him back on the Peacock throne, in which case the people of this country will obey him.

Khomeini then attacked Shahpour Bakhtiar, the shah's last prime minister, "a person who claims to be Iranian [and] asks Carter to exercise economic boycotts against Iran. . . . He said that he was first Iranian and second a Muslim, a statement which constitutes in itself a blasphemy." The ayatollah concluded by saying, "We are neither afraid of military interference nor of economic siege, since we are Shiites and as Shiites we welcome any opportunity for sacrificing our blood. Our nation looks forward to an opportunity for self-sacrifice and martyrdom."

Indeed, the ayatollah and his followers were not afraid of U.S. retaliation. The banner across the gates of the seized American embassy read "Khomeini Struggles. Carter Trembles."

In June 1980, the newly installed Islamic regime convened an International Conference on the Crimes of the United States and the Shah, attended by scores of "delegates" from all sorts of leftist movements and terrorist groups. From the United States came former Attorney General Ramsey Clark, who recognized the "wrongdoings" of his country. He then knelt down in the middle of the conference hall and asked pardon of the Iranians. Meanwhile, the 52 hostages remained in the custody of the radical students. They remained captive for 444 days, and President Carter lost his bid for reelection.

Upon the return of the hostages in January 1981 after long negotiations through third parties, A. M. Rosenthal, then executive editor of *The New York Times*, wrote, "It was a national humiliation."[2] Many Americans felt that their government was powerless in a new world. Some attributed the "mess" to a "lack of guts" in the White House. To Muslims, it was a "victory": The ayatollah had won against a superpower. Muslims exulted: It was possible to confront the big powers. After almost two centuries of domination and humiliation, Muslims felt proud and confident. A surge in terrorist activities followed.

Why such animosity against the West in general and the United States in particular? After all, embassies have always had spies and operatives on their diplomatic staffs. Actually those of the Islamic Republic of Iran have even participated in terrorist activities in countries where they were stationed. The ayatollah referred to "50 years" of "killings and plunderings." In fact, animosity against the West has existed for centuries. It was brewing even before the discovery of the Americas by Columbus.

ROOTS OF ANTI-WESTERN FEELINGS

From its beginnings, the nascent Islamic Empire acted as a rival of Western Christendom (Byzantium). Arab armies conquered many territories that were part of the Christian Empire known to them as *Roum* (the Roman Empire). Muslims were convinced that theirs was the "final" monotheism that had superseded the partial truths revealed by God to Moses and Jesus. Their classical jurists divided the world into two parts, the House of Islam and the House of War (inhabited by infidels who should convert or live under the flag of Islam).[3]

The Crusades and the establishment in Jerusalem of a Frankish kingdom stunned and disconcerted the Muslims. This was the first wound inflicted on them. Despite the defeat and the ensuing expulsion of the Westerners by Saladin, the Crusades left a deep scar in the psyche of Muslims in general and Arabs in particular.

The second injury to their pride came in the fifteenth century with the "reconquista" and the humiliating expulsion of the Arab "masters" from Iberia. The successful jihad conducted by the Ottomans in the same century in eastern Europe compensated to a degree for the loss of Andalusia, enabling Muslims to regain their confidence in Islam's superiority.

The failure of the second siege of Vienna in 1683, however, sounded an alarm. The treaty of 1699, the first to be imposed by a victorious enemy on a sultan-caliph, marked the beginning of a complete reversal of fortune.

At first, the Ottomans thought that they would easily reestablish parity by acquiring European military technology. But they continued to suffer one defeat after another. Moreover, the West was undergoing a scientific and industrial revolution that put it far ahead of the Muslim world.

As Professor Bernard Lewis put it, since the seventeenth century, Muslims have known "three stages of defeat."[4] First, they had to admit their loss of world domination to Western powers. Second, they could not stop the invasion of ideas, laws, ways of life, foreign settlers, and even colonial rulers. Finally, the incomprehensible forces of change accompanying the infidels started to "pervert" their societies and even their homes where wives, daughters, and sons flouted "paternal" authority. The hatred became an "outbreak of rage."

As they became more and better acquainted with the West, Muslims were overwhelmed by what they saw and heard. In 1593, for instance, a British ambassador arrived in Istanbul with credentials signed by a queen, Elizabeth I. Muslims stood aghast. How could a woman reign over men? How could a sovereign govern with a powerful parliament elected by the people? How could women and men intermingle in public places? And, above all, how could infidels be more advanced and powerful than the faithful? Indeed, the West was a "satanic" domain, worse than Sodom and Gomorrah. What worried most was the possibility that the "superior" Islamic civilization would be infected by an "inferior" culture studded with a myriad of temptations. Muslims assumed a defensive reaction (which reflected jealousy, envy, and profound hatred).

Wheras the upper classes admired some of the Western achievements and thought of acquiring them, the masses remained perplexed. A deep feeling of humiliation gripped the Muslim world because of its growing awareness of the inadmissible superiority of the infidels. Indeed, not only had the West gradually come to dominate the Middle East since the end of the eighteenth century, but it also had imposed its own order on the world at large. Never had the Muslim world, despite its greater civilization, been able to achieve such universality. Discussions naturally took place among the elites as well as among the masses. Remedies were suggested and sometimes tried: nationalism, militarism, secularization, and now militant fundamentalism, but to no avail. Behind all the vaunts of successive leaders and movements, feelings of shame and rage continued (and continue) to linger.

THE IMPACT OF SHAME

As Amir Taheri noted: "By the end of World War I, all the Middle Eastern countries had become colonies or protectorates of Britain and France or had imposed on them basic political options that had been devised by outsiders, in spite of their ostensible independent status. The state apparatus came to be seen by the masses as an instrument of the infidels who were determined to humiliate Islam and plunder the natural resources of the region. Modernity came to mean defeat for Islam and ascendency for Christendom, whereas tradition evoked the golden days of Islamic glory."[5]

The humiliation and shame felt by the Muslim masses call for compensation that has been offered in the long-winded speeches of charismatic leaders (the effect of which rapidly wanes). Over the past two or three centuries, according to a specialist, a pattern has manifested itself in the "codes of shame, honor, and power" developed by an ever-present tribal and religious tradition that has ensnared Muslims in a "closed circle."[6]

At any rate, feelings of shame and humiliation constitute a segment of the roots of the present Muslim antagonism toward the West. It often emerges from the leaders' utterances. Thus General Neguib, who led the Free Officers in the 1952 overthrow of the Egyptian monarchy, wrote in his memoirs, "I was ashamed of the low esteem in which Egyptians were held by Britons and other foreigners, and I was determined to show to our cynical rulers that something could and would be done about it."[7] On May 29, 1967, a week before the Six Day War that deepened Arab humiliation, Gamal Abdal Nasser delivered a major speech in which he said, "We are confronting Israel and the West as well, the West which created Israel and which despised us Arabs and which ignored us before and since 1948. They had no regard whatsoever for our feelings, our honor, our hopes, our rights. . . . We are now ready to confront Israel. . . . If the Western powers disavow our rights and ridicule and despise us, we Arabs must teach them to respect us and take us seriously."[8]

More recently an Arab publisher in Jordan wrote, "We will not suffer in perpetuity a degrading and imposed political order which served the colonial interests of Great Britain and France after World War I and then, after

World War II, the security interests of Israel and the commercial interests of American-led western oil companies, weapons manufacturers, corporations, and banks."9

The impact of Western-style reforms in the 1920s created in Muslim societies a thin upper layer of wealthy people and a small middle class aping the ways of life of Europeans—a complete rupture in the traditional customs of the masses. The masses, in turn, considered them agents of the infidels. It is therefore not surprising that many Muslims listened to the militant fundamentalists who were telling them that their salvation resided in fighting against the poisoned European-inspired reforms and harking back to the traditional ways that represented the "true path" that God had prescribed for the faithful.10 After all, the Koran, the last message of God, contains all that Muslims need for their transitory stay on Earth.

Moreover, the success of Khomeini in Iran and his ability and willingness to stand up against the United States inspired confidence and hope in Muslims.

To the foregoing should be added the feeling of Muslims that they were betrayed twice by the infidels. First, during World War I, the British promised independence to the Arabs if they revolted against their Ottoman masters. But once the hostilities were over, they reneged on their promise. Similarly, the partition of Palestine and the creation of Israel constituted a "true stab in the back." Arabs asked, Is that the way to treat us after we helped them against Muslim Turks? Westerners, as perceived by Arabs, lack any sense of honor.

A LONG LIST OF GRIEVANCES

To Muslims, the wrongs of the West against Islam are innumerable. They range from political to cultural. Obviously, Muslims reproach the United States and its allies for their unflinching support of Israel, which is a "foreign" element artificially imposed in the Muslim Middle East. They also accuse the West of helping maintain corrupt Muslim leaders who "confiscated" power and systematically abuse people and cling to office in order to continue to plunder the riches of their countries.

In 1955, as a UNESCO staff member, I attended a conference on television and culture in Tangier, Morocco. Because I know Arabic, a group of American and European delegates asked me to accompany them to the souk (bazaar) of Tetouan, a mountain resort that we were visiting during a recess. The delegates wanted to buy Moroccan leather goods. The owner of the shop at which we stopped was enchanted to meet an Iranian speaking his language. He granted a sizable discount. But when he saw me distributing the products to the Westerners, he erupted into a tantrum: "What are you doing? The low prices are for you, not for these pigs. They have looted us for so long. They should pay ten times the real price!"

Muslims complain bitterly about their exploitation at the hands of colonialists and imperialists who often were in cahoots with local leaders. Such leaders enriched themselves by helping the infidels plunder Islam's natural resources. A Jordanian publisher expressed a general feeling when he wrote, "We will not continue to suffer the grotesque personal wealth of the fantastic superrich, unelected, unaccountable, and often corrupt Arab so-called elites."[11] It is well known that Persian Gulf emirs and princes are profoundly despised by the masses and challenged by their own people. Muslims at large accuse the West of protecting those "thieves." Many Muslims remain convinced that the West introduced its capitalist system in Muslim countries in order to impoverish people and dominate them.

Cultural and moral grievances are even more acute. Muslims believe that "permissive" Western societies are the worst possible example and model for their youth. Through cinema, radio, television, tapes, records, books, and now the Internet, the West has set out to poison young Muslims and destroy Islam. These are "satanic" weapons invented by the "enemies of God." In Khomeini's view, for instance, the gravest crime of the shah was of giving women equal rights with men. This and other so-called reforms were dictated by the shah's Western secularist masters.

Many Muslim writers, for example, Sayed Qutb, the executed Egyptian leader of the Muslim Brotherhood, have expressed their disgust for or at least their reservations about Western culture. But two Iranian intellectuals seem to have exceeded other Muslims in their criticism of Western civilization. Ale-Ahmad, a fellow traveler of the Tudeh party, born to a religious family, coined the phrase "West-toxication" in the mid-1950s. In a pamphlet of the same title that he published in 1958, he attacked the "invasion" of Iranian culture by Western thought. A decade later Ali Shariaty[12] wrote in one of his books, "Come friends, let us abandon Europe. Let us leave behind this Europe that always speaks of humanity but destroys human beings wherever it finds them."[13]

Khomeini wrote in 1942 in his *Kashf ol Asrar* (Discovery of the Secrets), "Europe's ideology consists of nothing but blood-sucking, man-eating, and the burning of countries. Its only aim is to live a depraved life of anarchy in which lust rules supreme." His disciples have taken his criticisms of the West much further. Militants in Iran as well as in other Muslim countries see the West as a civilization of lazy people obsessed with longevity, material success, and imperialism. A member of the Iranian "Party of God," who spent several years in California, characterized the West as a "collection of casinos, supermarkets, and whorehouses linked together by endless highways passing through nowhere."[14]

One can go on almost indefinitely in citing militant fundamentalist grievances against the West. In the last instance, they come down to what is said at the beginning of this chapter as well as in other parts of this book, namely, that militant fundamentalists believe that Muslims have been entrusted with the "last message" of God. Because it represents the "ultimate truth," it must be imposed everywhere. Therefore, Muslims should not allow the "enemies of God" to contaminate the House of Islam with their sacrilegious culture. In other words, the West is trying to destroy Islam, which raises the question, Why single out the United States?

18

The "Great Satan"

At first sight, it seems that the United States is the principal, if not the sole, target of militant fundamentalists. To explain this, some specialists invoke Washington's unwavering support of Israel. It is true that the United States was the only Western power that often used its veto power in the UN Security Council to stop anti-Israeli resolutions. But Europe remains as committed as Washington to its support of Israel. Moreover, militant fundamentalists and Arab radicals have denounced other countries at times. Thus in 1990 the leader of a pro-Iranian terrorist group exclaimed at his trial in a Paris courtroom, "My name is death to the Western world!"[1] Qaddafi, while on a state visit to Ruwanda in 1985, affirmed, "Christianity is the religion of colonialist agents, of the French, the Belgians, the Germans, the Americans, the Jews [sic], . . . in short, of our enemies."[2]

If the name of the United States is invoked most often as the biggest enemy in the vocabulary of militant fundamentalists, it is because Washington is the leader of the West. In a way, America represents all the values of the West. It is also the most powerful economic and political center of the free world. Under the circumstances, it seems normal that the United States has "inherited" all the grievances of the Muslim world.

THE HAWALI TAPES

In 1995, an American journalist visiting Hamburg's Islamic Center (an Iranian fundamentalist front organization in Germany) met a citizen of the Islamic Republic who told him in anger, "If you had a cat, backed it into a corner, beat it, and abused it, then the cat would strike back. This is what the West and America are doing to the Muslims of the world."[3] Similarly, in 1993, a Somali, praying in a mosque, told an American reporter, "Americans are here to destroy our religion."[4]

Immediately after the Persian Gulf War, one of the most respected Wahhabi theologians of Saudi Arabia, Dr. Safar al-Hawali, dean of Islamic studies at the prestigious Ummal-Qura University of Mecca, delivered a series of speeches and sermons denouncing the deployment of American troops. The tapes of his critique were widely circulated. The United States, said al-Hawali, had long been planning to occupy Saudi Arabia. Kuwait's invasion was only a pretext. The theologian mentioned Nixon's memoirs in which the late President insisted on the necessity of a "permanent" American presence in the Persian Gulf. Carter concurred and created an airborne division to defend American interests. That was the division that Bush sent first to Saudi Arabia.

Dr. al-Hawali also quoted the prophet as warning his companions and followers that "Roum [Rome, specifically the Byzantine Empire] will attack you [the Muslims] in many forms." The Crusaders, the British and French colonialists, and now the Americans are all "forms of Roum." In al-Hawali's view, the Americans and the Soviets spent years arming Iraq and pushing it to invade Kuwait. Not only is the presence of American soldiers sacrilegious, but Muslims joining with infidels against other Muslims is forbidden. Al-Hawali accused his fellow Muslim intellectuals of committing "impiety" and even idolatry. "When the Mujahiddin drove the Russians out of Afghanistan, you did not say: 'Allah helped them.' You said: 'America helped them.' Now when we are threatened by war, you do not say: 'Allah will protect us.' You say: 'America will protect us.' America has become your God."

In his speeches, Dr. al-Hawali stopped short of calling for the overthrow of the House of Saud, but he concluded, "The real enemy is not Iraq. It is America and the West."

Islamic cassette shops that sell a variety of anti-American sermons at very low prices are proliferating in Saudi cities. One of them is called Supergun (an allusion to the long-range canon that Iraq was trying to build). It attacks the Saudi royal family and calls America "the atheist enemy of Islam."

In another cassette entitled "America as I Saw It," a preacher describes the United States as a country in which "men marry men, sons and daughters abandon their parents in hunger, women have fatherless children, naked people jog in the streets; and so on." In short, the United States is a country that Allah will certainly destroy, as He did Sodom and Gomorrah.[5]

THE CONSPIRACY PHANTASM

In 1987, pirated cassettes of a documentary aired on British Independent Television flooded the black market of Cairo. Called *The Sword of Islam*, the program described the surge of militant Islamic fundamentalism in Lebanon and Egypt. It praised Islam as a major monotheism and condemned the terrorist activities of Hezbollah, the Muslim Brotherhood, and other activist groups. Cairo's semiofficial daily *Al-Ahram* condemned the documentary as "trash that distorted the image of Islam and Muslims," whereas fundamentalist spokesmen referred to a vast Western conspiracy against Islam, even though the program criticized Israel for its air raids against civilians in southern Lebanon.

Indeed, Muslims remain preeminent promoters and consumers of conspiracy theories. For centuries such theories have been a major feature of Middle Eastern societies, where, in the absence of the free flow of information, the public is left at the mercy of rumors and fantasies. In my childhood, people used to "see" the "hidden hand" of the British Intelligence Service or the French Deuxième Bureau even in the most trivial occurrences of daily life such as a neighborhood or family quarrel. Obviously, this phenomenon, called the "conspiracy phantasm" by the French scholar Maxime Rodinson, is not exclusive to the Middle East. Before World War II and during the Cold War, Europeans and Americans searched for communist conspiracies. Nazis spoke at length of Jewish "plots." Conspiracy theories are still discussed in the United States, for example, about President Kennedy's assassination. In the autumn of 1973 and early 1974, a very strong rumor took hold of European capitals and was reflected in press articles and even editorials. It asserted that in order to deflect attention from the Watergate scandal and at the same time impair Europe's and Japan's economies, Washington had deliberately provoked the Yom Kippur War (October 1973) and the oil embargo.[6] In a poll conducted in France in 1986, a majority of people affirmed that Islam was a "prowar religion."[7]

Notwithstanding the variety of examples cited, the conspiracy phantasm is more widespread in the Middle East than in any other region. In 1967, I witnessed a curious conversation between the shah and King Faisal of Saudi Arabia, who was on his way to the Arab summit in Khartoum after the disastrous 1967 war. His jet had stopped in Tehran's airport where he had lunch with the Iranian monarch. Faisal explained that the occupation of the Sinai and the West Bank was the first phase of a larger Zionist plot to conquer the whole world and establish a universal Jewish government. He "brotherly" urged the shah to take necessary measures to counter the Zionist conspiracy.

During their eight-year war, Iran and Iraq kept accusing each other of secretly conspiring with the United States and Israel to destroy Islam. In the 1990–91 Persian Gulf crisis, Saddam Hussein regularly referred to the Saudi–U.S. coalition as an "American–Zionist conspiracy against the Arab nation." In 1994, all militant Islamic fundamentalist groups condemned the UN World Conference on Population, convened in Cairo, as an "American plot to dominate the Muslim world" by spreading Western "immorality." (Curiously, the pope joined forces with militant Muslims.)[8]

The conspiracy phantasm provides both rulers and masses with an excuse to escape responsibility for what has happened. Nasser, in 1967, accused the Americans of having sent their planes to support Israel in the Six Day War. The shah, in 1979, blamed the oil companies for his predicament. At the same time, the conspiracy phantasm induces a ray of hope, for it asserts that Muslims lost their superiority only because their leaders strayed from Allah's commandments; therefore, submitting again to Allah's will will retrieve "lost might." Accordingly, the militant fundamentalists propose their "wonder" cure: overthrowing corrupt leaders; reimposing the sharia; assembling an arsenal, including weapons of mass destruction; and waging internal and external jihad.

Because some of the objectives of the militants cannot be put into effect immediately, Muslims cannot yet prepare to wage an open war against the United States and other Western countries. But they can and should respond blow for blow to all the wicked moves of the infidels. Such was the response of the Gameat al-Islamia (an Egyptian splinter of the Muslim Brotherhood) to the condemnation of Sheikh Omar Abdal Rahman by an American court. In a communiqué, the group proclaimed, "The Americans have chosen war with Islam. The 'Gameat' vows to Allah that it will respond by targeting American citizens and interests."

AMERICA, THE "TOTAL" ENEMY

In 1979, a young Tunisian intellectual, musing on Khomeini's success in Iran, confided to a French journalist, "The Muslim world can become once again a center of literature, the arts, and science. Will that be an 'ill' for the West? Each time we raise our heads, America and others force us down by brandishing the 'Islamic scarecrow.' We do not agree with Tehran's summary executions or with hostage takings. But we admire the way in which Khomeini overthrew tyranny without firing a single bullet. . . . For once a popular movement was able to determine the future of a whole nation."[9]

Indeed, Khomeini's rapid rise to power and the way in which he stood up to the American superpower stirred the pride of Muslims around the world. To them, the old and frail ayatollah opposing the powerful United States constituted a metaphor for the plight of all Muslims. Despite the particularities of Shiism and Iranian culture, Muslims identified with the Qum cleric and, following in his footsteps, concentrated all their hatred of the West on one country: the United States. America became a kind of scapegoat for all infidels.

World events after 1979 seemed to confirm and to compound the grudges of Muslims against the United States, despite the latter's help in arming and training the Afghans against Soviet aggression. The killings in Sarajevo after Yugoslavia's breakup provoked a general outrage in Muslim countries. Although Europeans bore the main responsibility, the militant Islamic fundamentalist groups incited anti-American feelings among the Muslim masses. In this respect, a sort of competitive emulation began to characterize the behavior of radicals and local Muslim governments. State-run media likened the Serbian assaults on Sarajevo to the Crusades; the West, they said, is unconcerned about the spilling of Muslim blood. A Saudi daily, *Al-Ryadh*, called the Bosnian situation a "prelude to the war between Islam and the West." Calls for a jihad against the Serbs sounded in every corner of the Muslim world. Malaysia's prime minister proposed declaring war on the Serbs. Iran's president expressed the opinion that the Serbs should be denounced and that help to the Bosnians should be stepped up. All Muslim countries condemned the West and particularly the United States, "the leader of the free world."[10]

As time goes on, the chasm between the Muslim world and the United States will continue to deepen. Today even Saddam Hussein appears to Muslims as a victim of America's anti-Islamic policies. The feeling that the United States opposes the reemergence of a strong and prosperous Islamic world is gaining currency among the faithful. More and more the United States appears to Muslims as the "absolute" or "total" enemy of Islam. From the standpoint of militant fundamentalists, it is indeed the Great Satan.

In fact, it is obvious that the United States does not harbor anti-Muslim designs (nor, for that matter, is it opposed to any other religion). The condemnation of Sheikh Abdal Rahman and his coconspirators had no anti-Islamic undertones; it was directed against terrorists and acts of sabotage.

Actually, the United States has shown restraint in many cases of anti-American activities—even when they resulted in the loss of lives. Muslims in the United States enjoy the same rights and freedoms as those exercised by all other religious or ethnic communities.

One can find several reasons for the prevalence of anti-American rhetoric in the Muslim world. First and foremost, militant Islamic fundamentalist propaganda targeted the United States as far back as the 1960s. Sayed Qutb, the Muslim Brotherhood leader, in his writings, presented the United States as a land of sin. Fundamentalist groups, both religious and secular, need to identify some powerful enemy. Communists, before the collapse of the Soviet Union, used to demonize the United States almost in the same manner as Ayatollah Khomeini did in 1979.

One can also cite a certain fickleness in Washington's foreign policy toward Muslim countries. In some cases, America supports "modernizers" (Egypt, the shah, and others) and in other cases, fundamentalists (Saudi Arabia, Afghan Mujahiddin, Pakistan, and others).

Finally, in a way, it is customary for unsatisfied groups or countries to blame the United States for their shortcomings. After all, it is the only remaining superpower.

19

A Global Danger?

"I am the evil spirit that moves around only at night, causing nightmares. . . ." Who spoke those uncanny words? Fantomas? Fu Manchu? They were actually uttered by a real person: Sabri al-Banna, alias Abu Nidal, the well-known master terrorist of Palestinian origin who won fame in the 1970s by organizing massacres at airports in Rome and Vienna.[1] He added in the same context, "I am Abu Nidal, the answer to all Arab sufferings and misfortunes."

It is true that Abu Nidal's assertion of invincibility was reflected in the belief of many Arabs in those days. But things have changed since Khomeini's revolution. Today militant Islamic fundamentalists are different from their terrorist predecessors. They do not seek personal renown. They are not for hire. They are actors in an eschatological drama. They sacrifice their lives for the triumph of Islam. They are believers in the service of Allah. Their reward awaits them in the hereafter: a place in paradise. Contrary to the terrorists of the 1960s and 1970s, they do not strike at random. They are members of organizations that pursue lofty objectives. They are committed to their leader, generally a cleric. They are ready to die for the cause. They are a far cry from the ordinary terrorist. They are reminiscent of soldiers enlisted in special "hit" units. In a way, they are much more dangerous than the Abu Nidals and Carloses (the notorious terrorist of the 1970s, a.k.a. the Jackal). But do they really represent a destabilizing force in "global politics"? Let's turn to the facts.

A LONG LIST

It is obviously impossible to enumerate all the deeds of contemporary militant Islamic fundamentalists. A few striking examples will suffice to assess their force and their impact. In 1979, a whole group of fundamentalists occupied Mecca's grand mosque, the holiest of Islam's shrines; they were dislodged after a long battle. In 1980, a group of fanatics attacked the American Cultural Center in Karachi (Pakistan). In 1981, Iranian fundamentalists arranged the murder of an opponent in Washington, D.C. In 1983, a suicide bomber detonated a truck full of explosives at the entrance of the American embassy in Beirut (Lebanon). In the same year, other trucks exploded at the U.S. Marine headquarters, killing 294 servicemen. In the same year, a suicide bomber partially destroyed the American embassy in Kuwait. In 1984, in Paris, a terrorist trained by Iran tried to kill Bakhtiar, the shah's last prime minister. Another murdered the president of Beirut's American University. Five American citizens were kidnapped by Hezbollah activists. Every other year, fundamentalists staged unsuccessful coups against Bahrain's ruler. Similar plots were discovered in Malaysia and a number of Muslim countries. In Sudan, non-Muslims are being slaughtered by the thousands in a civil war waged by the fundamentalist government. Suicide bombers of Hamas (the Gaza Strip fundamentalist organization) operate in the West Bank as well as inside Israel. Hezbollah regularly bombs Israel from southern Lebanon. Let's add Algeria's daily mass killings, subway and other vicious attacks in Paris, the bombing of Pan Am Flight 103, Sadat's assassination, numerous hijackings and abductions, the New York Trade Center blast, and so on.

The terrorist activities of militant Islamic fundamentalists should not obscure their long-term goal: the establishment of an international Islamic world order.

Given the foregoing, an affirmative answer to the question concerning the destabilizing effects of militant fundamentalism seems inescapable. As early as 1985, Nathan Adams, testifying before a Senate panel, said, "In my opinion, there is no greater threat to world peace today than state-supported terrorism and the potentially deadly sequence of events that can be set in motion by a single incident."[2] Professor Zonis of the University of Chicago affirmed that "the message of resurgent Islamic fundamentalism must be considered one of the two greatest ideological innovations of the twentieth century, the first being the Bolshevik Revolution."[3]

A WARNING

At this point in my narration, I feel compelled to clarify confusion that unfortunately has blurred the rational examination of the question of Islamic militant fundamentalism. Since the occupation of the American embassy in Tehran and the hostage taking of its fifty-two diplomats, a trend has developed in the West that equates Islam and terrorism. (This trend, which had begun to ebb, resurfaced at the time of the Trade Center blast.) Obviously, it does no one any good. If we want to analyze the possible dangers of militant fundamentalism, we must, as I have indicated in earlier chapters, draw a clear line between Islam and religious fundamentalism, on the one hand, and militant Islamic fundamentalism, on the other. The latter, a manifestation of what scholars call political Islam, despite its Islamic underpinnings, does not represent Islam as one of the major monotheisms. Its aggressive nature and its vocal and sometimes deadly manifestations have nurtured growing anti-Muslim feelings in the West. This certainly is an inappropriately excessive reaction. Obviously, all Muslims are neither activists nor militant fundamentalists. Mainstream Islam became fundamentalist around the twelfth century. But neither the bulk of the faithful nor the majority of clerics approve of terrorism and violence.

What is striking is the long period of time it took Western experts and governments to discern the aggressive nature of militant Islamic fundamentalism that gained momentum after Khomeini's rise in Iran. Indeed, the ayatollah made no secret of his views. As early as the 1960s, he insisted that the clergy seize power and denounced a "Western–Jewish conspiracy" as the main source of troubles in Muslim countries. Succumbing perhaps to the brandishments of a few Western-educated people in the entourage of the ayatollah during his brief exile in France and to the reassuring statements of their own experts, Western governments chose to accept a sanitized version of a "moderate" Khomeini. (Such a blunder is not without precedent: Prime Minister Chamberlain, coming back from Munich, described Hitler as a "gentleman.") Andrew Young, then the U.S. ambassador to the United Nations, labeled the ayatollah a "twentieth-century saint." The French philosopher and social scientist Michel Foucault wrote that Khomeini was "introducing a spiritual dimension to politics." Professor Richard Falk of Princeton asserted that "the entourage of Khomeini has had considerable involvement in human rights activities and is committed to a struggle against all forms of oppression. . . . A noncommunist Islamic Republic will probably be a stabilizing element geopolitically, both in the region and in the third world [sic]."

Such misreadings have not ceased. Until very recently American administrations, one after the other, continued their illusionary searches for moderates among the fundamentalists (an oxymoronic exercise). Academics did not fare better. Professor Edward Said of Columbia University called the Islamic threat phony. In a recent book, Professor John Esposito tried to lessen American fears. Referring to the West's past exaggeration of the "communist menace," he contended that militant fundamentalist movements have been seen by Westerners as more disturbing than they really are.[4] Robert Kaplan, author of a book entitled *The Arabists*, wrote, "If we knew a little more about Jalal-ad-Din Rumi, the thirteenth-century Turkish founder of the *tariqat* (fraternity) that was associated with the whirling dervishes, Islam might not seem incompatible with democracy and Islamic fundamentalists might not seem so monolithic and threatening. . . . Rumi dismissed immature fanatics . . . and consistently spoke against tyranny. . . . Indeed, Turkey's democratic system has incorporated [his ideas] . . . the great Sufi *tariqats* have defined Islamic identity in Turkey and in the Balkans [sic]."[5]

The examples I have quoted show the extent to which confusion exists about Islam in governmental as well as in intellectual circles. It is true that Sufism is admirable, tolerant, and open to pluralism, but it represents only a tiny minority among Muslim sects and is rejected, if not completely condemned, by mainstream ulemas. Moreover, Rumi was Persian and wrote in Farsi; if his ideas "defined Islamic identity in Turkey," how could the Ottomans have ruled so oppressively and, among other things, committed the 1915 massacre of the Armenians (not to speak of today's violations of human rights in Turkey)?

At any rate, Sufism and "moderation" are on the wane today, and a groundswell of aggressive fundamentalism is swaying the Muslim world. It was triggered by Khomeini's accession to power in Iran and, contrary to what many people believe, is more political than religious. Thus in Saudi Arabia, a staunch theocracy based on Wahhabi fundamentalism, the regime is challenged by other fundamentalists. Their aim is certainly not to enforce the sharia, which is strictly applied. What they want is to seize power.

DANGER IN THE PERSIAN GULF

The anti-Saudi activists belong in general to Shiite minorities (although some are well-known Wahhabis). In recent years, Sunni opponents have multiplied. They are the offspring of official religious institutions or part of a strain of the current Wahhabi fundamentalists who participated in the Afghan war against the Soviets. Whatever their roots, they aim at over-throwing the ruling family whom they accuse of straying from the tenets of their religion. The leader of the group that bombed an American-run train-ing center in Riyadh in November 1995 recalled in a televised confession before being beheaded, "I did travel to Afghanistan [where] I met people of various nationalities who charged rulers and scholars with blasphemy. [With three friends] we decided to carry out an act of jihad inside Saudi Arabia."[6]

The challenge to the royal family continues both inside and outside the country. The authorities shut down the Committee for the Defense of Le-gitimate Rights, which was founded in 1993 by six activists. The leader, Muhammad al-Masri, managed to escape and to continue his attacks from his London-based residence. Another fundamentalist, Usama bin Ladin, scion of a wealthy merchant family, was stripped of his Saudi citizenship; he took refuge in Sudan from which he funds many fundamentalist institu-tions and militant groups. Cassettes of impassioned sermons and other anti-government material circulate more or less freely. The authorities arrested two prominent religious scholars, including the famous al-Hawali.

Saudi Arabia is also subjected to Iranian efforts at subversion. Tapes, books, and other propaganda materials are smuggled into the country through Persian Gulf coastal areas, and Saudi citizens are trained in camps in Iran and Lebanon.[7]

In Bahrain, the large Shiite community nurtures militant fundamental-ist movements. In 1979, after Khomeini seized power in Iran, their at-tempts to create an Islamic republic were rapidly subdued. In 1981, another attempted coup was thwarted. According to police reports, it was master-minded by Hojat-ol-Islam Modaressi, a high-ranking Iranian cleric; a letter signed by Khomeini was found. It gave him "responsibility for Bahrain and the Persian Gulf Emirates."[8]

Serious disturbances continue to rock the island-state. The authorities accuse Iran of helping local Shiite militant fundamentalists. Shiite and Sunni opposition groups based in London regularly call for change in Bah-rain.[9]

In Oman, Iran's efforts to unseat the sultan remain largely unsuccessful. In the summer of 1992, a group of local fundamentalists tried to overthrow the regime. But the coup was promptly thwarted. In Kuwait after the 1983 blasting of the United States embassy by Khomeini-backed terrorists, the government received threats of more attacks and decided to drop charges against Iran. Local militant fundamentalists have been inactive since the 1990–91 war, but nonviolent criticism of the authorities continues.

After the Islamic Republic was instituted in Iran, activists tried to export their revolution to Pakistan. But they soon found themselves bogged down in the local traditional Sunnite–Shiite infighting that has plagued Pakistan since its creation in 1947. They shifted to another policy: funding local revolutionary groups or opponents based in London.[10] At the same time, Iran's militant fundamentalists undertook efforts to spread their brand of Islamic activism among India's Muslims. Since 1982, they have expanded their activities to the Philippines, Malaysia, and Indonesia.

In the Middle East, Iranians have gained a solid footing in Lebanon through the Hezbollah and friendly relations with Syria. They also provide financial and other material assistance to a score of militant groups in other parts of the Middle East. Khomeini's indirect influence must also be stressed inasmuch as his example has given rise to renewed efforts on the part of Sunni militant fundamentalists. The most spectacular effect of such an indirect influence became evident in Egypt in 1981 with Sadat's assassination and in Syria with the Muslim Brotherhood revolt in Hama and its subsequent dramatic suppression. (Whole neighborhoods were bulldozed, and more than 10,000 people were killed.)

Iranian militants have also been active among Muslims in Africa as well as in Europe.[11] The idea behind these policies is to create progressively a vast network of Islamic republics and militant fundamentalist "fifth columns" that will be unleashed in the prelude to the "final" jihad. Indeed, for these militants, the Crusades never ended. In 1986, an Iranian fundamentalist theorist wrote, "The Crusades never stopped. . . . Allah sent us our great leader, Khomeini, the smasher of idols, who is going to end the Crusades forever with the victory of Islam."[12]

THE "WESTERN FRONT"

Experts usually attribute Muslim hatred of the West in general and the United States in particular to their support of Israel. This is true only to a very small degree. In fact, militant fundamentalists consider Israel a "Trojan horse" implanted in the House of Islam by their main enemy—the West.

Ayatollah Morteza Motaheri, one of Khomeini's closest aides, who was assassinated in 1981, wrote,

The West represents the last attempt by Satan to destroy monotheism on Earth. It tells man that God is dead and you are the masters of the universe. Yes, the Western man can vote, can abolish divine laws, can even live without churches and priests. He can devote all his time to pleasure and to debauchery. . . . Now it is difficult to find a man who would deliberately abandon the possibility of such a life in favor of a life of prayers, pilgrimages, penitence, poverty, and unquestioning obedience to divine law. The satanic ideas of the West, which have their origin in pagan ancient Greece and Rome, have already finished off Christianity in all but name. Allow these ideas to reach the realm of Islam and the faith of Muhammad will also be in danger. May Allah never allow that day to dawn.[13]

The destruction of Western civilization is therefore the duty of the true believer. And this is not only a Shiite tenet. Indeed, Usama bin Laden, the Saudi billionaire businessman who funds many Sunnite militant organizations, has proclaimed, "The Americans are the main enemy."[14]

According to experts, by the end of 1993, more than fourteen militant fundamentalist military groups—involving many thousands of individuals—were functioning in the West, where they can live more easily than they can in their own totalitarian homelands. The success of Khomeini and the fundamentalists who were sponsored by the United States in Afghanistan has led militant fundamentalists to believe that they can bring America to its knees.[15]

The first trial involving growing militant Islamic fundamentalist groups in France ended in January 1997 with the sentencing of eight members of an organization based in France that had attacked a tourist hotel in Marrakesh, Morocco. The trial showed how young Frenchmen of Islamic descent have become susceptible to the appeals of militants to wage jihad.[16] Indeed, many Islamic radical organizations operate in or around major French cities and carry out bombings both inside and outside France.

As for the United States, Steven Emerson, who has been investigating the matter for years, remarked in a 1995 article, "The vast majority of Muslims in America are peaceful and law abiding and do not condone violence. But in recent years an extremist fringe of militant Islamism has taken root here. To avoid raising suspicion and to take advantage of civil liberties protection, these militant groups reconstitute themselves as research, charitable, or 'civil rights' institutes." Emerson cited a former FBI official, Oliver Revell, who said, "They [these organizations] are ultimately committed to waging a holy war [jihad] both in the Middle East and in the world at large."

He then gave a detailed account of some of these organizations and their activities. In addition to fundraising for activist groups such as Hamas (in Gaza), they conduct sustained propaganda and invite lecturers from the Middle East. One of the latter, Bassam al-Amoush, a member of the Islamic Coalition in the Jordanian parliament, told a gathering in Detroit that it certainly was possible to defeat America, as the Vietnamese had demonstrated. He also declared America to be the "number one enemy" and "the Great Satan."[17]

To some observers, the numerous attacks on American targets and all the anti-Western rhetoric are tantamount to a declaration of war. But before assessing the degree of danger represented by militant Islamic fundamentalism to the West in general and to America in particular, we should clarify one last point. The 1993 World Trade Center bombing in New York City not only constituted the transplantation of militant Islamic operations to American soil but showed that the leaders or representatives of more than five groups (Islamic Jihad, Hamas, the Sudanese National Islamic Front, the Pakistan-based al Fuqrah, and other groups funded by Persian Gulf donors) were directly or indirectly involved in the plot. In addition, Sheikh Omar Abdal Rahman, the blind Egyptian cleric, had been hosted or sponsored by approximately half a dozen Islamic charitable and religious organizations in the United States.[18]

The foregoing raises the following question: Is there a centrally coordinated command above all the militant organizations? Some writers who coined the phrase "Khomeini International"[19] suggest that this is so.

A COORDINATED COMMAND?

One afternoon in June 1996, in the hazy heat of Tehran's Mehrabad International Airport, a group of deadly serious Arab-speaking men deplaned from the Iranair flight that originated in Damascus, Syria. Most of them had untrimmed beards and wore crumpled suits without ties. Some wore military fatigues. All displayed surly dispositions. They were spirited away in limousines by a squad of Revolutionary Guards who were waiting on the tarmac.

They were the leaders of several Middle Eastern militant Islamic fundamentalist organizations backed by Iran. They had been invited to participate in a secret meeting on coordinating their actions and on determining new targets for terrorist attacks. Among them were Ahmad Jabril, head of the General Command of the Popular Front for the Liberation of Palestine (PFLP), a suspect in the bombing of Pan Am Flight 103; leaders of the

Lebanese Hezbollah; representatives of the Egyptian branch of Islamic Jihad (which is loyal to Sheikh Omar Abdal Rahman); and delegates from
several other terrorist groups.[20]

This was not the first meeting of this type. Militant Islamic fundamentalists frequently attend coordinating conferences and training sessions in
Iran. Immediately after Khomeini's seizure of power, leaders of Muslim
revolutionary movements flocked to Tehran. The PLO's chairman, Arafat,
was among the first to embrace the ayatollah and obtain financial support
from Iran. In September 1981 Khomeini ordered the founding of the High
Council of the Revolution, whose task was to plan a strategy for activating
surrogate terrorist movements and undertaking activities in the Persian
Gulf and elsewhere.[21] At its start, the Council focused its efforts on uniting
under one command the Iraqi revolutionary groups that had sought refuge
in Iran after Saddam Hussein invaded Iran. Later on, the Council created
several committees and subcommittees to take charge of different regions.
In 1986, a number of organizations were supported or coordinated by the
Council. Among them were the Islamic Revolutionary Organization in the
Arabian Peninsula; the Islamic Front for the Liberation of Bahrain; Islamic
Da'wa; Islamic Amal and Mujahiddin of Iraq; Takfir wa Hijra and Islamic
Jihad of Egypt; Party Islam of Malaysia; Moro National Liberation Front of
the Philippines; and others. Some of those organizations have dissolved or
changed their names, as often happens in the shifty world of militant fun-
damentalism.

Since 1989, after militant fundamentalists overtook Sudan, similar conferences cosponsored by Iran were held in Khartoum. It is remarkable that
Shiites and Sunnites have been able to cooperate so closely in the universe
of militant fundamentalism, despite their deep-seated and often irreconcil-
able theological differences. This is one more proof of the political character of militant fundamentalism. Indeed, the Sunnite Muslim Brotherhood
and the Shiite Islamic fundamentalists of Tehran share the same goals:
overthrowing local "corrupt" governments and creating a one-world Muslim state.

Such conferences underline the community of aims subscribed to by or-
ganizations as different as Turabi's Islamic Front; Iraq's al Da'wa; Jordan's
Muslim Brotherhood; Pakistan's Jamiati Islami; Egypt's Islamic Jihad;
Lebanon's Hezbollah; Tunisia's an-Nahda; Algeria's FIS; Hekmatyar's
Hizbi Islami (Afghanistan); and other groups.

Actually, a feeling of political solidarity tinged with religious overtones
has existed among Muslims in their revolutionary movements since World
War II. A case in point is the Organization of the Islamic Conference

(OIC), which binds all Muslim countries despite their political, ideological, and economic differences. The idea of instituting the group was aired as early as 1965 by King Faisal of Saudi Arabia and King Hassan of Morocco. But Egypt's Nasser opposed it because Washington was encouraging Islamic alliances as a bulwark against communism and local nationalism.[22] The OIC was created after Nasser's demise. Moreover, Muslims have always considered themselves part of the "umma," the community of believers created in Medina by the prophet (no matter the divisions between their elites and leaders). Although the "community" never completely materialized, it remains a compelling dream in the psyche of Muslims. By proclaiming it as one of their goals, militant fundamentalists have struck a chord among the masses. Indeed, from its beginning, the Muslim Brotherhood presented itself as open to all Muslims. It called itself an international organization and rapidly constituted chapters in many countries.

Local organizations operating inside Western countries emulate Tehran and Khartoum interfundamentalist conferences. They hold occasional (and sometimes annual) conventions in hotels or conference centers. For example, in the United States, the Muslim-Arab Youth Association (MAYA), founded in 1974 with petro-dollars and headquartered in Indiana, invites top militant fundamentalists to address its annual meetings.[23]

The least one can say is that militant fundamentalist groups collaborate closely and that some of them take their cue from Tehran or Khartoum.[24] It is also true that Iran has been recognized by all militant Islamic organizations as the first country in which the shared goal of seizing power was achieved. But no hard evidence has been found to show that these numerous activist groups are centrally coordinated. Despite common goals and common enemies, ideological and national considerations divide them. Even the Lebanese Hezbollah, created with the material and financial help of Iran, does not always follow Tehran's direction. As a result, some experts tend to minimize the danger of militant fundamentalism for the West. But others have conluded that terrorist incidents in Europe and the Americas as well as anti-Western rhetoric have provoked anti-Islamic feelings in the West. Some commentators even speak of a coming "clash of civilization," whereas others think that a "green peril" is replacing the "yellow peril" of yore and the "red peril" of the past four decades. The feeling of possible danger is sustained by the continual use by militant fundamentalists of the word *jihad* against the West.

20

Holy War (*Jihad*)

Jihad has become a household word in the West thanks to its continual use by journalists. Similarly, it is invoked continually in the political discourse of Muslim countries. Some radical groups have chosen it as the title of their organizations. Top officials often brandish it as a threat against the "enemies of God."[1] Militant fundamentalists believe that they have resumed the holy war begun by the prophet and his companions in order to spread Allah's "latest and last message."

AN AMBIGUOUS NOTION

Because the term "jihad" tends to be equated with militant fundamentalism, terrorism, and the killing of innocent people, some Muslim intellectuals and statesmen have reacted with outrage. They accuse the Western media of presenting a tainted image of Islam and Muslims. They insist that *jihad* denotes a moral and spiritual quest rather than a military campaign.

It is true that some Western writers, journalists, politicians, and filmmakers have gone out of their way to besmirch Muslims and to suggest that Islamic politics inevitably leads to the use of terror. It is equally true that the word *jihad* has several meanings in the Arabic language and involves different obligations as articulated in the Koran. But, obviously, the militants focus on "holy war" rather than on the other meanings of the word. Thus as early as 1926, Abul Ala Mawdudi, the Indo-Pakistani fundamentalist who inspired militants throughout the Muslim world, affirmed that *jihad* meant "revolutionary struggle." More recently (October 1991) at the International Conference convened in Tehran in support of the Islamic Revolution of Palestine, the delegates from the Middle East, Africa, and Asia continually invoked the word in its military sense.[2] *Jihad* was also the catchword of Sheikh Ahmad Yassin, the founder of Hamas. Moreover, the majority of Muslim classical jurists understood *jihad* as "holy war."[3]

Nevertheless, many Muslim intellectuals and politicians, trying to soften the military meaning of *jihad*, insist on considering it as a "spiritual striving." This bandying of definitions befuddles the public and kindles confusion about Islam in the West.

In current Arabic, *jihad* means "effort," "striving," and "struggle." All these different meanings appear in the Koran. In its nonmilitary connotation, "jihad" refers to the obligation of each Muslim to live up to the tenets and the commandments of the religion. It can be used for peaceful purposes; thus in the summer of 1979, Khomeini called for a jihad to reconstruct the country.[4] These are some aspects of jihad that many Western scholars tend to ignore or minimize, probably because the hadith gives prominence to the military meaning.

JIHAD IN THE KORAN

The Koran does not make *jihad* as "holy war" an "article of faith," a designation that is used to refer to the "five pillars of Islam" (*shahada*, prayers, alms, fast, and pilgrimage). In the past, only one sect—the Kharijites in the eighth century—raised jihad to the level of a "sixth pillar." Today most militant fundamentalists consider it an essential duty of the "true" believer. Ayatollah Khomeini continually emphasized the sacrificial aspects of jihad such as martyrdom. In his message to Pope John Paul II, he declared, "As Shiites we welcome any opportunity for sacrificing our blood. Our nation looks forward to an opportunity for self-sacrifice and martyrdom. Now let us suppose that Mr. Carter [the U.S. President] should agree to send military forces here. . . . We will go to battle with all these 35 million [the population of Iran in 1979] and once we have all been martyred, then our enemies can do whatever they want to do with this country. We are not afraid of such an encounter. We are men of war; we were born to struggle."[5]

Because jihad is not an article of faith, it is not "obligatory." It is more of a communal than an individual obligation. The incentive for jihad lies in the immediate access to paradise that will be granted in case of martyrdom. The right to call for jihad belonged to the highest authority, the caliph. After the first jihad—begun by the prophet and continued by the first four caliphs and some members of the Ummayad dynasty—the continuous raids against Byzantium and the Abbassids, the incursions in India by the Ghaznevids, and the conquest of part of Eastern Europe by the Ottomans were sanctioned by jihad. In the eighteenth and nineteenth centuries, the seizures of European ships by the local authorities of Tripoli, Tunis, and Algiers, which were dubbed acts of piracy by the West, were considered by Muslims to be "naval jihad." The last call for a universal jihad against non-Muslims was sounded by the Ottoman caliph-sultan in the autumn of 1914. It was a failure. Leaders' appeals to jihad are not binding, as administrative orders are: The caller must convince the faithful.

In this respect, Tabari—the great Muslim historian of the ninth–tenth centuries—recounted a telling incident that took place under Caliph Umar in the seventh century. To induce the tribal chiefs to join in the holy war, Umar told them, "O Muslims, God has promised to his prophet the conquest of Syria, the country of Roum [Byzantium] and Persia. God never fails His promises. . . . Go to Iraq!" Nobody answered Umar's appeal. The next day he again addressed the tribal chiefs, "Who is ready to sacrifice his life and possessions in the Path of Allah?" No one turned up. On the third day, Umar recited verses from the Koran and added, "O Muslims, since Hejaz came to life, we have traded with Syria, Iraq, Abyssinia, and Yemen. That is how we earned our livings. . . . But today the whole universe is our enemy. If you do not want to fight your enemies, it is necessary to conclude peace with them. Otherwise, you cannot stay here, you would starve and sink into poverty." The audience was moved. The chiefs, convinced by Umar's reasoning, agreed to join the jihad.[6]

To mobilize the masses, Khomeini declared Islam to be in danger in Iran. For years he criticized the shah's reforms as straying from the sharia. But, as in the case of Umar, he had to add economic incentives to his appeal. After the oil boom of the 1970s, he accused the shah and his family of squandering the national riches and dangled before the people the prospect of distributing among them all the superprofits derived from oil.

JIHAD IN CLASSICAL THEORY

During the first two centuries of Islam, jurists developed what can be considered a theory of international relations that can be summed up as follows: From the fact that there is only one God in the heavens, it follows that there can be only one ruler on Earth. Because the Koran is the final message of God and Muhammad is his last prophet, Islam supersedes all religions and must rule the planet. The jurists divided the world into two sections: the House of Islam and the House of War. In this respect, Professor Majid Khadduri noted, "The territory of war was the object, not the subject, of the Islamic legal system, and it was the duty of Muslim rulers to bring it under Islamic sovereignty whenever the strength was theirs to do so."[7]

Therefore, at least in theory, a "permanent state of war" exists between the two houses. Truces, not permanent treaties, are allowed. That is why only armistices were concluded after each Arab-Israeli war since 1948. This theory has shaped the mind-set of Muslims throughout the centuries. Thus a recent study carried out among Lebanese Muslims (as well as Syrians and Palestinians living in Beirut) by Professor Hilal Khashan of the American University of Beirut concluded that those who approved of peace negotiations between the PLO and Israel saw them merely as a truce before another military confrontation.[8]

When most Arab governments envisaged lifting the boycott imposed on companies dealing with Israel by the end of 1994, Saudi rulers solicited the country's highest religious authority to endorse the move. Sheikh Abdal Aziz Bin Baz, the grand mufti, issued a *fatwa* (a religious decree or edict) affirming the right of the government to pursue normal economic relations with Israel. He cited a verse from the Koran: "If the enemy moves toward peace, you shall too, placing your dependence on Allah." Recalling the prophet's willingness to declare a truce with his enemies in the battle for Mecca, Sheikh Baz wrote, "It is proper for the ruler to agree to a truce if he sees there is a benefit in that." Critical reaction from some Arab theologians prompted Sheikh Baz to issue additional explanations in which he specified that peace with Israel cannot be made as long as Jews occupy Muslim lands; accommodation with Israel "dictates making the land their property temporarily until the temporary truce expires or Muslims gain the strength to drive them out by force. . . . And so they must be fought when possible until they convert to Islam or pay tribute. . . ."[9]

In any case, the majority of Muslims are convinced that one day, sooner or later, all humanity will live under Islam's banner. This deep-rooted belief stems from the religious interpretations taught to Muslims for more than a thousand years. It is true that in today's world environment many Muslims do not dream of war and conquest. Instead, they think that Islam will expand peacefully (as, for instance, it is doing in Africa). They believe that the infidels will finally come to understand the superiority of God's "final message." But militant fundamentalists think otherwise. To them the instrument that would wipe out the House of Unbelief or War is jihad in the military sense, an obligation imposed by Allah on all Muslims. Only an armed confrontation can achieve God's sovereignty on Earth.

Consciously or not, Iran and Iraq's quest for mass weapons of destruction (including nuclear devices) is part of their dream of reconstructing the strength of the Muslim world. What militant fundamentalists question is the world order that has been imposed by the West since the nineteenth century. Turkish columnist Fehmi Koru recently wrote,

> In fact we are now, after the fall of communism, observing the creation of a new "world order" with important implications for Western–Muslim relations. The "old order" arose from two world wars and had very little respect for the values of the Muslim world. . . . Positivism, rationalism, materialism, and imperialism were the undercurrent values of the "old order." On those terms the Muslim world was not in a position to attract respect; it remained aloof from the "old order" and, of course, was left out of it. But the proposed "new order" is completely different in outlook and its announced values are not alien to the Muslim world. . . . But whereas the "old order" was primarily circumspect toward the Muslim world, the "new order" is careless. There is a growing unease among Muslims that the "new order" has identified Islam as the enemy to replace communism.[10]

The militant fundamentalists seek to impose their own world order. They do not hide their ultimate aim. In 1981, the foreign minister of the Islamic Republic of Iran addressed the UN General Assembly in these terms:

> We are determined to build a new world on the basis of the sublime teachings of Islam for the salvation of mankind and to offer humanity that thirsts for justice a new framework of human values. . . . In conclusion, I, as a representative of the Islamic Republic of Iran, announce to the oppressed and the deprived in the world that today a billion Muslims are rising throughout the world and that Islam is once again bringing its blessed liberating forces to the world scene, and our faith tells us that the movement of this ocean of oppressed humanity will destroy world imperialism headed by the Great Satan, the United States of America.[11]

The minister's words sound like a declaration of war on the West. They describe the objective and the ways of jihad that most militant fundamentalists envisage. In a recent study of jihad, the jurist Patrick Moore affirmed:

The rules of Islamic law on jihad and the permanent state of war with the non-Muslim world are still in effect. . . . What we must realize is simply that the world of Islam is not the same as our world, the world of Western civilization and the Judeo-Christian heritage. . . . Our reactions to the world of Islam must not be automatically confrontational, but we should not shrink from asserting our rightful interests. Perhaps we must recognize that "containment" is the hallmark strategy of Western strategy which has proven eminently successful in defeating another and even less congenial ideological opponent in the past.[12]

Some academics have gone beyond Moore's conclusion and suggest the coming of a "clash of civilizations" between the world of Islam and the West.

21

A Clash of Civilizations?

In 1993, Professor Samuel Huntington of Harvard University published an important and controversial essay in the summer issue of *Foreign Affairs*. He contended that world politics was entering a new phase in which the major source of conflict would be neither ideological nor economic but cultural.

WAR OF CULTURES

According to Professor Huntington, "the fault lines between civilizations will be the battle lines of the future."[1] It will be "the West against the rest" and especially against "resurgent" Islamic fundamentalism. In his view, as the ideological division of Europe has faded away, the "cultural division" between Christianity and orthodox Christianity and Islam has re-emerged. "Conflict along the fault line between Western and Islamic civilizations has been going on for 1,300 years. These centuries-old military interactions are unlikely to decline."

Moreover, Professor Huntington sees anti-Western cooperation in the "connection" between Confucian and Islamic states. While the West is at the peak of its power, a "return-to-the-roots" phenomenon is in progress in the non-Western world: "Asianization" in Japan; "Hinduization" in India; "Re-Islamization" in the Middle East.

In proposing a way of evaluating the future, another academic, Professor Benjamin Barber of Rutgers University, published a provocative book entitled *Jihad Versus McWorld*. Barber went one step further than Huntington in offering an interpretation of the whole modern world. In his vocabulary, *jihad* means "bloody holy war on behalf of partisan identity that is metaphysically defined and fanatically defended." McWorld, on the other hand, is "a product of popular culture driven by expansionist commerce. Its template is American." Jihad is also a rabid response to colonialism and imperialism and their economic children, capitalism and modernity; McWorld abets jihad and vice versa.

In his study of jihad, quoted in the preceding chapter, Patrick Moore followed a more or less similar line of reasoning. Indeed, he cited a 1937 book[2] in which Hilaire Belloc remarked that "the West has progressively lost its religion" and worships "a particular economic arrangement believed to be the satisfaction of social justice." Belloc added in the quoted passage that Islam has, in the main, preserved its "soul": "Islam has not suffered this spiritual decline [as the West]; and in the contrast between the religious certitudes still strong throughout the Mohammedan world . . . lies our peril." Patrick Moore concluded:

> The fact is, just as Belloc pointed out more than half a century ago, while American and other western nations [following the moral and political fall of communism] seem to be increasingly rejecting their own traditional values and ideas of moral existence and political life, people in another area of the world are increasingly calling for an ostensible return to their traditional moral and political values both in opposition to and criticism of the West, i.e., in a number of third-world and Middle Eastern Muslim countries. Whether we like it or not, it appears that the Judeo–Christian West and the world of Islam may once again be engaged in what Edward Gibbon called the "world's debate."[3]

"World's debate," "world competition," "world conflict," "clash of cultures or civilizations," and so on, in my opinion, are literary metaphors that do not help us understand the real challenges posed by militant Islamic fundamentalism. First, what we call Islamic civilization is something of the past. We can still see and appreciate its products and its magnificent artistic and architectural achievements. But it has produced nothing "new" (or comparable to its own past) since the eighteenth century. We admire its literature, poetry, and philosophy, but the greatest part of this artistic achievement was elaborated in the first four or five centuries of Islamic civilization. And a large part of it was rejected and condemned by the clerics of the Middle Ages. The old fatwas against the bulk of the work of philosophers and scientists such as Ibn Rushd (Averroës) or Ibn Sina (Avicenna) have not been canceled. What we call Islamic civilization is not "alive." In recent years, intimations of an artistic and literary renaissance have emerged timidly in some parts of the Muslim world, despite material difficulties and severe censorship. But they have not yet been implanted solidly. What is still with us are mores, ways of life, and religious rites.

The word "culture" is in itself ambiguous. It sometimes refers to the values of a society and sometimes to the traditional habits of people. Considered a "way of life," Muslim culture is significantly different from the culture of the West.

THE LIVING AND THE DEAD

I read in the press a story about a Turkish woman who had become a naturalized German.[4] Her father died in 1981, and she buried him in the Muslim section of west Cologne's cemetery. When she visited the tomb approximately fifteen years later, she found a sign indicating that the ground was to be leveled. She hurried to City Hall where the official in charge of cemeteries told her that the site that she had chosen was qualified for burial only for fifteen years. Similar Christian tombs (and those of other religions) were also slated for leveling. She fought the decision, arguing that it was contrary to Islamic ways. City officials contended that with only 55 cemeteries and an average of 10,000 deaths per year, the entire country of Germany would soon become one huge cemetery if everyone had a permanent grave. The problem had nothing to do with faith or the rights of immigrants.

Other complaints, in different domains, have been made on behalf of the two million Turks who live in Germany. They concerned, among other things, the slaughter of sheep, the use of head scarves in schoolrooms, public swimming pools for both men and women, and the like. On the Christian-German side, educators registered concern that students who fasted during the whole month of Ramadan lost the mental energy needed for following the courses in German schools.

A journalist who reported on the conditions of Turks in Germany mentioned these examples as "signs" of a "clash of cultures that is spreading across Europe as Islam, imported by immigrants, takes root." But can such events be equated with a clash of cultures or a war of civilizations? It seems to me that they involve problems of adjusting to a different environment.

They have nothing to do with a confrontation between the Western and Muslim worlds. Since the Iranian Islamic Revolution, militant fundamentalists have infiltrated Muslim communities in the West and have become discontented about the inconveniences that have arisen from living different ways of life.

What is really happening on the cultural front is not a clash with the West but a withdrawal—a refusal to compete and to adapt to a changing world. As happened in the twelfth century (and in other moments of history), Muslim culture, in a way, is recoiling on itself. What is challenging the West is not Islamic "culture" but militant Islamic fundamentalism, a revivified brand of "political" Islam.

Let us put aside such catch phrases as "clash of civilization" and "cultural war" and deal with facts. The real dread in Western societies concerns the expansion of terrorist acts. Westerners see jihad in terms of terrorism. They wonder whether the present wave of militant fundamentalism constitutes a serious threat to them.

A WORLD THREAT?

In 1985, Ayatollah Khomeini met in Tehran with a number of Muslim radical leaders from other countries. He told them,

> Brothers do not sit pretty at home, so that [enemies feel free to] attack. Move onto the offensive, and make sure that they retreat. . . . Do not content yourselves with teaching people how to pray and how to fast. The rules of Islam are not limited to that. . . . Why don't you recite the surat of *Qital* [killing]? Why should you always recite the surats of mercy? Don't forget that killing is also a form of mercy. . . . There are ills that can be cured alone by burning. The corrupt in every society should be liquidated. . . . The Koran teaches us how to treat those who are not Muslims: It teaches us to hit them, throw them in jail, and kill them.[5]

By "those who are not Muslims," Khomeini meant the Christians of the West and the Israelis. He did not need to be precise. Muslims everywhere had become used to hearing him curse the United States—the superpower behind most of the hated governments from the Atlantic to the Indian oceans—almost every day. In his testament, which was broadcast immediately after his demise, he renewed his loathing of the Great Satan, a "basically terrorist" nation. He referred to the Saudi rulers as "American valets" and King Hussein of Jordan as a "criminal tramp." In his words, Morocco's King Hassan and Egypt's President Mubarak "did not miss an opportunity to betray their own people in the interest of the United States and the Zionist regime [Israel]." He concluded by calling on Muslims to unite and added: "If Muslims would unite, they would represent the greatest power in the world."

His message did not fall on deaf ears. Militant fundamentalists everywhere identify the West and its leader, the United States, as the enemies of Islam and as the targets against whom the ultimate jihad will be directed. But they know that no militant fundamentalist government is in a position to wage a successful "classical" war against any European country, let alone the United States. They therefore bide their time and prepare thoroughly for the "final" confrontation. In this respect, they must pursue three major objectives: seize power in Muslim countries whose rulers are pro-Western and train and equip modern armies; stall the Middle East peace process and eventually destroy Israel, which is the West's Trojan horse in the Muslim world; and finally, weaken Western societies as much as possible and frighten their people through terrorism and sabotage.

22

Preparing for the "Final Round"

A busy downtown Tehran street bears the name of Sadat's assassin, Khalid Istambuli. In 1991, ten years after that event, Algeria, Egypt, Jordan, Saudi Arabia, Tunisia, and many other Muslim countries (as well as Israel) were battling militant Islamic movements that had mushroomed since Khomeini's seizure of power in Iran in 1979. The officials of those countries were (and are) unanimous in accusing Iran and Sudan of fomenting unrest. Their intelligence services have disclosed evidence that Iran is arming, training, and financing militants from many Arab and non-Arab countries in ideological and military camps in Iran, Lebanon, and Sudan. Iran and Sudan also offer havens and other facilities to fundamentalists.

DOUBLE TALK

Iran and Sudan denied involvement and attributed the unrest to domestic discontent. But, as I have discussed in previous chapters, militant fundamentalists systematically use deception and dissimulation. Double talk is widespread among mullahs and militants. The scholar Khalid Duran noted in a recent study that a leader such as Sudan's Turabi continually denies "what he said a day earlier before a different audience" and that "he has ever written things so progressive that an eminent scholar such as Professor John

Voll seriously questioned if there were any differences between the positions of Turabi and Mahmud Taha (a progressive intellectual executed in Sudan)." Duran added, "The problem is that neither Turabi nor Abbas Madani [Algerian militant leader] nor, for that matter, Khomeini and Khamenei [Khomeini's successor] can be judged by what they say or write but solely by what they do."[1]

A Jordanian security officer described Iran's ambitions as a "very big plan which we are all [Arabs] treating as an actual war being waged from Tehran."[2] Moreover, it is no secret that Iranian-supported Hezbollah and Hamas are continuing their efforts to derail the peace process between Israel and the PLO; that violence in Algeria, Bahrain, and elsewhere continues; and that concerned authorities have accused Iran. Although there is no hard evidence of an "Islamic International" run by one leader, active cooperation among numerous militant organizations is a fact. Their aims are also clear: overthrowing regimes that cooperate with the West and the United States. Their targeting of tourists and any other "alien" presence is obviously aimed at "unifying" Muslim societies and getting rid of possible "fifth columns" and spies in preparation for the ultimate stage, the spread of Islamic rule in the House of War. Thus in his 1990 invasion of Kuwait, Saddam Hussein had clearly in mind the goal of monopolizing Middle East oil. Had he succeeded, he undoubtedly would have tried to destabilize the Saudi grip on Arabia and reinstall the Hashemites (King Hussein) in Mecca. He would then have been in a position to stand up to the West and the United States.

BUILDING ARSENALS

In 1977, I was present at a meeting between the Iranian foreign minister and a high-ranking Soviet delegation to the United Nations. At that time the shah was buying sophisticated fighters from the United States and his army was said to be ranked fifth or sixth in the world. André Gromyko, the Soviet foreign minister, said, "We are wondering in Moscow who the shah has in mind? Your Arab neighbors are no match. . . . Could it be us?" Today Iran continues to spend a large part of its oil revenues to amass both classical and sophisticated armaments: missiles from China and North Korea, submarines from Russia, and so on. Libya is in the process of creating a strong chemical weapons industry. Pakistan has already developed nuclear capacity. In 1992, Robert Gates, then CIA director, said that Tehran could pose a threat to the United States and its allies "within three to five years"; Iran is quietly developing a nuclear infrastructure that will eventually give it the option of a bomb.[3] Professor Graham Allison of Harvard considers it only a matter of time before a terrorist detonates a nuclear device in America.[4]

Indeed, fundamentalist and other radical Muslim governments are apparently preparing for the future by building up huge and sound military capacities. They are also training and maintaining large units for guerrilla warfare as well as individual terrorists and saboteurs. In this respect, the Vietnam and the Algerian wars proved that guerrillas with their moving bases, flexible strategy, and use of time pose a formidable challenge to regular and sophisticated armies. Ho Chi Minh once told a French journalist, "If we have to fight, we will fight. You will kill ten of our men, and we will kill one of yours, and in the end it will be you who will tire of it."[5]

As for terrorism, the Trade Center blast underscored the vulnerability of the United States. According to an expert from the Rand Corporation, the "message" read like this, "Four 'amateurs' with readily available commercially produced materials can build a bomb for under 400 dollars that kills six people, causes untold millions of dollars in losses, and generates endless publicity. . . . Anybody can be a terrorist." In July 1994, a series of events (an attack against a Jewish center in Argentina, a Hezbollah bombing of Israel from southern Lebanon, and several explosions in London) drew the following comment from a senior Israeli intelligence officer: "Whoever is capable today of organizing such a worldwide cluster of murderous attacks, in perfect timing, from his standpoint, of being successful in all of them, and then of withdrawing all of his personnel safely will tomorrow be able to overthrow governments. It is clear to us . . . that there was one hand directing or assisting the car bomb in Buenos Aires, the Hezbollah attack in southern Lebanon, and the two car bombs which blew the next day in central London. We also know that compared to the Iranian hand, the old known international terrorism is becoming a child's play."[6]

Moreover, as Matthew Wald remarked in an article, "terrorism need not involve bombs or even violence. An opponent bent on widespread disruption rather than symbolism might try computer sabotage. Recalling a computer glitch at a New York bank (in February 1994) that debited depositors' accounts twice for each withdrawal they made, [an expert] suggested [that] a terrorist could find a smart computer programmer and wreak havoc. . . . The system is not safe from domestic hackers, let alone trained foreign agents."[7]

WEAKENING THE WEST

Sometimes terrorist acts are intended to punish a government that helps the "enemy." Thus the Algerian FIS attacks targets in France because Paris gives assistance to the Algerian militias. In general, the aim of fundamentalist terrorism is to weaken Western societies by increasing the cost of security, by causing serious damage, and by giving rise to feelings of fear and vulnerability. The West's law enforcement agencies cannot easily handle the growing global network of militant Islamic fundamentalists who have killed people and sabotaged installations from Paris to Buenos Aires.

In addition to terrorist acts perpetrated inside the Western world, militant fundamentalists resort to another tactic. They attempt to tie the West's hands by creating and multiplying trouble spots around the world. The philosophy behind such a strategy is based on the belief that the West cannot act in several places at the same time. Accordingly, militant fundamentalists, sponsored by particular states, nurture violence and unrest wherever possible. Obviously, the West cannot involve itself in many places. But in some cases it has to intervene for "humanitarian purposes." Fundamentalists, by their actions, hope to force the United States and others to scatter their forces and efforts in as many spots as possible. Once this goal is attained, they will be able to begin to carry out a destabilization plan against Muslim regimes friendly to the West. Indeed, the United States and other Western governments, being "busy" elsewhere, would not be in a position to intervene effectively.

A "GREEN PERIL"?

Militant fundamentalists turn to Tehran for help. According to experts, not only did Iran send arms to Sudan, but it also concluded a barter deal with South Africa, exchanging Iranian crude oil for arms sent by Pretoria to Khartoum. Moreover, a detachment of Revolutionary Guards proved more effective against the "freedom fighters" of southern Sudan than thousands of soldiers of the local army.[8] Activists travel with diplomatic passports to kill opponents and commit terrorist acts. At home, militant fundamentalists use a vast array of tactics: demonstrations, riots, attacks by urban guerrillas, mosque sermons, and so on. Foremost among those tactics is the subversive use of charitable and other nonprofit foundations. Mosques and charitable institutions are also widely used in that way in Western countries.

Most important to them is to take advantage of local constitutional freedoms and media opportunities in the West. In Muslim countries, freedom of speech is severely limited, and governments control the media. In the West, however, fundamentalists are able to speak openly and have easy access to the media. Thus the Trade Center blast offered an opportunity to Sheikh Omar Abdal Rahman to appear on television and to give interviews. His messages were instantly transmitted to all Muslims living in the United States and Canada. Moreover, this exposure (and, indeed, free publicity) enhanced his stature at home and in other Muslim countries where Western media, because of their independence from government, enjoy a great amount of prestige. Anti-Western militants see no contradiction in taking advantage of the tolerant climate of Western democracies. Tunisia's al-Ghannushi, in exile in London, once said: "We Islamists may have a lot of criticism of Western values, yet we are seeking refuge in such atheist states because we appreciate the benefits of freedom and the value of democracy" (which they deny to their own people when they seize power, as was done in Iran and Sudan).[9]

According to Khalid Duran,

Islamism is, in certain ways, a successor to Soviet communism. This is not an invention of the leaders of xenophobic parties in Europe and America. The Khomeinists themselves say it loudly. They relish nothing as much as to be called "Green Danger." And they curiously emulate the Soviets in a number of ways. One of those is to use Western terms and give them a totally different meaning. Few people have been as eloquent as Khomeini in upholding the "lofty position of women." But what he meant by that was entirely different from what most Westerners would understand by equal rights for women. The closest parallel can be found in Nazi Germany with its mass mobilization of women for the war effort. . . . The "Association of German Girls" in retrospect appears like a blueprint for "Al Akhawat al Muslima" in Turabi's Sudan.[10]

For years American strategists dreamed of a "green belt" around the Soviet Union to contain communism. The invasion of Afghanistan by the Red Army gave them the opportunity to translate their idea into reality. They even regretted their criticism of Khomeini in connection with the hostage crisis and the occupation of the American embassy in Iran. Some went as far as to attribute the whole case to Soviet agents (among the students were a few former Marxists). They encouraged all Muslim countries to send volunteers to fight alongside the Afghan Mujahiddin. Many young Muslims from around the world rushed to the CIA training camps established in Pakistan. The United States and Saudi Arabia poured in billions of dollars, which enriched feudal and tribal fundamentalists. Afghanistan was destroyed, and hundreds of "terrorists," who are now operating in many countries, including the United States and other democracies, were let loose.

As Judith Miller recalled in her recent book, even before the Afghan case, the United States and its allies were encouraging militant fundamentalists as a bulwark against communism and Arab secular nationalism.[11] Obsessed by the "red peril," the West turned a blind eye on the dangers involved in playing the "Islamist" card.

THE BRIDES OF BLOOD

In his book *Holy Terror*, Amir Taheri described a gathering in a Beirut mosque to honor a group of young virgins, "brides of blood"[12]—candidates for suicide bombings. Their aim was to "avenge the blood of Imam Hussein," the grandson of the prophet, who was martyred in Karbela in the seventh century at the behest of the first Ummayad sultan. The ceremony was held on March 25, 1986. The ayatollah who delivered the sermon said that in the hereafter Imam Hussein himself would choose their husbands among "the most pious and shapely of young men." The women candidates to martyrdom were members of special female brigades of the Lebanese Hezbollah. During the ceremony respects were paid to two martyred "brides." One, Suraya Saad, drove a bomb-car into an Israeli position in southern Lebanon in 1985; her mother and brother were invited to Tehran where a street was named after her. The second, Sana Muheidly, drove a bomb-car into an Israeli convoy and became a heroine praised in many poems and stories.

Khomeini, who received the parents, called their dead daughters "soldiers of Allah" in the "last stage of the historical Crusades." To Khomeini and his followers, the Crusades never ended. There was a period of dormancy, which came to an end. In an address delivered to militants from thirty countries who had gathered in the courtyard of his residence, Khomeini said in December 1984: "Allah be praised, our young warriors are putting His command into effect. They know that to kill the infidels is one of the noblest missions Allah has reserved for mankind."[13]

Khomeini's view of war and his slogan ("Kill and Be Killed"), which appears on the walls of many Muslim cities, seem to confirm Patrick Moore's analysis of "the five critical aspects" of jihad: "Finally jihad is and must be permanent. Jihad is a permanent obligation upon the entire Muslim community. It may pass into periods of dormancy, but the obligation of jihad can never end short of the complete subjugation of the non-Muslim world."[14]

Militant fundamentalists try to establish toeholds among Muslims living abroad. I reiterate Steven Emerson's conclusion that an "extremist fringe of militant Islamism has taken root [in the United States]" in the guise of charitable or civil rights organizations.[15] Kenneth Timmerman, who founded the Foundation for Democracy in Iran, affirmed that the "Iranian government is operating in the United States under many guises. Through the [Alavi] Foundation [in Manhattan] and a variety of other front organizations operating on the orders of Iran's permanent mission to the United Nations and supervised by its Interests Section in Washington, the Islamic Republic keeps its finger on the pulse of American politics."[16] Both writers are of the opinion that "to the extent we tolerate such groups, we are laying the groundwork for local tragedies such as the World Trade Center bombing."[17]

Given the views of militant fundamentalists on jihad and the "continuation" of the Crusades as well as the blanket condemnation of the West as the "enemy" of Islam, one wonders whether the institutions they have created in the West are not part of a "fifth column" or "Trojan horse" implanted for other purposes. At any rate, they seem to be able to take advantage of all mistakes committed by the West. Thus, for example, when the Clinton administration in 1994 decided to turn a blind eye on Iranian arms shipments to Bosnia, Tehran immediately established a militant Islamic-Iranian base. "Iran quickly established a terrorist center and dispatch point and a political haven in Europe in the most unstable area of the continent."[18] Not only did Iranians send arms, but they also provided trainers and fighters.

From the standpoint of an armchair strategist who calculates numbers without taking into account local circumstances and differences in mindsets, the future may look ominous. Militant Islamic fundamentalism seems to have expanded and grown stronger. The precarious position of Muslim governments friendly to the West, facing increasing opposition and violence, provokes dread. What if Egypt, the largest and most significant Arab country, succumbed to fundamentalism? And what if the house of Saud collapsed? And what about Turkey? and so on.

Is militant Islamic fundamentalism really a major danger to the West and the world? Is it really preparing for the "final" jihad against the non-Muslim world?

In the preceding pages, I have tried to analyze some of the strong elements and some of the weaknesses of militant Islamic fundamentalism. Having garnered all the information, it is now time to ask ourselves whether this brand of political Islam can succeed in carrying out its world ambitions.

23

Can Militant Islamic Fundamentalism Succeed?

The American theologian Reinhold Niebuhr once said that we must never forget "the depth of evil to which individuals and communities may sink particularly when they try to play the role of God to history."[1] To Iranian as well as non-Iranian Shiites, Ayatollah Ruhollah Khomeini was not an ordinary leader: He represented Allah's will on Earth. It was sufficient for him to open his mouth to be instantly obeyed. Thus in the suicide bombing of the American marine barracks in Beirut in October 1983, he gave no direct orders but expressed in a radio statement that true Muslims should put an end to the "shameful" occupation of Lebanon by Christian infidels. A couple of days later, the attack against the American marines and the French paratroopers took place.

Khomeini's demise has not basically changed the picture. Indeed, the ayatollah emphasized Allah's will in his writings and numerous speeches that have been made available at either very low prices or gratuitously in books and pamphlets and on cassettes.

THE GRAND DESIGN

Like his archenemy, the shah, Khomeini harbored a vision of the future. Whereas the shah aimed only at the restoration of Iran's ancient empire as one of the world's powers, the ayatollah envisioned the resurrection of the Muslim empire of yore as some sort of a loose federation of Muslim republics that would wage the ultimate jihad and hoist Islam's flag over the whole planet under the leadership of the clergy. (We have seen in earlier chapters that he ordered the gradual creation of an army of twenty million.)

Because he knew that such an endeavor would require many years to achieve, Khomeini proclaimed regional hegemony as the immediate objective. He was convinced that a confrontation with the Great Satan and the destruction of Israel were prerequisites to the success of his overall project. The war with Iraq only partially delayed his enterprise. In a fiery sermon delivered in July 1982, while the war with Iraq was still raging, he affirmed, "Muslims should unite and defeat America. They should know that they can do this [because] America and the West's lifeline is [the oil of] this region."[2]

He defined the first stage of his grand design in a threefold "plan": the establishment of a Persian Gulf–Mediterranean axis through alliances with the Shiites of Syria, Lebanon, and Iraq; "the exportation" of the revolution to other Muslim countries, especially those in the Middle East and North Africa; and the launching of a worldwide "terrorist" campaign against Muslim dissidents and Western interests.

Some of these objectives have been achieved more or less completely: alliance with Syria; control of the Lebanese Hezbollah; carrying out terrorism as far away as the Americas; cooperation with Sunnite militant fundamentalists; establishing an Islamist republic in the Sudan. As for executing the final phases of the grand design, Iran is quietly building up a powerful army and acquiring sophisticated armaments. In May 1991, one of the top mullahs, Mussavi-Khoeniha, openly declared, "If we obtain the nuclear ability, the waves of Islamic revolution will get new power, and liberation movements throughout the world will look at the Islamic Republic of Iran as a new superpower with all its ideological potentials."[3]

THE SPREAD OF TERRORISM

As for terrorism, things seem to have developed according to the wishes expressed by Khomeini and his followers as well as by Sunni fundamentalist leaders. The 1983 Beirut car bombings against American and French servicemen opened the way.

On April 17, 1986, in London, Hindawi, a young Jordanian, accompanied his pregnant Irish girlfriend to Heathrow where she was to board an El Al flight to Tel Aviv. Her carry-on luggage passed through the X-ray machine without incident. But an Israeli agent, noting its unusual weight, opened it and found three pounds of plastic explosives set to be detonated by a small hand computer. Hindawi fled to the Syrian embassy but was arrested. The inquiry proved that the Syrian ambassador and members of his staff were involved. Britain broke diplomatic relations with Syria, and Damascus responded in kind, describing the bomb plot as an "Israeli–American" ploy staged to embarrass Arabs. Later, other terrorists, with the help of Libya, succeeded in blowing up Pan Am Flight 103 over Scotland. In 1995–96, there was a series of horrible cases, among them the October 1995 bombing of a Paris subway station; the November 1995 bombing of the National Guard building in Riyadh; the May 1995 car bombing at the Jordan-Syria-Saudi border; the June 1996 attack on American servicemen near Dahran; and numerous massacres in Algiers and other capitals.

On May 11, 1995, an intelligence report presented evidence that Iran provided more than $100 million every year to terrorists in a sustained campaign to kill its enemies and to derail the Middle East peace process. The report also reaffirmed that Iran financed the Lebanese Hezbollah. A *New York Times* commentator wrote: "Of the seven countries cited by the State Department as sponsoring terrorism [Iran, Iraq, Libya, Syria, the Sudan, North Korea, and Cuba] only Iran now plays an active role in promoting terrorism aimed at the United States and its allies. . . . The Sudan provides a haven for religious and [secular] terrorists . . . and Iran sees the Sudan as a launching pad for radical groups throughout North Africa."[4] The authors of the same report indicated that the Hezbollah had infiltrated the Shiite community living near the common border of Paraguay, Brazil, and Argentina. In June 1996 Bahrain discovered an Iranian-inspired plot to overthrow its government. Iran was dubbed "terrorism's *de facto* global headquarters."[5] In April 1996, the United States expelled some Sudanese diplomats attached to the mission to the United Nations. Intelligence officers of Iran, Iraq, Syria, and Sudan often meet in Khartoum.[6]

In the United States, the World Trade Center bombing was not an isolated incident. Four months later, a ring of terrorists (some of them from the Sudan) was discovered in New York, and members of the Abu Nidal group were arrested in St. Louis (Missouri), Ohio, Wisconsin, and Illinois. Moreover, new movements, spurred by the World Trade Center example, emerged from different sources (ethnic, sectarian, and others).[7]

It seems that terrorism will grow in the near future because the oil-rich Arab countries cannot help as they used to do. As a result, the welfare programs that kept the lower stratas of societies in check will stop. A mass of idle and poor young people will fall prey more easily to fundamentalist propaganda and recruitment efforts.[8]

At first glance, the future appears grim and full of dangers. Khomeini's grand design seems to be progressing steadily toward its final goal. Modern Cassandras predict the "end of Western civilization," but such prophecies are not new.

Since the sixteenth century, astrologers and soothsayers have reopened Nostradamus's book of predictions and reinterpreted his quatrains. According to some of them, the old French physician predicted the domination of the West (and the rest of the world) by "Mahommedans."

THE HOPKINS MANUSCRIPT

Such prognostications remind me of a curious book that I read in the 1940s when I was a high school student, *The Hopkins Manuscript*. Although it somehow related to history and Islam, it was neither an archeological trove nor a learned study by some anonymous Muslim scholar of the remote past. It was an "anticipatory" work of fiction (one would say science fiction today). The author, R. C. Sherriff, a British playwright and Hollywood scenarist who died in the mid-1970s, wrote the novel to mock his countrymen's mores.

The story starts sometime in the twenty-third century (or later). Europe has been wiped away for some unknown reason and its history completely forgotten. The archeologists of Abyssinia, the most advanced country of the time, know that Europe once harbored a brilliant civilization: After finding some monuments and inscriptions on stones, they reconstitute some of its languages such as Latin and English. They learn through deciphered inscriptions that a certain Caesar invaded Gaul and the British Isles. An archeological mission to England brings back a small stone carefully kept in Addis Ababa's state museum, and savants discuss the meaning of its inscription: "Pelham, five miles." They send teams to regions whose "bad" climate probably led to the destruction of all books and papers. Nevertheless, one of the missions unearths a thermos bottle containing a manuscript, the twentieth-century diary of a Mr. Hopkins, Esquire, who apparently was an English gentleman involved in the poultry business. He lived in a London townhouse and was a member of several clubs and of the Royal Society of the Friends of the Moon. One day he was summoned to an extraordinary meeting of the society to receive an ultrasecret communication: For some unspecified reason, Earth's satellite, deflected from its orbit, was hurtling toward the planet and would fall in the Atlantic. In order to avoid panic, the information would be kept from the public. Hopkins did not change any of his habits but did start a diary.

On the night of the event, he went to bed as usual at ten o'clock. The next morning he found a yacht in his garden, projected probably by the uncontrollable tides caused by the fall of the moon. After breakfast, he sat at his desk and typed a letter to the editor of the London *Times* complaining about the annoyance and asserting that the government should immediately remove the craft from his courtyard. From his daily notations, we learn that geologists were discovering many rare metals in the lunar soil and that the United States and Canada as well as European countries had begun to bicker about the apportionment of those riches. The disagreements and wranglings went on for years and completely divided the West.

In the meantime, a Muslim preacher in India exhorted the impoverished masses to revolt against the colonialist and imperialist exploiters. He organized a "march" against the enemy—the rich countries of the West. Billions of people from Asia, the Middle East, and Africa invaded Europe and, like locusts, destroyed everything in their path. Then, appalled by the cold and unhealthful climate, they returned to their homes. . . .

In the 1940s, Malthus's theories were almost completely forgotten, and nobody had yet articulated the population time bomb and other kinds of ecological worries. Could Sherriff in the 1930s have foreseen events of the 1980s and 1990s? Could he have imagined characters like Khomeini and Mawdudi? Did he possess powers of divination? Will his prediction come true, and will *The Hopkins Manuscript* become a prescient text? It is true that Khomeini's ancestors migrated to India. It is equally true that Mawdudi was an Indo-Pakistani. It is true that both were preachers who railed against the West and singled it out as the enemy of Islam and the third world. It also is true that they called for jihad against the infidels. But resemblances to Sherriff's story stop there. Brooding about the decline and the ultimate demise of Western civilization began at the dawn of the twentieth century with writers such as Spengler, not Sherriff.

FACTS VERSUS DREAMS

In the minds of militant fundamentalists, final victory over the infidels is certain. Thus Sudan's Turabi boasts that "the West is even more apprehensive about Islam than it was about communism because although it knows how to deal with material challenges, it has no idea how to go about facing a spiritual challenge."[9]

But the fact is that all Muslims are not fundamentalists and all fundamentalists are not militants. Actually, the majority of Muslims disapprove
of violence and random killings, even if they seem reluctant to condemn
them in public. On the other hand, militant fundamentalists have failed to
achieve unity among themselves. Sectarian and other differences continue
to divide them, and there is no concrete evidence of a militant Islamic International manipulated by one hand. Finally, the excesses of the Iranian
and Sudanese regimes as well as the massacres committed by the Algerian
militants and the killings performed by other groups have turned many
Muslims against them. Generally speaking, the people are not in favor of
militantism, even when they vote for its candidates. In many cases, they
follow the "militant trend because of the inefficiency of existing political
parties (as in Turkey, for instance) or because of the repressive character of
many Muslim countries in which only the pulpits of the mosques can be
used to express dissent."[10] At any rate, when the Sudanese dictator Nu-
meiry imposed his own version of "hard and pure" Islam in 1985, a series of
popular demonstrations against his rule took place in Khartoum and its
twin city, Omdourman, where shouts of "Down with the sharia" reverber-
ated in the streets. As the writer Amir Taheri noted: "For the first time in Islam's contemporary history, tens of thousands of Muslims openly rejected
life under the law of the Koran, preferring Sudan's traditional legal system."[11] As for the Algerian Islamic Salvation Front, its systematic killing of
journalists, teachers, and intellectuals deprived the country of a much
needed class of educated citizens.

Trying to isolate Muslim societies from the rest of the world to "protect"
them from the "contamination" of the "satanic" Western culture is noxious
as well as ineffective. It not only deprives Muslims of the cultural and scientific benefits of the West, but it also fails to stop the flow of the less valuable
"entertainment" products from reaching the younger generations. The
wares of Madonna, Michael Jackson, and other rock singers and dancers
continue to pour into environments dominated by the sharia. Communication satellites and the Internet do not need passports to cross frontiers.
Tapes can be easily smuggled. As a journalist noted, "The West does keep
creeping in."[12] The splendors of the "golden age" of Islam, which militants
continually summon up for the masses, only confuse the issues, as did the
mirage of Arab unity conjured up by nationalists in the 1950s and 1960s.
The promise obfuscates the basic problems of inadequate resources, anach-
ronistic social structures, and essential reforms. A renaissance in Muslim
societies is possible but certainly not through the return to a dead past. The
present mess in Afghanistan and Sudan as well as the negative balance

sheet of Iran's Islamic Republic after eighteen years of existence constitutes sufficient proof of the terrible price of militant fundamentalism.

THE UNBEARABLE COST OF FUNDAMENTALISM

On November 13, 1992, *The New York Times* ran an article entitled "Tehran Journal: Sophistication Sets In: Head Scarves by Chanel." According to the report, "music plays from loudspeakers in hotel lobbies, at homes, and in taxis. Sales of videotapes and music cassettes are booming. People line up at movies and amusement parks. . . . Restaurants around town [are always full] and serve nonalcoholic Islamic beer . . . . This account of life in Tehran incensed a reader whose letter to the editor was published on December 1:

This narrow view of present-day Iran masks the dramatic plunge in the standards of living of Iranians during the last decade, a period in which the local currency lost 95 percent of its dollar value. You could have described how people on fixed incomes are coping with the inflation. What is it like to be required to bring your medical supplies for surgery in a hospital? What is the true nature of quasi-official corruption visitors complain about? Who are the beneficiaries of the "private foundations" holding billions of dollars of confiscated properties with accountability to no one? To what extent is the political arena the exclusive realm of the clergy, their relatives, and their associates? As far as we know, even former Prime Minister Bazargan . . . and his Islamic group are barred from publishing their newspaper and participating in the elections.

The fate of secular opposition has been much worse. Those not executed are in prison or have been terrified into silence. Opposition leaders living outside Iran are being systematically eliminated.

This angry reader of *The New York Times* provided a list of politicians assassinated in Germany, France, and Switzerland in 1991 and 1992. (The 1996 trial in Berlin of the murderers of one of them linked the case to Iran's supreme leaders.)

Western observers (including many *New York Times* reporters) confirm the grim account provided by the reader. As a senior expert wrote in *Foreign Affairs*,

To understand the likely course of fundamentalism in power, we can do no better than look at Iran, the first and most important state to be overwhelmed by militant Islam. Fifteen years after the regime's jubilant beginnings, the verdict is clear. Iran's revolution has failed, dismaying its people and bankrupting its coffers. . . . The decomposition of Iran's Islamic Revolution is striking even among the revolutionary hard core.[13]

Judith Miller, who has visited Iran several times since 1979, wrote in her recent book, "The cost has been enormous. . . . Almost two decades of mismanagement, administrative chaos, state murder, repression, corruption, [and] unnerving unpredictability have caused many of the most talented to flee and many others who stayed to despair. The pauperization of the middle class and the educated elite continues to alienate young Iranians from the regime, from Islamic government, even from Islam itself."[14]

THE GREAT LEAP BACKWARD

Eighteen years after the seizure of power, the Iranian mullahs are facing huge problems in all economic and social fields. Iran is now facing mass unemployment, double-digit inflation, falling productivity (both in industry and agriculture), and a massive foreign debt. The national currency fell from 75 rials to the dollar (in 1978) to more than 5,000 at a point in 1996. The per capita GNP is now less than half its 1977 level. Foreign debt has reached $40 billion. Problems continue to pile up: the population explosion (it has doubled in eighteen years); the dire consequences of the eight-year war with Iraq, which cost hundreds of billions of dollars (one million people maimed and injured, half a million dead; reconstruction estimated at $200 billion); and the importation of food ($14 billion each year). Iran's oil-export capacity, which was more than 5 million barrels a day before the Islamic Revolution, is now less than 3.8 million barrels.

In the political and social domains, things continue to worsen. In 1995 and 1996 a number of industrial strikes, antigovernment demonstrations, and even riots occurred in Tehran and other major cities. Lawyers, doctors, bazaar merchants, retired officers, intellectuals, and journalists took swipes at the regime and its policies. Today Iran is diplomatically isolated. In the past eighteen years, the only European heads of state who visited Tehran were Romania's Ceascescu (a few days before his execution) and the controversial Kurt Waldheim of Austria.[15]

Ibrahim Yazdi, the American citizen who helped Khomeini and took over the leadership of the Freedom Movement after Bazargan's demise, regularly denounces the "despotic one-party system": "We disapproved of Khomeini's authoritarian philosophy. . . . We reject an electoral system in which the government must approve each candidate. . . . Nepotism, crony-ism, and corruption are rampant. . . . Inflation has soared to nearly 100 per-cent. Public industries are bloated. . . ."16

Even senior ayatollahs in the past two years have asserted their opposi-tion to the government and have called for new leaders capable of strength-ening the economy and ending the nation's isolation.

The regime survives through several layers of repression: in addition to the ordinary police force, the secret police headed by a cabinet minister; the Revolutionary Guards; and the *Bassijis* (a supplementary law-enforcement group recruited among slum dwellers and failed students). These groups continually harass all dissenters and critics. Moreover, the government (like Saddam Hussein in Iraq) has its assassins who physically eliminate in-ternal and external opposition. Like other dictators of the century—Hitler, Stalin, Saddam Hussein, Qaddafi, and others—the mullahs intimidate the people who complain in secret and wait for the emergence of a savior.

Sudan, the other country where militant fundamentalism is in power, has not fared better than Iran. Not only has its Islamic government failed to solve the many problems facing it, but it has rekindled the civil war with the non-Muslims (Christians and animists) of its southern regions, which entails a cost of $1 million per day in a country beset by famine, economic bankruptcy, flooding, and infestations of crickets and locusts. The funda-mentalist government stops at nothing in order to retain its sway. Turabi's National Islamic Front had infiltrated the administration and the army long before the coup that brought the militants to power. After the coup, Turabi's Front replaced key jobholders with its own supporters. Milton Viorst wrote in *Foreign Affairs* that the National Islamic Front "extended its dominion over the economy by taking control of banks, foreign trade, and much of farm and industrial production. Moreover, it has penetrated the entire culture with a program of Islamic indoctrination."17 All visitors con-firm that the economy is in shambles, crippled by a near triple-digit infla-tion and a staggering foreign debt of $16 billion.

The regime has mercilessly suppressed dissent in the army as well as among civilians. It put down protests with its "riot" police. Viorst con-cluded his article with the following assessment: "There is also disillusion with Islamic rule, which is no better than the rule it replaced. . . . Clearly popular dissatisfaction with the Islamic state runs deep, but Turabi and his followers have entrenched themselves so skillfully . . . that it may be impossible to get them out." Judith Miller, in her recent book, qualified the regime as "brutal": "The level of violence seemed one of the few rising indicators. . . . Once uncommon in Sudan, torture was now widespread."[18] As is done in Iran, the regime is brainwashing children and young people. In 1994 a Sudanese citizen, at an Islamic horse race (without betting, at least openly), told *New York Times* reporter Chris Hedges, "This government is squeezing all of us until we suffocate. We have to do everything now, from betting to drinking, on the sly. It is not much of a way to live, but we hang on. They haven't yet figured out how to ban human nature."[19]

Both Iran's and Sudan's experiences underline the high price the people have paid for Islamic governments. The way the superfundamentalist Taliban are acting in Afghanistan bodes ill. The producers and directors of these tragedies often retort to critics that they need time. In 1980, Bruce Van Woorst, *Time* magazine's Middle East bureau chief, confronted Khomeini: "The economy has not revived. The poor in south Tehran are as poor as ever. . . . There is no normal political activity. In light of this, is it not fair to say that the revolution has failed?" The ayatollah answered that the revolution could take twenty years to complete.[20] Almost twenty years have passed since Khomeini's answer, but the premises on which the journalist based his question remain unchanged. Militant fundamentalism has proved to be a costly failure. It has hurt Muslims badly. It has separated them, as it were, from their past glories and their no longer expected future progress. Indeed, the Islamic society that militant fundamentalists propose to create is a far cry from even the palest copy of the Abbassid heyday when Charlemagne and his peers looked toward Bagdad with envy. It offers only a dull and repressive environment conditioned to kill forever even the slightest manifestation of humor, let alone culture and science. In 1994, for instance, an Iranian cartoonist and his publisher were arrested and condemned to long prison terms for creating and publishing a drawing of a soccer player that "religious authorities asserted bore a shocking resemblance to the late Ayatollah Khomeini." That same year, in the Turkish city of Sivas, thirty-six liberal artists and writers perished when fundamentalists burned down their hotel.[21] Many intellectuals and artists are fleeing into exile in the West. Indeed, militant fundamentalism amounts to a great leap backward.

24

A Challenge to the West and the World?

In a mid-1980s thriller, one character says to another: "Do not make the error of thinking of the Muslim militants as lunatics. They are anything but. . . . They know they have their hands on the throat of the developed world, and they intend to keep them there."[1] Indeed, Khomeini affirmed that Muslims can defeat America because its lifeline is the oil of "this region."[2]

Yet it is difficult to consider normal the militant fundamentalists who look forward to martyrdom. During the Iran-Iraq War, an East European journalist who witnessed one of the "human wave assaults," in which tens of thousands of Iranian children and adolescents went willingly to their deaths, could hardly believe what he was seeing as the small boys were hurled in the air by the explosion of land mines.[3]

In fact, these children as well as the young suicide-bombers had been (and still are) carefully trained. The training includes religious indoctrination by clerics who focus on all the verses of the Koran that refer to the "glory of dying for God." They describe at length the promised paradise as a "carefree garden replete with magnificent palaces, scrumptious food, and beautiful virgins awaiting the martyrs." A fifteen-year-old trainee, who was arrested in 1995 in Gaza, told reporters that his training had started when he was ten years old: "They taught me about the heroes of Islam who were killed as saints and how they are now in heaven beside God." They are buried in mock graves to erase from their minds the fear of death. Before going to their "ultimate mission," they spend several days chanting relevant verses from the Koran.[4]

Many Westerners tend to see all Muslims as young suicide bombers who are committed to fight against them. This is not correct. As I have already indicated, the majority of Muslims are not militant fundamentalists. Frustrated members of the faithful, facing the tides of change and the problems of the modern world, might be temporarily deceived by distorted historical references and empty slogans that sound sagacious because of Koranic quotations taken out of context, but sooner or later the mistaken premises of fundamentalism are bound to emerge.

OPIUM AND MILITANCY

Another source of deep concern in the West is the link between drug trafficking and militant fundamentalism, especially in Afghanistan. As Andrew Meier, a *Time* magazine reporter, recently noted, "The *opium standard*, one of the enduring legacies of America's opposition to the Soviet Union's occupation, lives on."[5] Indeed, the use of fundamentalism as a "cold-war" weapon has resulted in the rise of both heroin supplies and "wandering" terrorists in the West.

Before and after the Soviets withdrew, tens of thousands of Islamic radicals from approximately forty nations went to Afghanistan to learn the "lessons of jihad." They have taken their war abroad to Algeria, Azerbaijan, Bangladesh, Bosnia, Burma, China, Europe, Egypt, India, Morocco, Pakistan, Saudi Arabia, Sudan, Tajikistan, Tunisia, the United States, Uzbekistan, and Yemen. Noor Amin, a commander of the Islamic party, proudly boasts, "The whole country is a university for jihad."[6]

Afghanistan now produces roughly a third of the heroin that reaches the United States. Hundreds of tons of heroin are shipped via Pakistan, Turkey, and new routes in Central Asia and the Balkans. The Taliban, who control almost two thirds of the country, have proclaimed their intention of cracking down on drugs but are doing nothing of the sort. On the contrary, they encourage the cultivation of opium: "Last summer farmer after farmer bore witness to the persuasive powers of Kalashnikovs in the service of the Koran. 'Even if we wanted to grow just wheat, they wouldn't allow us,' said one elderly grower. . . . 'Maybe they haven't studied anything but the Koran,' he said, 'but they have learned how much profit opium brings.' The new overlords not only tax the poppy harvest—taking a *zakat* of 25 percent, . . . but they even distribute fertilizer."[7]

The general situation in Afghanistan seems grim. An American expert recently wrote, "Since the Taliban captured Kabul on September 27, 1996, and extended their rule over two thirds of Afghanistan—imposing their ultraconservative form of Islamic rule, confining women to their homes, banning girls from schools, requiring men to grow beards, and outlawing soccer, kites, chess, and music—the United States has remained curiously passive. . . . Thus far there is little indication that the international community is prepared to offer any alternative to the fighters and the opium growers."[8]

Taken at face value, the training of suicide bombers and jihad fighters as well as the swelling of heroin production might seem ominous and suffused with danger for the West. In fact, the risks involved should not be exaggerated. For one thing, the Taliban are at odds with Iran's fundamentalists and other Islamic militants. Moreover, despite their claims to the contrary, they need Western assistance if Afghanistan is to survive its present predicaments.

To be sure, terrorist activities conducted by militant Islamic fundamentalist groups can cause damage and claim human casualties. But, in my opinion, they do not constitute, at least for the time being, a perilous challenge to Western countries. The Muslim world remains steeped in underdevelopment: Oil wealth, nationalist fervor, modernizing efforts, and now renewed fundamentalist militantism have not been able to lift it. It seems that the leaders and the elites, religious or secular, moderate or radical, in striving to reach parity with the West, have developed a mistaken view of the ways in which Europeans achieved their present advance.

A MISTAKEN VIEW OF THE WESTERN ADVANCE

In the eighteenth and nineteenth centuries, the Ottomans attributed the superiority of the West to its weaponry. They acquired arms from European weapons dealers who were only too happy to enter into profitable contracts. With the help of Western experts, the Turks even created an armament industry. But their efforts did not prevent further setbacks and the rapid rise of Western domination. Nevertheless, almost all Muslim countries continued to follow in the footsteps of the Ottomans, spending fortunes on military equipment and training. As Professor Bernard Lewis noted in a recent study: "Even after the departure of the West, [their efforts] have not sufficed to restore even a semblance of parity in the effective use of military power. The efforts of some states to acquire weapons of mass destruction—Western inventions all—are attempts to remedy this disparity. Such attempts may achieve mutual destruction, but they will not achieve victory or even parity."[9]

Like many secular leaders of the past and the present, fundamentalists believe that power resides in weapons and in submission to Allah's law rather than in the technoscientific power and economic progress characteristic of "civil societies." In short, they completely overlook the basic conditions that allowed the West to forge ahead: continuous endeavors to understand and quantify the physical world (which was abandoned by Muslims after the triumph of fundamentalist interpretations around the twelfth century); improvements in techniques of industrial and agricultural production; printing with movable type (which was rejected by ulemas until the mid-nineteenth century); the transition from feudalism to capitalism; the gradual promotion of a new mind-set; freedom of speech; consequent criticism and discussion of ideas; enforcement of equality and individual rights; the rule of law; the establishment of favorable conditions for economic development; the emergence of "civil society"; and other factors.

Technology can be bought, but its underlying scientific knowledge can only thrive in an environment of freedom of thought and discussion, which allows the promotion of new ideas and inventions. Recently economists such as Paul Romer of Stanford University have refurbished theories that highlight the role of ideas and technological discoveries as "driving engines" of economic growth. It is obvious that militant fundamentalism does not promote new ideas. The only invention in recent years in Iran was an adaptation of the guillotine for severing hands according to the Islamic criminal code. Robin Wright, who was at first supportive of the Islamic Republic of Iran, recently wrote: "Iran is now moving to stifle the exchange of ideas in universities, cultural circles, the media, and even at mosques." She quotes Abdol Karim Sorouch, an Iranian professor who helped Khomeini but later turned against fundamentalism, "The clergy is always talking about the duties of the people, but they never speak about people's rights."[10] Until Muslims establish the conditions for economic growth and civil societies, the Muslim world will have no chance to become an alternative to the ruling principals in the West.

STATUS OF WOMEN

Another underlying condition of economic and social development is the improvement of the status of women. In Muslim societies, women are not on any sort of equal footing with men. Like the "protected" non-Muslims, they are "second-class" citizens consigned to perform "lower tasks" (in the case of women, child bearing and domestic work). Many educated Muslims are aware of the effect of this situation on the general underdevelopment of their countries. Thus Nawal al-Saadawi, a woman who exceptionally became the director of a section of the Egyptian Ministry of Health, wrote in her autobiography, "It is no longer possible to escape the fact that the underprivileged status of women, their relative backwardness, leads to an essential backwardness of society as a whole."[11] Fundamentalists do not agree. They even accuse the advocates of women's rights of promoting anti-Islamic Western values.

One of the first things that Khomeini did after seizing power was to void all the advantages accorded to women by the shah's "white revolution." It is true that Iran and Sudan continue to send veiled women to international conferences, and it is equally true that Rafsanjani's daughter was "elected" to the Islamic parliament. But these special appearances are nothing more than "window dressing."

Muslim feminists in a multiethnic and multireligious society such as Malaysia, where some degree of individual freedom exists, have articulated their own slogans against both militant fundamentalists and mainstream ulemas, such as: Blame Men, not Allah! One of them recently affirmed, "For fourteen centuries, the Koran has been interpreted almost exclusively by men. Only in the past two decades have women begun to say, 'Let us look at the text and come up with our own conclusions.' "[12]

Militant fundamentalists would consider such expressions of self-confidence on the part of women sacrilegious. In Afghanistan, the Taliban have closed girls' schools and forbidden women to work in offices or shops. Confronted with international criticism, one of their spokesmen said bluntly, "We are following the rules of the Holy Koran. A woman's work is to take care of the house and the child."[13] Yet many of the "rules" concerning women were developed long after the death of the prophet. Thus Professor William Cleveland remarked that early Arab conquerors adopted the practice of veiling from Mesopotamia, where high-class women used to veil to distinguish themselves from the lower orders of society. He also underlined that the Koran set forth guidelines intended to improve the status of women in seventh-century Arabia by giving them the right to own material possessions and limiting the number of wives to four instead of the previous unlimited polygamy.[14]

THE ROLL OF THE DICE

Another factor accounting for the West's advance is linked to the notion of risk. In a recent book, Peter Bernstein argued that the idea of risk permeates our modern world. We talk about risk, measure it, hedge it; we insure almost everything; we forecast weather; we calculate the resistance of bridges and buildings; we prolong our scientific investigations with "guesses" (theories) that we submit to tests. Our world, Bernstein continued, is different from that of our ancestors who resigned themselves to the mercies of a wholly unpredictable universe. In his opinion, by understanding the problem of risk, humanity liberated itself from the "caprices of the gods" and gradually put individuals in their own hands: Understanding risk, uncertainty, and probability made the modern world possible.[15]

Bernstein notes that the first serious consideration of probability occurred during the Renaissance and was inspired by games of chance. Decades before him, the nineteenth-century Swiss historian Jacob Burckhardt underlined in his *History of the Renaissance* the importance of chance games in the overall development of the West. In his opinion, the Muslim world had missed the coach, as it were, because chance games were forbidden by the Koran. The Muslim imagination was, as a result, pushed toward the discovery of "hidden treasures" and not the undertaking of risk to create wealth.

Curiously enough, in the heyday of the reign of the Ummayads and the Abbassids, elites were very much attracted to predictions and forecasts—the caliphs had their own private astrologers. But scientists were not allowed to address problems of probability: It is sacrilegious to "question" Allah's will. Science could develop only in the West.

A GREATER DANGER TO THE MUSLIM WORLD

From the foregoing it appears that instead of creating the basic conditions of progress, Muslim leaders undertook programs of development "from the top" by devising state economies that did not encourage individual entrepreneurship. Egypt's Nasser, Iraq's Saddam Hussein, Libya's Qaddafi, and Iran's Muhammad Reza Pahlavi tried to transform their countries into military powers (at least regionally). The shah's army crumbled at the start of the Islamic Revolution; Iraq's troops failed to unseat Khomeini in the 1980s and to stand up to the U.S.-led coalition in 1990–91; Qaddafi could not conquer Chad; Nasser's army, together with the Jordanians and the Syrians, did not resist for more than six days in the war against Israel.

It seems a safe bet to say that militant Islamic fundamentalists cannot fare better. A change in the world balance of power is unlikely in the near future. Unless they get hold of weapons of mass destruction (including nuclear ones), militant Islamic fundamentalists will remain a limited threat to the rest of the world. (With arms capable of mass destruction, the action of any one person or small group anywhere, taken in the name of any cause, could have horrible consequences.)

If, despite all its anti-Western rhetoric, militant Islamic fundamentalism is not a major threat to the West, it might prove a fatal one to the Muslim world itself. In saying that, I do not have in mind the fate of the so-called secular leaders of countries "friendly" to the West but that of all Muslims at large. Indeed, as already indicated, militant fundamentalism amounts to a "great leap backward" at the moment when the advanced world is literally soaring ahead with its new scientific and technological revolution.

The first wave of militant fundamentalism that swept the Muslim world some eight centuries ago resulted in its steady decadence and led to its present underdevelopment and weakness. The new wave triggered by Khomeini's successful seizure of power in Iran might delay its reemergence for many more centuries. Indeed, Muslims have had difficulty adjusting to the world that was shaped by the nineteenth-century industrial revolution. Militant fundamentalism is digging a deep chasm. At any rate, so-called religious revivalist movements have dangerously delayed the Muslim world's march toward democracy, the rule of law, and civil society. They stifle curiosity about the past and an interest in assessing the present that alone can open the gates of the prison to which Muslims were consigned by the triumph of fundamentalist doctrines in the twelfth century.

Conclusion: The "Past Shock"

The spectacular overthrow of the shah of Iran by Ayatollah Khomeini became a kind of metaphor for the widespread debate about "modernity" that was (and is) going on in many countries in the third world and in the West. Indeed, the shah was in the process of introducing in Iran Western standards and ways of life. In contrast, the ayatollah reasserted the old medieval mores. Their confrontation also, in a way, reflected continuing discussions in the West concerning the "erosion of values" brought about by the accelerating changes associated with uninterrupted scientific and technological breakthroughs.

I witnessed in my childhood the disturbing impact of the "novelties" that the British and French colonial powers were introducing in the Middle East. Years later, when I moved to Europe, I found myself caught in the vortex of another kind of speedy modification that triggered a heated and unceasing controversy in the media as well as in intellectual circles. Some pundits questioned the "rationality" and "positivism" that had dominated Western thought since the eighteenth century, whereas others defended them fiercely. A new wave of conservative thinkers cast doubts on the concept of progress and increasingly demanded a return to moral limits.

FUTURE AND PAST SHOCKS

In the 1960s and 1970s, many writers, experts, and journalists belabored the theme of "the total" transformation or "mutation" of humanity. Alvin Toffler coined the phrase "future shock." In his book, *Future Shock,* which became an instant bestseller, he argued that change was sweeping the highly industrialized world with waves of ever increasing speed and unprecedented impact: "A new culture is superimposing itself on an old one, hence a future shock." Some went so far as to speak of a "crisis of civilization" or of "the end of an era."

The transformation that occurred in the West rippled over the planet and reached the Muslim world where the processes of modernization had already been initiated by reformist leaders, provoking a more or less acute clash between a "new" and an "old" culture. Because of this aspect of change in Muslim countries, which recalled Toffler's diagnostic of the West, many experts concluded that a crisis was shaking the entire universe. In fact, what was happening in Muslim countries was quite different. When Khomeini's name appeared in the headlines, Muslims were beginning to emerge from their medieval environment, whereas Westerners were jumping from one level of modernity to a more advanced and sophisticated one. Khomeini, if anything, took Iranians back to the Middle Ages. His effect resembled a "past shock."

In fact, our world is in the throes of two different crises that present some similarities because of their inevitable interaction in an ever shrinking and interdependent planet. It would be a mistake to equate militant Islamic fundamentalism's rejection of modernity with the criticisms of Western observers.[1]

The rise of modernity in Europe was triggered by the Renaissance and its increasing reliance on reason, free inquiry, and empirical science. Modernity, almost immediately, faced a powerful and sometimes "militant" opposition by fundamentalist clerics of the Catholic church. Institutionalized by the Council of Trent (1545–63), the movement culminated in the first Vatican Council of 1870.

As Professor Colin Williams aptly remarked in a 1981 paper, "Khomeini's militantism had a great deal in common with this initial Western response to modernization."[2] The "shah-ayatollah" metaphor mentioned above is inaccurate. The "modernity" of the shah and the "traditionalism" of Khomeini do not fit with the concepts at the core of the debate in the West. Moreover, it is also a mistake to consider the rise of militant fundamentalism as a sign of religious revivalism.

RELIGIOUS REVIVALISM?

After the ayatollah's seizure of power in Iran, a great number of books, articles, and learned papers reached bookstores and libraries bearing such titles as *Return of Religion, Religious Revival, God's Revenge, Resurgence of Faith, New Age of Spirituality*, and titles of a similar nature. This abundant literature—despite warnings, qualifications, and clarifications by the authors—created widespread confusion in distinguishing religious revivalism from militant fundamentalism. It also promoted the mistaken idea that before Khomeini, religion had been in regression for some time. Religion never left our world, and so it could not make a return with people, including people like Khomeini. In the 1970s, when Khomeini came to prominence, Harvard University theologian Harvey Cox underlined religon's endurance in *Religion in the Secular City*. Even in the officially atheist Soviet Union, a large majority continued to practice religion. In the Muslim countries, the muezzins never stopped calling the faithful to prayer five times a day. Hundreds of millions of Hindus and other people continued to honor their gods.

What is relatively new is not a return of religion, but a resurgence of militant fundamentalism and violence linked to faith. To be sure, there are some resemblances between mainstream religions and fundamentalism: Both have reasserted themselves as the custodians of moral values and demand respect in society; both also seem to utter the same lines. To mention only one example, Catholic and other Christian churches condemn abortion, but they do not encourage the use of violence as some antiabortion activists seem to endorse.

Beyond the similarity of moral principles and sacred references, religion and militant fundamentalism are often at odds. In the case of Islam, Dr. Mahatir Muhammad, the prime minister of Malaysia, affirmed recently that "people who are usually described as fundamentalists are far from following the fundamental principles of the Islamic religion. On the contrary, they are the people who reject the teachings of Islam or who deviate from them."[3]

MUSLIMS ARE NOT TERRORISTS

Although Khomeini played a prominent role in publicizing the present wave, terrorism around the world cannot be attributed solely or even principally to Muslim radicals. The Oklahoma City bombing, which claimed more victims and produced more material damage than the New York World Trade Center blast, has been linked to white supremacist activists.

Christian prolife killers (without oxymoronic irony), Indians who use violence in their campaign for a Hindu nation, and Orthodox Jews pelting people driving through their neighborhoods on Saturdays are not followers of Muhammad's faith. Nor are the Sri Lankan Sinhalese Buddhists who are waging a bloody war against Tamil separatists.

Despite the fact that the word *fundamentalism*, as used today, refers to a certain type of politically motivated religious radicalism, one should not forget that secular extremists using political ideologies can be considered fundamentalists. Indeed, the radical interpretation of religion is not the only platform on which fundamentalists base their claims. Race, language, culture, and political differences may also serve as banners to fundamentalist groups.

Another point that should be stressed is that fundamentalism is not necessarily militant and reprehensible. Many people live by the strictest exigencies of their beliefs without impinging on others' rights and freedoms. In democracies, antagonist political parties and different ethnic and religious communities live side by side and participate in the political, social, cultural, and economic life of their countries. In contrast, *militant* fundamentalism nurtures intolerance and violence. Even when it is swathed in religious or secular ideological garb, it remains essentially a political movement. It aims at seizing power and, if successful, at imposing totalitarian rule (as Hitler and Stalin did in the 1930s, and Khomeini and Turabi did in the 1980s).

It is therefore essential to draw a clear line between religion and nonviolent fundamentalism and militant fundamentalism. The latter, either religious or secular, is basically intolerant and resorts to violence in order to impose its views. Because of that, it presents dangers to societies and justifies measures of defense on the part of concerned majorities.

Because of its confrontational nature, militant fundamentalism requires one or several adversaries whom it brands with vocabulary borrowed from the Koran. Thus the names of the designated enemies become at once familiar and impressive: "corruptors on Earth" for local leaders and "Great (or lesser) Satan(s)" for Westerners.

THE WEST AND MILITANT FUNDAMENTALISM

Since the establishment of militant fundamentalist regimes in Iran and Sudan, terrorism (especially state-sponsored terrorism) has dramatically increased within and without the Muslim world. As previously indicated, radical Muslims consider Western democratic secularism and most Muslim leaders their worst enemies.

The West, up to now, has responded to terrorism by mobilizing its law-enforcement agencies; retaliating against selected targets; imposing sanctions against "rogue" states; and engaging in what it euphemistically calls critical dialogue. None of these approaches has so far yielded any positive result.

Although the question of countering militant fundamentalism lies outside the scope of this book, I would be remiss if I completely avoided the subject. In the late 1960s, I read an interview of Jorge Luis Borges conducted by an American journalist. It was, if I am not mistaken, in the Sunday *New York Times Book Review*. Asked why Latin Americans disdained North Americans, the famous Argentine writer said, in this paraphrased version of his comment: We have great consideration for militaries, but the United States sends us only businessmen! This was obviously a witticism, but it contained a certain amount of truth. Indeed, the tendency is widespread in the West to put the "cash register" before everything else. Often trade concerns supersede principles. Although this might be understandable in this world of high unemployment and deficits, it is all the same regrettable.

The issue of whether concern for human rights is outweighed by economic interests is not new. Very often Western governments have continued to pursue normal relations with rogue states while exerting diplomatic pressure. Such a policy, which might yield some short-term economic advantages, nevertheless has two adverse results. First, it discourages (if it does not destroy) internal opposition to tyrannical regimes. Second, it strips the West of all credibility. In the eyes of militant fundamentalists, Western countries, including the United States, are "paper tigers" who would go to any length to obtain economic profit. At any rate, history bears witness that whenever the West transgressed its own values for short-term gains, it invited serious problems.

It is as if the West were forgetting that all theorists and supreme guides of militant Islamic fundamentalism, from Hassan al-Banna to Ruhollah Khomeini (and their successors), have always proclaimed that the main threat to Islam is the propagation of Western ideas. (Incidentally, that is why they fiercely fight against the use of satellite dishes in their countries.) As one of them stated bluntly, "The West cannot destroy Islam by its bombs or its economic might and technology. Its deadliest weapons are its pagan ideas such as legislation by mortal men in defiance of divine law."[4] The West can trade with fundamentalist countries; it can create treaties with them; it can help them acquire and operate modern technology. But the West will always be considered their ultimate adversary, the one that must be finally eliminated. The militants, in this respect, capitalize on the basic distrust of the West that characterizes the attitude of all Muslims.

The challenge posed by militant Islamic fundamentalism to the West is not solely "military." What it primarily contests is the Western democratic and secular ideology. It wants to appropriate Western technology without embracing its ethos. In short, the battle waged against the Great and lesser Satan(s) possesses an important sociocultural dimension. Therefore, the response of the West should also have such a cultural dimension. It should, for example, involve explanations about the benefits of democratic institutions and their compatibility with Islam (and other religions). The West should demonstrate to Muslims that it does not harbor anti-Islamic feelings; it should counter the propaganda that it intends to destroy Muhammad's faith.

MUSLIM POLITICIANS AND MILITANT FUNDAMENTALISTS

In the view of militant Islamic fundamentalists, the danger to Islam represented by the West is compounded by the policies of the present Muslim leaders who have strayed from the "true" principles of their religion and are squandering the resources of their nations in cahoots with the infidels. These leaders and their supporters have "confiscated" political power. Therefore, the only way open to the true servants of Allah is to seize power and reestablish the rule of the sharia. Hence the resort to violence and the increasing use of terrorism and other means by Islamic fundamentalists in most Muslim countries.

To this challenge, local governments respond by instituting repressive measures. They deploy their police and armed forces and curb not only fundamentalist groups but also secular opposition. These governments accuse foreign states of encouraging the actions of fundamentalists. They point fingers toward Iran, Sudan, and other countries that directly or indirectly help the militants or sometimes give them havens. They criticize the West because it gives asylum to fundamentalist leaders who take advantage of civil and political liberties in order to launch their propaganda and direct terrorist operations.

It is true that many oil-rich Muslim countries have financially helped militant groups. It is equally true that Iran and Sudan have training camps and offer haven to terrorists. It is also true that many exiled militant leaders live in the West where they pursue their agendas. It is true that the West, particularly the United States, assisted and trained fundamentalists from all Muslim countries during the war against the Soviets in Afghanistan. Yet external causes alone cannot account for the surge of violence inside Muslim countries. Their authoritarian nature plays a great role inasmuch as it does not allow any peaceful expression of dissent. Moreover, the leaders of these countries court mainstream clerics whose interpretation of the Koran is not different from that of the militant fundamentalists. The ulemas gain access to the media, and their television and radio programs, in a way, complement the militants' propaganda, thus helping them recruit followers. At the same time, concerned governments stifle their own secular intelligentsia, not allowing a much needed public debate to take place.

All this accelerates the cycle of violence and results in obfuscating the real and urgent problems facing Muslims at the threshold of the twenty-first century. One of the most important questions facing them concerns their place and role in the new world order that is rapidly taking shape. In the last decades of the nineteenth century and during the twentieth century, while emerging from their long slumber, Muslims were wondering how to adapt to the changes that had taken place around them without losing their religious identity. Until the 1960s and 1970s, leaders such as Reza Shah and his son, Muhammad Reza, in Iran; Mustafa Kemal Atatürk in Turkey; Nasser in Egypt; Qaddafi in Libya; Bourghiba in Tunisia; and others tried to modernize their societies "from the top down." The all failed, at least partially. And this failure gave a boost to the fundamentalists who fiercely oppose modernization. (Even in Turkey, where secularism was pushed further than in any other Muslim country, we are witnessing an "Islamist" resurgence.) The reason, in my opinion, is that reforms cannot be imposed by decree; they need some sort of participation on the part of the people before they can be accepted. Reform should begin from the bottom up. To succeed it needs to be bolstered by a sustained campaign of information and education, if not of persuasion. In other words, reform cannot take root in the absence of a democratic atmosphere, which was not allowed to flourish by the modernizers of the Middle East and North Africa.

TIME IS RUNNING SHORT

The strict application of the sharia by a government of clerics supported by militant fundamentalists is certainly not the right solution for Muslims. On the contrary, it might accelerate their descent into backwardness, underdevelopment, and isolation. If one could set aside the question of the sharia and the involvement of clerics in government, it would be apparent that the militant fundamentalists are not so far away from the modernizers. Fundamentalists also think that improving standards of living and buying new technologies will bring them to parity with the West. They ignore (or fail to understand) that the main obstacle on the road to real development is their mind-set and that of their coreligionists. Indeed, the fundamentalist interpretations of the Koran that triumphed in the twelfth century have, in a way, trapped all Muslims in that remote period of time. They have, as it were, "locked" their minds, preventing them from continuing along the path of their predecessors of the first four centuries of the faith—a path marked by progress and the acquisition of knowledge.

Obviously, the unlocking of the chambers of the mind is neither an economic matter nor a military one. It will require a basic cultural effort that the intelligentsia alone can provide. Muslim intellectuals have to find a new Islamic language that will be capable of uniting the elites and helping the masses wake from the slumber that was induced by militant fundamentalism eight centuries ago. The failure to create a modern Islamic symbolism will widen the gap between Muslims and the rest of humanity.

While asking people to abide by age-old traditions, methods of thinking, and ways of life, militant Islamic fundamentalists are engaged in introducing the latest organizational structures and processes of the West and importing the most advanced technologies, which often violate the beliefs that they claim protect society from erosion. In a sense, they invite Muslims to drive their cars on a twenty-first century road without redirecting their sight away from the rearview mirror. Such driving instructions would only provoke deadly accidents. It is true that militant fundamentalists are not afraid of death, as Khomeini, in his 1979 message to the pope, affirmed. Obviously, a death wish cannot help Muslims enter the twenty-first century. Unlocking their minds will allow them to look toward the future and avoid the lure offered by the mirage of past glories.

At any rate, time is running out. The global economy of the nascent new world order is developing at increasing speed. Experts are warning that nations or regions that fail to make the necessary adjustments now to get a market share and obtain enough capital are likely to remain permanently poor.[5] Militant fundamentalism does not offer any possibility of responding to the exigencies of our time. On the contrary, militant fundamentalists take advantage of the deep sense of distress and disorientation that enervates the Muslim masses in order to isolate them from the rest of the world. They inculcate paralyzing feelings of nostalgia and frustration.

Nostalgia is a powerful sentiment but a dangerous guide to politics. The seizure of power by militant fundamentalists proved catastrophic to Muslims. Conversely, the refusal of the so-called secular rulers to introduce the necessary democratic reforms produced bitter results. If Muslims do not face the realities of their ominous situation, it is possible that their world will become one of the "ghettos" of the "global community."

And, finally, a few closing lines to distill the essence of the arguments presented in this book: Militant Islamic fundamentalism is essentially a political movement, not a religious one. Although it may pose a threat to the West in general and to the United States in particular, it will certainly be lethal to the Muslim world.

Notes

INTRODUCTION

1. Amir Taheri, *Holy Terror, Inside the World of Islamic Terrorism* (New York, 1987).

2. For instance, the "units" grouped under the PLO's umbrella cannot be considered Islamic fundamentalists, although at some point their leaders were members or sympathizers of the radical Muslim Brotherhood. (For that organization, see chapter 3.)

3. Moreover, this appellation draws a clear line between contemporary activists and "mainstream" Islam, which turned to fundamentalism some eight centuries ago (see chapter 6).

4. Besides, juvenile gangs, drug dealings, drunk driving, and a host of other ills are often more harmful to Western societies than militant Islamic terrorist activities.

5. Robert McFarlane, who was at one point the national security adviser in the Reagan administration.

6. For example, a title such as *The Islamic Threat, Myth or Reality?* (Professor John Esposito) is misleading inasmuch as Islam, like any other religion, cannot be a "threat" by itself. Its use by militant groups can constitute a threat.

CHAPTER 1—FIRST ENCOUNTER WITH A MILITANT

1. See chapter 3.

2. A mufti is a jurisconsult and interpreter of Islamic law among Sunnis. His office exists officially in every Muslim Sunni country.

3. See Taheri, *Holy Terror*, p. 50.

4. I heard the rumor in Beirut where I was a student. It was also reported in books about this period such as *Arab Rebellion and Terrorism in Palestine* and *Arabism and Zionism in Palestine*, ed. Elie Kedourie and Sylvia G. Haim.

CHAPTER 2—THE IRANIAN CONNECTION

1. Cited by Daniel Yergin, *The Prize: The Epic Quest for Oil, Money, and Power* (New York, 1991), p. 271.

2. The holy month of fast, which is celebrated at varying times according to the Muslim lunar calendar. *Sawm* in Arabic. One of the five pillars of Islam.

3. See Taheri, *Holy Terror* pp. 63–65. A *fatwa* is an opinion of a mufti, a sheikh, or an ayatollah on an issue of canonical law.

4. This collection of the lessons that Khomeini gave in his religious seminar was published in book form after the revolution under the title *Islamic Government*.

5. A fatwa declaring somebody *mahdur-o-dam* [blood worthless] is tantamount to a death sentence.

6. The title *seyyed, seyed,* or *sayed* means "gentleman" in Arabic. In Iran it is reserved for those who claim direct descent from Prophet Muhammad. Seyeds wear black turbans. Non-seyed mullahs wear white turbans. Because record keeping did not exist in Muslim countries until the early twentieth century, it is difficult to assess the accuracy of the seyed claimants. On this matter, see Amir Taheri, *The Spirit of Allah: Khomeini and the Islamic Revolution* (Washington, D.C., 1986), pp. 27–28.

7. Kasravi's fiercely anti-Islamic theories incensed the mullahs. His books and articles are available in Persian. A summary of his ideas has been given by Taheri, *Holy Terror*, pp. 63–65.

CHAPTER 3—THE COMMUNITY OF DEVOTED FIGHTERS

1. The phrase is Taheri's; see *Holy Terror*, p. 46.

2. On Abdoh and al-Afghani, see chapter 8.

3. Hassan Banna, *Muzakerat ad-Da'wa wal Da'yah* (Conversations on the Calling and Its Preaching (Cairo, 1958), p. 73.

4. On the "just despot," see chapter 8.

5. On Hassan Sabbah, see chapter 5.

6. Bizri Bawab, "Le mouvement Ibad al-Rahman et ses prolongements a Tripoli," *Radicalismes Islamiques*, ed. O. Carré and P. Dumont (Paris, 1985), pp. 159–204.

CHAPTER 4—THE BEADS AND THE BULLETS

1. On Nasser, see Dewan Berindranath, *Nasser, the Man and the Miracle* (New Delhi, 1966) and Jean Lacouture, *The Demi-Gods, Charismatic Leadership in the Third World* (New York, 1970). On Saddam Hussein, see *Saddam Hussein, On Current Events*, trans. Khalid Kishtainy (London, 1977).

2. Taheri, *The Spirit of Allah*, chapter 2.

3. The twelfth Shiite imam (the descendant of Ali), who disappeared mysteriously in his childhood and whose return is awaited by Shiite "twelvers," is supposed to bring justice and equity on Earth. He is considered the only legitimate ruler. In his absence nobody can pretend to replace him. The shahs were only tolerated. On this question, Khomeini strayed from the views of the majority of ayatollahs.

4. On Navab Safavi, see *Navab va Yaranash* (Navab and His Companions) (Tehran, 1981).

5. Ibid.

6. In the Zoroastrian religion (which was Iran's religion before Islam), *Ahura Mazda* (the Wise Lord, God) presides over the continuous duel between the forces of Good and the forces of Evil. The forces of Evil are represented by Ahriman, the leader of demonic forces, who will be defeated at the end of the world.

7. See D. Yergin, *The Prize*, chapter 22.

8. Ibid., p. 457.

9. Navab Safavi, "Jame'eh va Hokumat-e-Islami" (Qum, 1980).

10. The "Hojatieh Society" was founded by Sheikh Mahmud Halabi (who later became an ayatollah). It devoted its energies to "returning" Bahais to the Muslim faith. Disbanded in 1984 by Khomeini, it went underground.

CHAPTER 5—SOME PRECURSORS

1. Judith Miller, *God Has 99 Names* (New York, 1996), p. 132.

2. Ibn al-Jawzi, *Naqd,* pp. 19–20. Philip K. Hitti, *History of the Arabs* (London, 1960), p. 441.

3. On Muslim sects, see Hitti, pp. 429–449; also, C. E. Farah, *Islam* (New York, 1970), pp. 174–195.

4. The principle of dissimulation under the name ketman became a part of Iranian Shiite theology. It is primarily used by Iranian and other Shiite clerics. It has also gained currency among Sunnite clerics. One can find a description in Gobineau's *Trois ans en Asie*.

5. It seems that Marco Polo confused Sabbah with one of his later disciples who lived in Syria and was nicknamed "the Old Man from the Mountain."

6. Quoted in Hitti, *History of the Arabs*, p. 429 et seq.

7. As translated by A. Taheri in *Holy Terror*.

8. See Christian Jambet, *La Grande Resurrection d'Alamut* (Paris, 1990), pp. 30–32.

CHAPTER 6—THE TURNING POINT

1. The symposium was held in New York City on October 23, 1996.

2. On Khalid ibn Walid's feats, see Hitti, *History of the Arabs*, p. 149 et seq.; Alois Musil, *Arabia Deserta* (New York, 1927), pp. 553–573, 570.

3. Hitti, p. 150.

4. Ibid., chapter 21.

5. See chapter 5.

6. *Makatib-e-Farsye Ghazali* (Ghazali's Letters in Persian), (Tehran, 1951). Among Ghazali's major treatises, one should mention *Revivification of Religious Sciences* and *Refutation of the Philosophers* (also translated under the title *Incoherence of the Philosophers*).

7. V. S. Naipaul, "Universal Civilization," *International Herald Tribune*, November 5, 1990.

8. Jdanov supported the "fake" agronomist Lyssenko against real scientists. As a result, there was a sharp fall in agricultural crops.

9. Quoted by Henry Corbin in "La Philosophie Islamique des Origines a la mort d'Averroes," *Histoire de la Philosophie*, tome I (Paris, 1969), p. 1193.

10. See my books *Que Veulent les Arabes?* (Paris, 1991), chapter 13; and *L'Islam Bloqué* (Paris, 1993), chapter 3.

CHAPTER 7—FUNDAMENTALISM FOREVER

1. There are four recognized schools of jurisprudence named after their founders: the "Hanafite," the most tolerant, adopted by the Ottomans and Asian Muslim countries; the "Malekite," more conservative than the Hanafite; the "Shafeite," in between the other two; and the "Hanbalite," the strictest. The latter was adopted by the Wahhabi (Saudi Arabia).

2. See Hitti, *History of the Arabs*; and Corbin, *La Philosophie Islamique*.

3. The imam in Sunni Islam is the one who stands before the faithful during prayers in the mosque. Among Shiites he is also a guide and a supreme leader.

4. On Wahhabism, see Hitti, *History of the Arabs*; C. E. Farah, *Islam*; and Georges Corm, *L'Europe et l'Orient* (Paris, 1989), pp. 152–158 and 174–192.

5. In Shiism the Mahdi is the awaited twelfth imam who disappeared in his childhood. The imam-Mahdi dogma is an essential part of the twelvers Shiite creed. In Sunnism the Mahdi-restorer of the faith does not occupy such a place. The belief in the coming of the Mahdi lent itself to the appearance of many pretenders in all periods of Muslim history.

6. See P. M. Holt, *A Modern History of Sudan* (New York, 1961), and *The Mahdi State, 1881–1898* (London, 1958).

7. Judith Miller, *God Has 99 Names*, pp. 131–133. The V-shaped gap between the Mahdi's two front teeth (like the prophet's) underlines the importance of resemblance to the prophet. Khomeini and others used the fact that Muham-

mad was an orphan brought up by his uncle to point to resemblance. See my discussion on the uncle syndrome in chapter 4.

8. *Le Monde* (Paris), May 20, 1984.

9. *The New York Times*, August 18, 1993.

10. Cited by Taheri in *Holy Terror*, following the contents page.

CHAPTER 8—THE ISLAMIC STATE

1. *Risalat Fusus al-Hikam* (Epistle on Wisdom); *Risalah Fi Ara Ahl al-Madinah al-Fadilah* (Epistle on the Opinions of the People of the Superior State); *Al-Syassah al-Madanyah* (Civil Politics).

2. Al-tarabi, *Al-Syassah*, p. 35.

3. Ibid., p. 42.

4. Reprinted by the quarterly *Al-Minar* (III, 577–582 and 600–607). I use here L. M. Kenny's translation in *Journal of the American-Oriental Society*, vol. 86, no. 1, March 15, 1966.

5. Daniel Lerner, *The Passing of Traditional Society, Modernizing the Middle East* (New York, 1958), pp. 281–282.

6. Philippe Aziz, *Les Sectes Secretes de l'Islam* (Paris, 1983), p. 118.

CHAPTER 9—FUNDAMENTALIST AGENDAS

1. Shariati was born to a family of devout Muslims and received both a religious and a modern education. He cooperated with the nationalists and after a few months in prison, in 1957, he became a teacher. From 1960 to 1964 he studied sociology in Paris and joined the anti-shah movements. He returned to Iran where he worked with religious dissidents and at the same time taught at Mashad University. In the 1970s he was imprisoned for the second time. After his release, he managed to escape to London where he died in 1977 of a heart attack. His books cover Islamic history and social studies. Among them the following should be mentioned: *Che Bayad Kard* (What Must Be Done?); *Mazhab akeyhé Mazhab* (Religion Against Religion); *Shiism; Hokumaté Haq* (The Just Government).

2. The handbook was first published in 1950 in Tehran.

3. In those days the "economy" was part of the Ministry of Finance.

4. "What Islam Stands For," in *The Challenge of Islam*, ed. Altaf Gauhar (London, 1978), pp. 2–15.

5. Ibid.

6. The phrase is Charles Adams's in, "The Ideology of Mawlana Mawdudi," *South Asian Politics and Religion*, ed. Donald Smith (Princeton University Press, 1966). See also O. Carré, *Radicalismes Islamiques*.

7. Fazlul Rahman, *Islam and Modernity* (Chicago, 1983).

8. Quoted by J. Miller, *God Has 99 Names*, p. 451.

9. See Amir Arjomand, *The Turban for the Crown* (New York, 1988), p. 104.

CHAPTER 10—ENTER KHOMEINI

1. See chapter 4.
2. See chapter 2.
3. See chapter 4.
4. See chapter 2.
5. Ibid.
6. See Taheri, *The Spirit of Allah*.
7. In a speech broadcast by Tehran Radio on January 2, 1984.

CHAPTER 11—THEOLOGIAN AND TACTICIAN

1. In an interview with Tehran Radio on February 20, 1979.
2. For example, Ghotbzadeh and Chamran, who became foreign minister and head of the Revolutionary Guards, were trained in Palestinian camps and held Syrian passports for some time.
3. Musa Sadr strayed once again from the shah around 1976 and became dependent again on Libya's funds. But Qaddafi wanted him to account for his use of the money. Sadr and his companions traveled to Tripoli in September 1978 on the occasion of the anniversary of the Libyan revolution. They never reappeared.
4. The first Russian prime minister after the tsar was deposed in 1917 and replaced by a provisional government. In October the Bolsheviks led by Lenin overtook the government, and Kerenski fled from the country.
5. International Commission of Jurists. Quoted by D. Yergin in *The Prize*, pp. 675–676.
6. Notre Dame University, May 22, 1977.
7. Richard Sale, "Carter and Iran: From Idealism to Disaster," *The Washington Quarterly*, autumn 1980.
8. Ibid.

CHAPTER 12—THE KINDLING OF THE REVOLUTION

1. Jay Haley, *Les Tacticiens du Pouvoir* (French translation, Paris, 1984).
2. I was told this by my brother in April 1978. He was at the time minister of the court.
3. In Arabic, *imam* means "mosque preacher," not "guide." See chapter 7, note 3.
4. In Taheri, *The Spirit of Allah*, p. 203.
5. Quoted by Taheri in *The Spirit of Allah*.
6. Bernard Lewis, "The Revolt of Islam," *The New York Review of Books*, June 30, 1983.

7. Michael Ledeen and William H. Lewis, "Carter and the Fall of the Shah," *The Washington Quarterly*," spring 1980.

8. Ibid.

CHAPTER 13—THE PARTY OF GOD

1. In Taheri, *Holy Terror*, pp. 86–87.

2. *Rah-e-Ma* (Our Path), booklet (Tehran, 1982), p. 11.

3. Muhammad Ali Hashemi, a theoretician of the Hezbollah, wrote in *Gharb-e-Gharib* (Exotic West), (Tehran, 1980) a justification of the use of children on the battlefield and accused Western scholars of artificially dividing human life into categories. He specified, "Children are expected and made to act childish while young people are forced to go out and become corrupt or run after a silly ball on the soccer field instead of cutting down the forces of evil on the battlefield."

4. "Religious Fundamentalisms and Global Conflict," *Foreign Policy Association—Headline Series* (New York, 1994).

5. See, for example, a collection of the Iranian monthly *Baseej*.

6. PFLP, DFLP, Hamas, and others.

7. Douglas Jehl in *The New York Times*, April 21, 1996.

8. Ibid.

9. FIS stands for "Front Islamique du Salut," the French name of the organization.

10. See chapter 1.

11. PFLP, PNLM, Abu Musa's faction of Fatah, IJMP, Hamas, Islamic Jihad, and others.

12. ADL, January 1995, p. 7.

13. *The New York Times*, February 1, 1993.

14. *The New York Times*, June 12, 1994.

15. On *ketman* or *taqiyah* (religiously accepted dissimulation), see previous chapters.

16. See J. Miller, chapter on Sudan.

17. Cited by J. Miller.

18. Ibid.

19. *The New York Times*, May 17, 1992.

20. Robert Fisk, "The Transformation of Hezbollah," *The Independent* (London), Sunday, April 21, 1996.

CHAPTER 14—THE STRETCHING SHADOW

1. Report by Georges O'Neil in *Le Monde*, September 14, 1986.

2. Ibid.

3. J. Miller, *God Has 99 Names*, p. 53.

4. *Time*, March 15, 1993.

5. *The New York Times*, May 6, 1994.

6. *Time*, March 15, 1993.

7. *The London Times*, September 1, 1996.

8. See interview with Madani in *Politique Internationale*, autumn 1990.

9. Ibid.

10. J. Miller, *God Has 99 Names*, p. 207.

11. *Le Monde*, March 29, 1987.

12. Taheri, *Holy Terror*, pp. 196–197.

13. *Le Monde*, July 12, 1986.

14. *The New York Times*, April 30, 1987.

15. *Le Monde*, August 7, 1979.

16. *The New York Times*, May 18, 1996.

17. General Hakki in *The New York Times*, January 1, 1996.

18. *Histoire des Moeurs*, tome III (Paris, 1991), p. 1272.

19. Celestine Bohlen in *The New York Times*, June 3, 1995.

20. Ibid.

21. Price-Jones, *The Closed Circle*, p. 144.

22. *Le Monde*, June 9, 1985.

23. *Le Nouvel Observateur*, July 19, 1990.

24. Robin Wright, *Sacred Rage: The Crusade of Modern Islam* (New York, 1985).

25. *The New York Times*, February 21, 1986.

26. Taheri, *The Spirit of Allah* and *Holy Terror*.

CHAPTER 15—THE CAUSES OF MILITANT FUNDAMENTALISM

1. *The New York Times*, August 21, 1996.

2. Ibid., April 12, 1993.

3. "Pour l'Amour d'Allah," GEO, November 1991, and "La Carte Islamique de Saddam Hussein," *Le Monde*, January 11, 1991.

4. Koran, XVI, 71; XVII, 21. See my contribution, "Social Justice in Early Islamic Society," in *Social Justice in the Ancient World*, ed. K. D. Irani and Morris Silver (Westport, Conn., 1995).

5. *The New York Times*, July 28, 1995.

6. Ibid., December 21, 1992.

7. See Khomeini's *The Islamic Government*.

8. François Burgalat in *Geopolitique*, no. 34.

9. On the Saudis, the "oil boom," and their fear of Nasser, see, among other studies, G. Corm's *L'Europe et l'Orient*.

10. Ibid.

11. Robert Fisk in *The Independent* (Sunday), London, April 21, 1996.

12. *Geopolitique*, no. 34.

13. See chapter 6.

14. See Gustav E. Von Grunebaum, *Studien zum Kulturbid und Selbstvertaendnis Des Islams* (Zurich, 1969), French translation: *L'Identité Culturelle de l'Islam* (Paris 1973).

15. Quoted by D. Lerner in *The Passing of Traditional Society*, p. 205.

16. Guy Sitbon in *Le Nouvel Observateur*, December 17, 1979.

17. Mohammed Zerrouki, member of the Bureau of the Pen Club.

18. Max Olivier Lacamp in *Le Figaro*, October 17, 1960.

19. *The New York Times*, June 3, 1995.

20. Fazlur Rahman, "Islam and Modernity," *Transformation of an Intellectual Tradition*, Chicago, 1983.

CHAPTER 16—THE BROKEN CRESCENT

1. See chapters 8 and 9.

2. Interview in *Le Monde*, October 17, 1978.

3. See *Le Monde*, November 28, 1979, and the Iranian daily *Ettelaat*, June 17, 1979.

4. Declaration of August 19, 1979 (as published in *Le Monde*, August 21, 1979).

5. See chapter 8.

6. Professor Jalal Matini, "Negating the Past," trans. Paul Sprachma, *Index on Censorship*, University of Chicago Library, no. 6, 1985.

7. *Le Monde*, December 8, 1978.

8. Article by Ali Laaridh, spokesman of Al-Nahda (Tunisian fundamentalist group), published in Tunis weekly *Le Temps-Hebdo*, quoted in *Le Monde*, April 18, 1990.

9. *Le Monde*, April 7, 1979.

10. Bordewich, "Fascism Without Swastikas," in *Harper's*, July 1980.

11. *Politique Internationale*, autumn 1990.

12. Appleby, *Religion, Fundamentalism, and Global Conflict*, p. 17.

13. Martin and Appleby, Introduction to *Fundamentalism and the State* (Chicago, 1993), p. 3.

14. Appleby, p. 33.

15. Laqueur, *Fascism: Past, Present, Future* (London, 1996).

16. Muhammad Said al-Ashmawy, *Al-Islam al-Siyasi* (Political Islam), (Cairo, 1987); French trans. Richard Jacquemond, *L'Islamisme Contre l'Islam* (Paris, 1989). In this book, al-Ashmawy, a senior Egyptian judge, argued that Muslims never established a clear distinction between spirituality and history, between "ethics and praxis"; this confusion was upheld by Muslim political authorities who, since the first caliphs until the last Ottoman sultans, pretended to be "God's vicars on earth." Their opponents claimed always that "sovereignty" is "God's property" and fought them on the pretext of establishing a "religious government." As a consequence, Islamic history appeared to Muslims as well as Western

"orientalists" as a long series of religious conflicts, while in fact it was dominated by political and tribal wars under the cover of religion.

CHAPTER 17—THE CASE AGAINST THE WEST

1. Ad page in *The New York Times*, November 18, 1979.
2. *The New York Times Sunday Magazine*, January 1980.
3. See also chapter 20.
4. Bernard Lewis, "The Roots of Muslim Rage," *The Atlantic Monthly*, September 1990.
5. Amir Taheri, *The Cauldron: The Middle East Behind the Headlines* (London, 1989), p. 189.
6. In Pryce-Jones's book *The Closed Circle: An Interpretation of the Arabs*, the author argues that the Arabs are caught in a closed circle defined by deeply rooted tribal, religious, and cultural traditions. He describes how the codes of shame, honor, and power challenging—underlying Arab societies for centuries—are alien to Western concepts of order, loyalty, and justice.
7. Muhammad Neguib, *Egypt's Destiny* (Cairo, 1955), pp. 19–20.
8. Gamal Abdal Nasser, *Egypt's Liberation: The Philosophy of the Revolution* (Cairo, 1955).
9. Rami G. Khouri, "The Arab Dream," *The New York Times*, December 15, 1990.
10. Bernard Lewis in *The Atlantic Monthly*, September 1990.
11. Khouri (see chapter 17, note 9).
12. See chapter 9.
13. "On the Sociology of Islam," quoted in J. Esposito, *Islam and Politics* (Syracuse, 1984).
14. Yahya Danesh, *Naqshe Imam dar Enghelah* (The Part of the Imam in the Revolution), (Tehran, 1982), p. 97.

CHAPTER 18—THE "GREAT SATAN"

1. *Le Monde*, January 31, 1990.
2. Ibid., May 25, 1985.
3. Chris Hedges in *The New York Times*, March 15, 1995.
4. *The New York Times*, January 15, 1993.
5. Youssef Ibrahim in *The New York Times*, March 9, 1992.
6. J. F. Revel, *L'Express* (Paris), January 21, 1974.
7. *The New York Times*, August 30, 1994.
8. *Le Monde*, October 17, 1986.
9. Guy Sitbon in *Le Nouvel Observateur*, December 17, 1979.
10. "Unholy War," *The Wall Street Journal*, September 10, 1992.

CHAPTER 19—A GLOBAL DANGER?

1. Yossi Melman, *The Master-Terrorist: The True Story of Abu Nidal* (New York, 1986).

2. Statement by Nathan Adams, senior editor of *Reader's Digest*, before the Senate Joint Foreign Relations and Judiciary Committee Hearings on Terrorism, May 13, 1985.

3. In a documentary shown on PBS television on June 3, 1986.

4. For references see my article, "L'intelligentsia Occidentale Face à Khomeini," in *Revue des Deux-Mondes* (Paris), January 1988. See also J. Esposito, *The Islamic Threat, Myth or Reality?* (London, 1992).

5. *The New York Times Sunday Magazine*, February 20, 1994.

6. Philip Shenon in *The New York Times*, July 14, 1996.

7. See chapter 18.

8. Taheri, *Holy Terror*, pp. 169–172.

9. Gregory Gause III, *Islamic Political Opposition in the Arab Peninsula Monarchies*, *Muslim Politics Report* (Council on Foreign Relations, no. 8, summer 1996).

10. *London Kayhan*, July 10, 1986.

11. See Taheri, *Holy Terror*; and articles by Steven Emerson and Kenneth Timmerman. See also my chapter 14.

12. *Yadnameh-ye-AYATOLLAH Mahalati* (Homage to Ayat. Mahalati), (Tehran, 1986).

13. *Seyri Dar Afkar-e ayatollah Motaheri* (A Journey into Ayat. Motaheri's Thoughts (Tehran, 1984), p. 39.

14. Philip Shenan in *The New York Times*, July 14, 1996.

15. Benjamin Netanyahu, *Fighting Terrorism: How Democracies Can Defeat Domestic and International Terrorism* (New York, 1995).

16. *The New York Times*, January 11, 1997.

17. Steven Emerson, "The Other Fundamentalists: A Look Inside the Radical Islamist Network," *The New Republic*, June 12, 1995.

18. Ibid.

19. Joseph Alpher, "The Khomeini International," *The Washington Quarterly*, autumn 1980.

20. Douglas Frantz, "Investigators Look at History of Terrorism," *The New York Times*, August 24, 1996.

21. Adams's testimony at the Senate, see chapter 19, note 2.

22. Khattar Abu-Diab, "Les Mutations du Monde Arabo-Musulman," *Geopolitique*, no. 42, summer 1993.

23. Emerson, see chapter 19, note 17.

24. Ibid.

CHAPTER 20—HOLY WAR (*JIHAD*)

1. For instance, Rafsanjani, while he was speaker of the parliament in 1984. The United States had sent its fleet into the Persian Gulf; Rafsanjani threatened

to call on all "friends" of the Islamic Republic in the world to wage a jihad against the interests of countries that were intervening unduly in the Persian Gulf. (AFP and Reuters, reproduced in *Le Monde*, May 20, 1984).

2. Voice of the Islamic Republic of Iran. First Program Network in Persian, October 21, 1991.

3. Bernard Lewis, *The Political Language of Islam* (Chicago, 1988).

4. *Ettelaat* (daily), Tehran, June 17, 1979.

5. Message to the Pope, ad in *The New York Times*, November 18, 1979.

6. Tabari, *The Four First Caliphs*.

7. Majid Khadduri, *The Islamic Law of Nations: Shaybani's Siyar* (Baltimore, 1966). See also my books, *Que Veulent les Arabes?* and *L'Islam Bloqué*.

8. "Are Arabs Ready for Peace?" *The Middle East Quarterly*, spring 1994.

9. Youssef Ibrahim in *The New York Times*, January 31, 1995. See also the *Middle East Mirror*, January 19, 1995.

10. Fehmi Koru, *Muslim Politics Reports* (Council on Foreign Relations) no. 9, October 1996.

11. Mir Hossein Mussavi Khamenei, United Nations General Assembly, October 5, 1981.

12. Patrick Moore, "Jihad and Conflict in the World of Islam" (Lecture at the Joint Armed Forces Intelligence Training/Seminar), *Low Intensity Conflict*, June 6, 1993. See also the same author, "From Cold War to 'Guerra Fria'?" *American Foreign Policy Interests*, vol. 16, no. 4, August 1994.

CHAPTER 21—A CLASH OF CIVILIZATIONS?

1. Samuel Huntington, "The Coming Clash of Civilizations," *Foreign Affairs*, summer 1993. See also his shortened version in *The New York Times*, May 6, 1993.

2. *The Crusades: The World's Debate* (Milwaukee, 1937).

3. Moore, "Jihad and Conflict." See also chapter 20, note 12.

4. Undated report by Alan Cowel in *The New York Times*.

5. Tehran's daily *Kayhan* (airmail edition), February 13, 1985.

CHAPTER 22—PREPARING FOR THE "FINAL ROUND"

1. Kalid Duran, "Islamic Prospects for Human Rights in North Africa," *Islamic Law Reform* (Oslo: Nordic Human Rights Publications, 1993).

2. *The New York Times*, December 21, 1992.

3. E. Sciolino in *The New York Times*, November 30, 1992.

4. A. M. Rosenthal, "Only a Matter of Time," *The New York Times*, November 22, 1996. See also Tim Wiener in *The New York Times*, July 29, 1993, reporting that the director of the CIA affirmed that North Korea had tested a missile of

more than 600 miles in range. With this missile "Iran could reach Israel and Libya could reach U.S. bases and allied capitals in the Mediterranean region."

5. Robert Asprey, "The Challenge of Guerrilla Tactics," *The New York Times*, July 13, 1975.

6. R. Ben-Yisha in *Yediot Ahronot*, July 29, 1994.

7. Matthew Wald in *The New York Times*, March 6, 1994.

8. Duran. See chapter 22, note 1.

9. Youssef Ibrahim, "An Islamic Fundamentalist Abroad," *The New York Times*, January 9, 1994.

10. Duran. See chapter 22, note 1.

11. Miller, *God Has 99 Names*, pp. 468–469.

12. A phrase used by Taheri as the title of one of the chapters of *Holy Terror*.

13. Taheri, *Holy Terror*, p. 216.

14. Moore, "From Cold War to 'Guerra Fria'?" See chapter 20, note 12.

15. In his article in *The New Republic*, June 12, 1995.

16. "Islamic Iran's American Base," *The American Spectator*, December 1995.

17. Steven Emerson in *The Wall Street Journal*, March 5, 1993.

18. A. M. Rosenthal, "What Clinton Wrought," *The New York Times*, April 26, 1994.

CHAPTER 23—CAN MILITANT ISLAMIC FUNDAMENTALISM SUCCEED?

1. Cited by Arthur Schlesinger Jr. in "The Worst Corruption," *The Wall Street Journal*, November 22, 1995.

2. Sermon of July 16, 1982, reproduced in the booklet *The Imam Versus Zionism*, Ministry of Islamic Guidance, Tehran, 1984.

3. Yossef Bodansky, "The Grand Strategy of Iran," *Global Affairs*, fall 1993. Since the summer of 1992, Iran had been expanding its capacity to launch antishipping missiles from several directions. To that end, it consolidated its hold on the Abu Musa and the two Tumb islands at the mouth of the Strait of Hormuz. It installed on them missile batteries and huge army and marine bases. It also activated a strategic communication network linked to the National Command Center in Tehran. In addition, it reaffirmed its "right of sovereignty" over Bahrain (which had been renounced by the shah in 1970).

4. Tim Weiner in *The New York Times*, May 12, 1995.

5. John Hannah, deputy director of the Washington Institute for Near East Policy, in *The Wall Street Journal*, September 15, 1993.

6. Chris Hedges in *The New York Times*, December 24, 1994.

7. Mark Edington, "Terror Made Easy," *The New York Times*, March 4, 1994.

8. Vahan Zanoyan, "After the Oil Boom, the Holiday Ends in the Gulf," *Foreign Affairs*, November-December 1995.

9. Quoted by Steven Holmes, "Iran's Shadow," *The New York Times*, August 22, 1993.

10. Chris Hedges in *The New York Times*, October 4, 1993.

11. Taheri, *Holy Terror*, pp. 223–224.

12. Anne Reinfenberg in *The Wall Street Journal*, September 25, 1996.

13. Edward G. Shirley, "Fundamentalism in Power: Is Iran's Present Algeria's Future?" *Foreign Affairs*, May-June 1995.

14. Miller, *God Has 99 Names*, p. 430.

15. The economic and political information was extracted from the Iranian press and articles published in European and American journals.

16. Quoted by Milton Viorst, "Changing Iran: The Limits of the Revolution," *Foreign Affairs*, November-December 1995.

17. *Foreign Affairs*, May-June 1995.

18. Miller, *God Has 99 Names*, p. 147.

19. *The New York Times*, December 12, 1994.

20. Quoted by Fergus Bordewich in "Fascism Without Swastikas"; see my chapter 16, note 10.

21. Garry Trudeau, "Drawing Dangerously," *The New York Times*, July 10, 1994.

CHAPTER 24—A CHALLENGE TO THE WEST AND THE WORLD?

1. Copple, *The Apocalypse Brigade*.

2. Sermon of July 1982. See chapter 23, note 2.

3. Cited by Terrence Smith in *The New York Times Sunday Magazine*, February 12, 1984.

4. Neil MacFarquhar, "Portrait of a Suicide Bomber," *The New York Times*, March 18, 1996.

5. *Muslim Politics Report*, January-February 1997.

6. Tim Weiner in *The New York Times Sunday Magazine*, March 13, 1994.

7. *Muslim Politics Report*, January–February 1997.

8. Barnett Rubin in *Muslim Politics Report*, January-February 1997. Rubin is director of the Center for Preventive Action, Council on Foreign Relations, and the author of several books on Afghanistan.

9. "The West and the Middle East," *Foreign Affairs*, January-February 1997.

10. "Silencing Ideas: The Crisis Within Iran's Theocracy," *Los Angeles Times*, December 31, 1995.

11. "The Hidden Eve," cited by Pryce-Jones in *The Closed Circle*, p. 130.

12. *The New York Times*.

13. Mullawi Yar Muhammad, governor of Herat, in *Newsday*, October 6, 1996.

14. William Cleveland, Professor of History at Simon Frazer University, Toronto, *History of the Modern Middle East* (New York, 1995).

15. *Against the Gods: The Remarkable Story of Risk* (New York, 1977).

CONCLUSION: THE "PAST SHOCK"

1. See my article.

2. Colin Williams, *Ethics, Religion, and Governance*, Aspen Institute for Humanistic Studies (New York, 1981).

3. Article in *The Diplomat*, London, vol. I, no. 2, June 1996.

4. Muhammad Khalil Zayyen, *Fi Sabil al-Allah* (In the Path of God), (Rome, 1985), p. 22.

5. John Page, the World Bank's chief Middle East economist, cited by Judith Miller in *God Has 99 Names*, p. 475. See also "Will Arab Workers Prosper or Be Left Out in the Twenty-First Century?" The World Bank, August 1995.

Selected Bibliography

Agha Khan. *The Memoirs of Agha Khan*. London, 1954.

Ajami, Fouad. *The Arab Predicament: Arab Political Thought and Practice Since 1967*. New York, 1982.

————. "The Vanished Imam." New York, 1986.

Amir-Arjomand, Said. *The Shadow of God and the Hidden Imam: Religion, Political Order, and Societal Change in Shiite Iran from the Beginning to 1990*. Chicago, 1984.

————. *The Turban for the Crown*. New York, 1988.

Appleby, R. Scott. *Religious Fundamentalism and Global Conflicts*. Foreign Policy Association. New York, 1994.

Arkoun, Mohammed. *L'Islam, Religion et Société* (with Bormans and Arosio). Paris, 1980.

Aziz, Phillipe. *Les Sectes Secretes de l'Islam*. Paris, 1983.

Barchand, David. *Turkey and the West*. London, 1985.

Bernard, Cheryl, and Zalmay Khalilzad. *The Government of God*. New York, 1984.

Brière, Claire, and Olivier Carré. *Islam: Guerre à l'Occident?* Paris, 1982.

Carré, Olivier, and Paul Dumont. *Radicalismes Islamiques*. Paris, 1985.

Carré, Olivier, and Georges Michaud. *Les Frères Musulmans*. Paris, 1983.

Charnay, Paul. *L'Islam et la Guerre*. Paris, 1986.

Corbin, Henry. *Trilogie Ismailienne*. Paris, 1961.

———. "Histoire de la Philosophie Islamique" (encyclopédie de la Pleiade). Paris, 1969.

———. En Islam Iranien. Paris, 1971.

Corm, Georges. Le Moyen Orient Eclaté. Paris, 1983.

———. L'Europe et l'Orient. Paris, 1989.

Critchfield, Richard. Shahatt, an Egyptian. New York, 1978.

Dietal, Wilhelm. Holy War. New York, 1984.

Entelis, John. Comparative Politics of North Africa. New York, 1980.

Esposito, John, ed. Voices of Resurgent Islam. Oxford, 1983.

———. The Islamic Threat, Myth or Reality? New York, 1992.

Essaid, Abdul-Aziz. Le Reveil de l'Islam. Marseilles, 1985.

Etienne, Bruno. L'Islamisme Radical. Paris, 1987.

Farah, Ceasar. Islam. New York, 1970.

Gauhar Altaf, ed. The Challenge of Islam. London, 1978.

Glass, Charles. Tribes with Flags: A Dangerous Passage through the Chaos of the Middle East. London, 1990.

Grunebaum, Gustav Von. Essays on the Nature and Growth of a Cultural Tradition. London, 1961.

———. Studien zum Kulturbid und Selbstverstaendnis Des Islam. Zurich, 1969 (French translation: L'identité Culturelle de l'Islam. Paris, 1973).

Hirsowicz, Lukasz. The Third Reich and the Arab East. London, 1965.

Hitti, Philip. History of the Arabs. London, 1970.

Holt, P. M. The Mahdi State, 1881–1898. London, 1958.

Hosaini, I. M. The Moslem Brothers. Beirut, 1969.

Hoveyda, Fereydoun. The Fall of the Shah. New York, 1981.

———. Les Nuits Feodales. Paris, 1983.

———. Les Miroirs du Mollah. Paris, 1985.

———. Que Veulent les Arabes? Paris, 1991.

———. L'Islam Bloqué. Paris, 1993.

Hussein, Assaf. Political Perspectives of the Muslim World. New York, 1985.

Iqbal, Muhammad. Knowledge and Religious Experience. Lahore, 1968.

Issawi, Charles. An Economic History of the Middle East. London, 1982.

Jambet, Christian. La Grande Resurrection d'Alamût. Paris, 1990.

Jansen, G. H. Militant Islam. London, 1979.

Kadar, Benjamin. Crusade and Mission: European Approaches Toward the Muslims. Princeton, N.J., 1984.

Kedourie, Elie. Afghani and Abduh. London, 1966.

Kedourie, E., and Sylvia Haim. Zionism and Arabism in Palestine and Israel. London, 1982.

Khadduri, Majid. The Islamic Law of Nations: Shaybani's Siyar. Baltimore, 1966.

———. Political Trends in the Arab World. New York, 1972.

al-Khalil, Samir. Republic of Fear. New York, 1989.

Lamb, David. The Arabs. New York, 1987.

Lanternari, Vittorio. *The Religion of the Oppressed*. New York, 1963.

Ledeen, Michael. *Perilous Statecraft: An Insider's Account of the Iran-Contra Affair*. New York, 1988.

Lerner, Daniel. *The Passing of Traditional Society: Modernizing the Middle East*. New York, 1958.

Lewis, Bernard. *The Emergence of Modern Turkey*. London, 1961.

———. *Islam and the West*. New York, 1984.

———. *The Political Language of Islam*. Chicago, 1988.

Magassouba, Moriba. *L'Islam au Senegal: Demain les mollahs?* Paris, 1985.

Marty, Martin, and R. Scott Appleby. *Fundamentalisms Observed*. Chicago, 1991.

———. *Fundamentalisms and the State*. Chicago, 1993.

Mawdudi, Abul Ala. *Islamic Law and Constitution*. Rome, 1984.

Melman, Yossi. *The Master-Terrorist. The True Story of Abu-Nidal*. New York, 1986.

Miller, Judith. *God Has 99 Names. Reporting from a Militant Middle East*. New York, 1996.

Mitchell, Richard. *The Society of the Moslem Brothers*. London, 1969.

Naipaul, V. S. *Among the Believers. An Islamic Journey*. London, 1981.

Abdal-Nasser, Gamal. *Egypt's Liberation. The Philosophy of the Revolution*. Washington, D.C., 1955.

Neguib. *Egypt's Destiny*. London, 1955.

Netanyahu, Benjamin. *Terrorism: How the West Can Win*. New York, 1986.

Nouira, Hedi. *The State and Social Transformation in Tunisia and Libya, 1830–1980*. Princeton, N.J., 1986.

Peroncel-Hugoz, J. P. *Le Radeau de Mahomet*. Paris, 1983.

Peters, Rudolph. *The Doctrine of Jihad in Modern History*. The Hague, 1979.

Piscatori, James. *Islam and the Political Process*. Cambridge, Mass., 1983.

Pryce-Jones, David. *The Closed Circle. An Interpretation of the Arabs*. New York, 1989.

Qutb, Sayed. *Social Justice in Islam*. Washington, D.C., 1953.

———. *Islam the Religion of the Future*. Lahore, 1976.

———. *Islam the Misunderstood Religion*. Rome, 1984.

Rahman, Fazlul. "Islam and Modernity," *Transformation of an Intellectual Tradition*. Chicago, 1983.

Rassam, Amal. *Peoples and Cultures of the Middle East*. New York, 1983.

Rodinson, Maxime. *Islam et Capitalisme*. Paris, 1966.

———. *Le Marxisme et le Monde Musulman*. Paris, 1972.

———. *Les Arabes*. Paris, 1979.

———. *La Fascination de l'Islam*. Paris, 1989.

———. *Mahomet*. Paris, 1961 and 1989.

Roy, Olivier. *L'Afghanistan, Islam et Modernité Politique*. Paris, 1985.

———. *The Failure of Political Islam*. Cambridge, Mass., 1994.

Ruthven, M. *Islam in the World*. London, 1984.

el-Saadawi, Nawal. *The Hidden Face of Eve: Women in the Arab World*. London, 1980.

Sablier, Edouard. *Le Fil Rouge*. Paris, 1983.

Schechtman, J. B. *The Mufti and the Fuhrer*. New York, 1965.

Scholl-Latour, Peter. *Les Guerriers d'Allah*. Paris, 1986.

Sivan, Emmanuel. *Radical Islamism: Medieval Theology and Modern Politics*. New Haven, 1985.

Smith, Donald, ed. *South Asian Politics and Religion*. Princeton, N.J., 1966.

Sole, Robert. *Le Défi Terroriste*. Paris, 1980.

Taheri, Amir. *The Spirit of Allah: Khomeini and the Islamic Revolution*. Washington, D.C., 1986.

———. *Holy Terror: Inside the World of Islamic Terrorism*. New York, 1987.

———. *Nest of Spies: America's Journey to Disaster in Iran*. London, 1988.

———. *The Cauldron: The Middle East Behind the Headlines*. London, 1989.

Tibi, Bassam. *Arab Nationalism*. London and New York, 1981.

Touré, E.H.C. *L'Etat Islamique, ses spécificités et ses caractéristiques*. Dakar (Senegal), 1985.

Viorst, Milton. *Sand Castles: The Arabs in Search of the Modern World*. New York, 1984.

Vocke, Harold. *The Lebanese War*. London, 1978.

Wardlaw, Grant. *Political Terrorism*. Cambridge, Mass., 1982.

Williams, Colin. *Ethics, Religion and Governance*. New York, 1981.

Yassin, Abdas Salam. *La Revolution à l'Heure de l'Islam*. Tunis, 1981.

Yergin, Daniel. *The Prize: The Epic Quest for Oil, Money and Power*. New York, 1991.

Zabih, Sepehr. *Iran Since the Revolution*. Baltimore, 1981.

Zeghal, Malika. *Les Gardiens de l'Islam: les Ulémas d'al-Azhar dans l'Egypte Contemporaine*. Paris, 1995.

BOOKS IN ARABIC AND PERSIAN

Alim-Naini, Mir Javad. *Hezbollah* (Party of God). Tehran, 1985.

Bakhtar, Sadruddin. *Hezbollah dar Lobnan* (Party of God in Lebanon). Tehran, 1986.

Fadlallah, Muhammad Hussein, Sheikh. *Islam wa Manteghal ghuwa* (Islam and the Logic of Force). Beirut, 1981.

Harb, Ragheb. *Din al-Islam Aqwa* (Islamic Religion Is the Strongest). Beirut, 1983.

Hashemi, Muhammad Ali. *Gharbé Gharib* (Strange West). Tehran, 1980.

Hilwan, Ubaid. *Thowrat al-Islamia fil Eraq* (Islamic Revolution in Iraq). Rome, 1983.

Itani, Muhammad. *Al Nizhal Mussalaha fil Islam* (Armed Struggle in Islam). Beirut, 1981.

Khomeini, Ruhollah. *Kashfol Asrar* (Key to the Secrets). Qum, 1961. Republished in Tehran under the title *Hokumaté Islami* (Islamic Government) in 1980.

———. *Tahriral Wassila* (Liberation of Means). Tehran, 1985.

Mubarak, Hisham. *Al Irhabyoun Ghademoun* (The Terrorists Are Returning). Cairo, 1995.

Navai, Abdul Ghaffar. *Nehzaté Islami dar Afghanestan* (Islamist Movement in Afghanistan). Peshavar, 1985.

Qutb, Sayed. *Mashahid al-Qyama fil Qur'an* (Signs of Resurrection in the Koran). Cairo, 1947.

Radhwan, Fath. *Al Jihad, Qanoun al Hayat* (Holy War, Law of Life). Cairo, 1973.

Safavi, Navab. *Jameeh va Hokumat Islami* (Society and Islamic Government). Qum, 1985.

Sidqi, Karim. *Al Harakat al-Islamyah: Qdaya wa Ahdaf* (The Islamist Movement: Issues and Goals). London, 1985.

Yazid, Abdul Aziz. *Ahdaf al-Thowratal Islamyah* (Goals of the Islamic Revolution). Beirut, 1983.

Zayyen, Muhammad Khalil. *Fi Sabil al-Lah* (In the Path of God). Rome, 1985.

Index of Names

Index of Subjects

Seljuk dynasty, 40, 41, 47
seyed, 21, 59; Khomeini as, 21, 77
sharia (Islamic law), 9, 25, 197
Shiism, 17, 21, 26, 31; beliefs of, 37–38, 79
Shiites, 17, 20, 38–39; and self-sacrifice and martyrdom, 154
Shiites and Sunnites: political cooperation between, 151; shared political goals of, 151; rift between, 29, 148
Siassat Nameh (The "Art of Politics"), 41
Signposts on the Road, 27
Six Day War, 76, 106, 133, 139, 140
Sudan, 2, 4, 53, 147, 151, 178; civil war in, 144, 181; consequences of the Islamic Revolution for, 181–182; role of, in fomenting unrest, 165, 175; supreme leader in, 122
Sudanese National Islamic Front, 150
Suez Canal Company, 23, 24
Sunni, 17, 38–39
Sunnism, 8, 19, 24; beliefs of, 37–38
Supreme Shiite Council, 79
Sword of Islam, 139
Syria, 2, 8, 13, 25, 116, 148, 175; and the Alawites, 39; and Hezbollah, 97; and Lebanon, 97

Tahir (Liberation), 106
Takfir wa Hijra of Egypt, 151
Taliban (Afghanistan), 182, 184–85; treatment of women by, 187
Terrorism (International Symposium), 43, 54
terrorist acts, 167–168, 175; Iran's hand in, 167, 175; and Syria, 175; by white supremacist activists, 193
theories of the Islamic state, 63–69; as developed by Ruhollah Khomeini, 71; as developed by Mawlana Adul Ala Mawdudi, 66–69; as developed by Navab Sa-

favi, 63–66; as developed by Ali Shariaty, 63
theory of a "permanent state of war," 156
Towzih-ol-Massayel ("Explanation of the Problems"), 73
Trans-Iranian Railway, 13, 19
Tudeh (Communist) party (Iran), 31, 32, 33, 88, 135
Tunisia, 105–106; and the idea of the model Islamic society, 124; and the Tunisian Islamic Tendency Movement, 105; and the Tunisian Section of Islamic Jihad, 106
Turkey, 4, 8, 16; human rights violations in, 146; Islamic fundamentalists in, 107–109; militant fundamentalism in, 108, 178; riots in, 108; and the Turkish Army, 107, 108

ulemas, 41, 42; book burning by, 48
umma ("Community of Islam" or of "Believers"), 20, 152
Ummayad dynasty, 155, 188
"uncle syndrome," 29–31, 72, 104
United Nations World Conference on Population, 140
United States: and Afghanistan, 141, 149, 197; and analysis of the Islamic Republic, 89–90; and the Anglo-Iranian Oil Company, 34; commercial interests of, 134; coup by, against Mossadegh in Iran, 35, 81, 116; criticism of the shah's human rights record, 87; impotence of, 116; Khomeini's indictment of, 129–131; and oil, 183; as a paper tiger, 90–91, 195; and the presence of American military and civilian advisers in Iran, 87; as a scapegoat for all infidels, 141; and the seizure of the American embassy in Tehran, 71, 90, 116, 129, 131, 145; and the spread of fundamentalism,

About the Author

FEREYDOUN HOVEYDA is a former Iranian Ambassador to the UN (1971–1978). Currently a Senior Fellow with the National Committee on American Foreign Policy, Dr. Hoveyda is a widely published author of fiction and nonfiction. His *Les neiges du Sinai* won the Leopold Senghor Award in 1973.

Date Due